THE
MIND

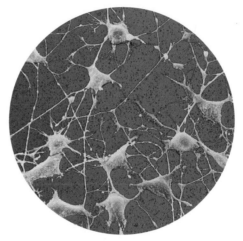

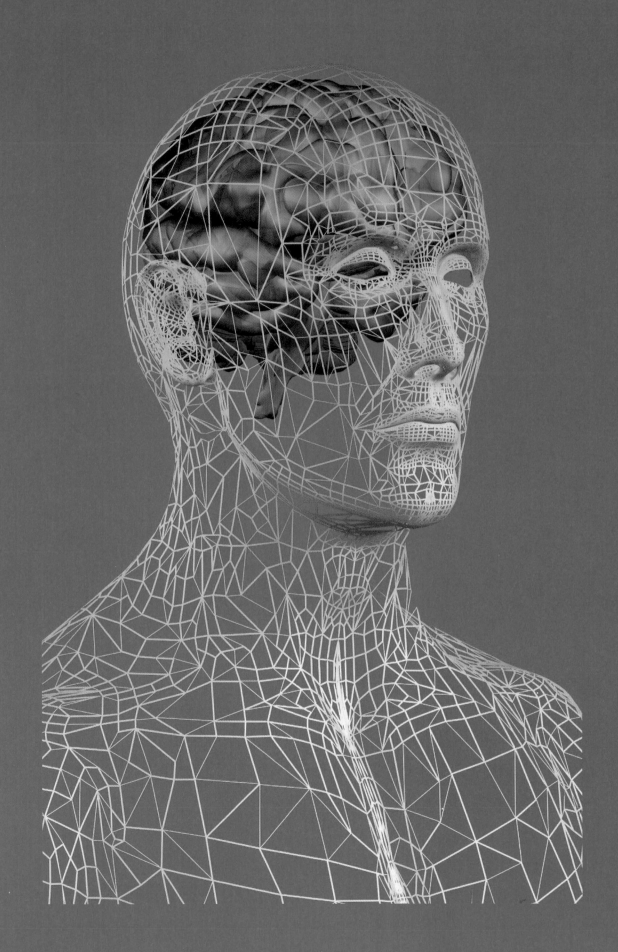

YOUR BODY YOUR HEALTH

THE
MIND

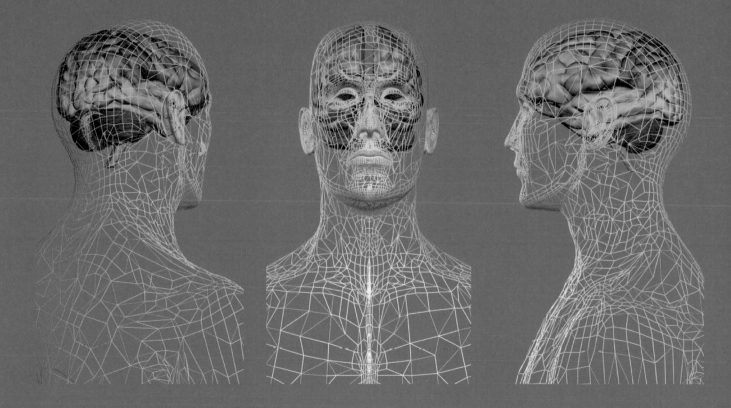

Reader's
Digest

The Reader's Digest Association Limited
London New York Sydney Montreal

The Mind

was created and produced by
Carroll & Brown Limited
20 Lonsdale Road
London NW6 6RD
for Reader's Digest, London

First English Edition Copyright © 2003
The Reader's Digest Association Limited
11 Westferry Circus
Canary Wharf
London E14 4HE
www.readersdigest.co.uk

Reprinted 2004

Copyright © 2003 The Reader's Digest
Association Far East Limited
Philippines copyright © 2003 The Reader's
Digest Association Far East Limited

ISBN 0 276 42879 X

Reproduced by Colour Systems, London
Printed and bound in the EEC by
Arvato Iberia

**The information in this book is for
reference only; it is not intended as a
substitute for a doctor's diagnosis and
care. The editors urge anyone with
continuing medical problems or
symptoms to consult a doctor.**

Managing editor
Anne Yelland

Managing art editor
Anne Fisher

Editors
Judy Fovargue, Marianne Canty

Art editors
Vimit Punater, Justin Ford

Series medical consultant
Dr Lesley Hickin, MB BS, BSc, DRCOG, MRCGP, General Practitioner

Specialist in Psychiatry
James Stone, BSc, MB BS, MRCPsych, Specialist Registrar in Psychiatry,
South London and Maudsley NHS Trust, London

CONTRIBUTORS

Joanna Bradley, BA, SRATh, Occupational Therapy Technical Instructor,
South London and Maudsley NHS Trust, London

Dr Wynnie Chan, BSc, PhD, Public Health Nutritionist

Katy Glynne, BSc, MRPharmS, Dip Pharmacy Practice,
Clinical Services Manager, Charing Cross Hospital, London,
Clinical Lecturer, The School of Pharmacy, University of London

Dr Michael T Isaac, Consultant and Senior Lecturer in Psychiatry,
South London and Maudsley NHS Trust, Guy's, King's and St Thomas' Medical School,
Institute of Psychiatry, London

Joel Levy, BSc, MA, Medical Writer

Brice Pitt, MD, FRCPsych, Emeritus Professor, Psychiatry of Old Age,
Imperial College. London

Pam Rigden, BSc, MA, YMCA Personal Trainer, NLP Master Practitioner,
Coach, Therapist and Trainer

Dr Michael Spira, MB BS, MRCS, LRCP, General Practitioner

Professor Peter Tyrer, MD, FRCP, FRCPsych, FFPHM. FMedSci, Professor of Community
Psychiatry, Head of Department of Psychological Medicine, Imperial College, London

For Reader's Digest
Series Editor Christine Noble
Art Editor Julie Bennett
Reader's Digest General Books
Editorial Director Cortina Butler
Art Director Nick Clark

The Mind

Awareness of health issues and expectations of medicine are greater today than ever before. A long and healthy life has come to be looked on as not so much a matter of luck but as almost a right. However, as our knowledge of health and the causes of disease has grown, it has become increasingly clear that health is something that we can all influence, for better or worse, through choices we make in our lives. *Your Body Your Health* is designed to help you make the right choices to make the most of your health potential. Each volume in the series focuses on a different physiological system of the body, explaining what it does and how it works. There is a wealth of advice and health tips on diet, exercise and lifestyle factors, as well as the health checks you can expect throughout life. You will find out what can go wrong and what can be done about it, and learn from people's real-life experiences of diagnosis and treatment. Finally, there is a detailed A to Z index of the major conditions which can affect the system. The series builds into a complete user's manual for the care and maintenance of the entire body.

This volume looks at the key feature that makes us who we are as individuals – the mind. It explains what is known about how the mind works, including the latest thinking on the mind–brain link, discoveries about the natural chemicals that direct our thoughts and feelings, what happens when we sleep, and the influence of gender, genetics and environment on personality and behaviour. Knowing what keeps the mind healthy helps in doing so, and the book examines the vital roles played by sleep, diet, relaxation and exercise – both mental and physical – in promoting mental agility and wellbeing. Threats to mental health such as stress, uncontrolled anger and low self-esteem are discussed, together with techniques and strategies to overcome any problem areas. Knowing when to seek help can make all the difference to quality of life, so clear descriptions of the major types of mental disorder are included, as well as symptoms, diagnostic techniques and treatment options, from talking and expressive therapies to medication and surgery.

Contents

How your mind works

Keeping your mind healthy

3

What happens when things go wrong

The life story of the mind

The most human thing about you is your mind. It is the wellspring and the core of your humanity – an extraordinary organ, unparalleled in the history of evolution on Earth, which is unfathomably complex and unique to every individual. Scientists are still unravelling exactly what the mind can – and cannot – do, and how and why it developed as it has.

Take almost any other organ or system in your body and you can find a close relation or parallel in the animal kingdom. Your heart is similar enough to a baboon's for that animal's organs to be used as a temporary replacement. Your liver is practically identical to a pig's (except that pigs don't drink alcohol). Your muscles and bones are very closely related to those of most other mammals, and an alien biologist might have trouble telling the difference between you and a shaved chimpanzee from your body parts alone. Even your brain looks superficially similar to a monkey's, and is made of the exact same material.

Only your mind is in a class apart. Many other animals clearly have minds, with personalities, emotions, desires and even degrees of intelligence, but not even a dolphin or a chimpanzee comes close to possessing the kind of mind that the most ordinary member of the human race can boast. We take for granted such human gifts as planning ahead, guessing what someone else might be thinking, learning a language or using it to lie to someone, but none of these abilities has a convincing parallel in the animal kingdom. These seem to be properties of the human mind and the human mind alone.

THE INTELLIGENT APE?

Humans, however, are part of the animal kingdom. We are descended from the same stock as the great apes, and DNA comparisons with our closest relatives, the chimps, show that we last shared a common ancestor around 6 million years ago. Fossils of human-like, or hominid, animals from after this split show that, slowly but steadily, the hominid brain increased in size. So did our minds simply evolve along with our bigger brains?

In fact the story is much more complex than this. Brain size is not directly linked to intelligence or other

The art of hunting
The oldest of the cave paintings discovered at Lascaux in the Dordogne region of France were created 17,000 years ago. In addition to proving that the human mind was capable of creating artistic representations of the world, the 1500 paintings of horses, bulls, stags, aurochs and other animals attest to the skills their creators possessed in hunting: observation, planning, memory and team work.

mental abilities, which means that the fossil record itself cannot tell us much about the evolution of the human mind. Only the products of the mind – art and artefacts – give an insight into its development, and a look at these products tells quite an unexpected story.

BRAIN BEFORE MIND

The first artefacts left by our early hominid ancestors are primitive stone tools that date back to around 3 or 4 million years ago. Although these represent a major mental advance, the use of tools is found elsewhere in the animal kingdom: chimps and birds, for instance, both use sticks to get at termites. The human toolkit changed very little for millions of years, and proof of more advanced mental abilities, such as art and ritual objects that show the presence of symbolic thinking, is entirely absent until around 50,000 years ago. By this time anatomically modern humans with anatomically modern brains had already evolved, yet it seems they did not have modern minds.

THE GREAT LEAP FORWARD

The emergence of advanced mental abilities around 50,000 years ago has been described as The Great Leap Forward. Over a comparatively short period of time (in evolutionary terms) humans developed the ability to think with symbols, probably at the same time as they learned to speak and understand symbols – in other words, language.

What led to this 'mental explosion'? It was probably a combination of factors. Changes in the environment and lifestyle of these early humans may have forced them to develop new methods of hunting and cooperating that benefited from advanced social abilities and language. As humans became more successful, they lived longer, so that family groups might have elderly members who could pass on their experience and knowledge. Culture became possible, and with it a flowering of mental abilities that led to the birth of magic, religion and art, as represented by the amazing paintings found in many European caves.

Renaissance Man
Leonardo da Vinci demonstrated the versatility of the human mind: he was one of the greatest artists and engineers of all time, and also an architect, astronomer, mathematician, geologist, botanist, inventor and musician. His notebooks include sketches from nature, a prototype flying machine and workings on the proportions of the human body (right)

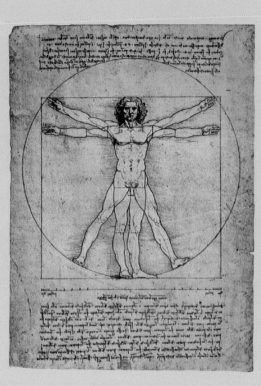

jokes, understand play acting, develop religion and culture, and do a thousand other things that we take for granted. Which makes it all the more strange that each human has to develop a theory of mind from scratch because it is one of a host of mental abilities that we are born without.

THE ABSENT MIND

Perhaps it is not surprising that babies are born with limited mental abilities, given that they have spent the last nine months developing in a state of sensory deprivation. Sound is one of the few stimuli that can reach the fetal brain, and tests on newborns suggest that babies can learn to recognise familiar tunes and other sounds while still in the womb. But most mental development takes place after birth, when the baby is suddenly plunged into a sensory riot of light, colour, sound, texture, taste, temperature and smell.

THEORY OF MIND

One of the most important mental abilities that these early humans developed was something that psychologists call theory of mind. This is the ability to imagine, guess or predict what another person (or other animal) might or might not be thinking or feeling. It's what allows us to interact with other people as people, rather than simply as objects or automatons.

For instance, if you were to see a dog pawing hopefully at a cupboard, you would probably surmise that he was hungry, even if you didn't know what was in the cupboard. As far as we know, and notwithstanding pet owners' high opinions of their animals, the dog would not be able to work out the same thing if your positions were reversed. He is not equipped with the mental ability to put himself in another animal's place and see through its eyes.

Humans had to develop theory of mind if they were to have meaningful social interactions, make alliances, do favours, fall in love, care for their children and parents, get

WIRING UP THE MIND

The mind is a product of the immensely complex web of connections and interactions between the neurons of the brain, but at birth very few of these connections exist. The vast majority of them are formed in the first few years of life, as the brain is wired up to produce a mind complete with a personality, intelligence and so on.

During the first stage of this process, babies are beginning to make sense of their body and senses, and through these the world around them. By touching, seeing, tasting, smelling and hearing, babies learn about the properties of objects and discover the difference between

At 12 months a child has a vocabulary of 3 words, which rapidly increases: by two years it is around 270, by four years 1540 and by the time a child starts school, around 6000. On average, some 3000 words are then added annually to reach about 45,000 by age 18 – about half the number of words in the English language.

self and non-self. Each interaction causes new connections to be made and old ones strengthened or discarded, as appropriate. The richer a baby's environment, the more information they will be able to derive from it and the quicker they will learn. Experiments with rats reared in environments rich in sensory stimulation as opposed to those reared in stark environments show that animals in the former group develop into more intelligent, responsive and happier rats, demonstrating that this early stage of brain development is vital for healthy mental development.

BABY TALK

At the same time as babies are developing this form of intelligence about the world around them, they are also developing a social and emotional intelligence through a bonding process involving interaction with caregivers.

This bonding is essential for future mental health, and helps to equip the infant mind with self-worth, confidence and empathy. It is also an essential part of the process of language acquisition, which begins when mothers start 'baby talking' to their children. By modifying what they say in response to their baby's actions and noises, they provide a feedback system that works together with 'programmes' built in to the baby's mind to produce language learning.

GET SMART

Acquisition of language helps to prepare the mind for the next stages of intellectual development, in which children use the processes of assimilation and accommodation to develop more sophisticated models for understanding the world. Assimilation is the process whereby children fit new information about the world into their existing mental

ONE LIFE, ONE MIND

A baby's intellect is not as developed as an adult's because the brain has still to be 'wired' through learning and experience. This process begins immediately and continues through adolescence. After that, a balanced and active life will help to keep the mind healthy into old age.

BABY

Baby face
Over the first six months or so, babies learn that they can influence the world through interaction with their caregivers. The mouth is a primary source of sensory information and toys are 'gummed' to learn about them.

*According to the World Health Organization, mental illness accounts for
25 per cent of all disability in Western Europe, the United States and Canada –
that is more than cancer and heart disease put together.*

structures and processes, while accommodation is how these structures and processes are altered to accommodate new information.

Very young children, for instance, have no concept of 'object permanence' – if an object vanishes from sight, it is as if it no longer exists. As they grow older, they assimilate the information that objects exist independently of their consciousness, and change their mental models about objects accordingly (accommodation). As they develop intellectually, children also develop emotionally and socially, developing a theory of mind and a personality, helped by

their status as a member of a family, which gives them identity. By the age of seven, a child possesses most of the mental skills of adults, although advanced abilities, such as logical thinking and problem solving, take longer to mature.

For most people, adolescence is the final stage of mental development, when the finishing touches are put to identity, personality and intellect. People continue to learn throughout their lives, but major changes in personality or intellectual ability are rare once we reach adulthood. But they are still possible, as life events can impact on the mind in unpredictable ways.

'You can't see me'
Until a child develops her own theory of mind, she believes that what she sees is what there is: if she can't see you – by covering or closing her eyes – then you can't see her either.

One of the crowd
At the age of 11 or 12 children want to be part of the crowd, dressing, looking and acting the same as their friends. Individual identity then gradually comes to the fore and is normally complete by the age of 16 or 17.

Time out
Adult lives can be stressful but regular time out helps, particularly getting out in the fresh air. Appreciating the beauty of the natural world may be enough to enable many people to keep things in perspective.

TEENAGE

PRE-SCHOOL

ADULT

Memory maker
A light micrograph of neurons in the hippocampus, part of the brain concerned with the formation of memories. The forging of neural pathways during childhood and adolescence makes memories rare before the age of four.

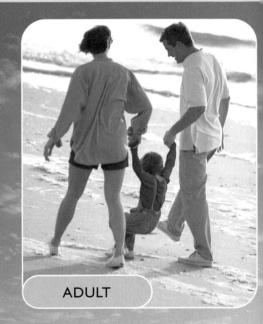

MENTAL HEALTH

Although some aspects of your mind were more or less fixed in form by early adulthood, the stability and health of your mind overall is by no means guaranteed throughout your lifespan. Like any other organ or system of your body, your mind is vulnerable to illness, injury and neglect. In fact mental illness is one of the fastest growing and most widespread health issues in the developed world.

Depression and anxiety are the most common types of mental illness, and conditions such as schizophrenia are also on the rise. Such illnesses can be life-threatening: suicide caused by severe depression is one of the biggest killers of young people aged 18–30. They also interfere with a person's career and relationship prospects and cripple quality of life in the long term.

OLDER

Keeping an active mind
Research suggests that active ageing – ensuring lifelong mental, physical and social opportunities – increases life expectancy and quality into old age.

MIND MATTERS

A new realisation is emerging that the mind can benefit from the same sort of preventative steps as other aspects of health. A combination of psychology research and common sense has determined a few simple rules for a mind-boosting lifestyle. These include getting good sleep, the need to tackle stress and learn to relax, and the impact of diet, exercise and substance abuse on the mind.

Techniques and interventions to help cure mental illness have also radically improved. Greater understanding of the physiological basis of mental illness has developed alongside drug treatments and diagnostic methods. Meanwhile, more than a century of psychology has produced a range of therapies, or 'talking cures': in the hands of a skilled practitioner, therapy provides powerful and effective tools for the restoration of mental health. Therapy can also benefit the mentally healthy, by promoting emotional stability and self-fulfilment.

BRAVE NEW WORLD

In the future it may be possible to unlock even more of this potential through revolutionary technologies such as genetics. Primary targets of genetic researchers are the genes that code for intelligence, a few of which have already been identified. An alternative route is being pioneered by British cybernetics researcher Professor Kevin Warwick, who seeks to augment human mental powers through computer technology. His dream is that mankind will one day be able to connect to, and make use of, the world of computers. For now we can only imagine what will happen to the human mind if – when – this dream comes true.

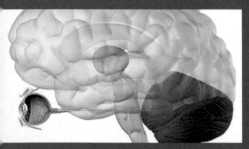

1

How your mind works

Your amazing mind

Your mind is the most versatile, ingenious and complex part of you. After centuries of study, however, we still can't properly describe it, and we are only beginning to learn how it relates to the rest of your body, including your brain.

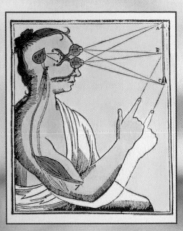

MIND AND BRAIN

Perhaps the first topic ever discussed in psychology was the mind–brain problem, first outlined in detail by the 17th century philosopher and scientist René Descartes. It is called a 'problem' because, to this day, no one can properly explain the relationship between the brain – physical matter that sits inside the skull – and the mind, with its collection of thoughts, feelings, memories and perceptions. The former appears to be a mass of cells like any other organ in your body, while the latter has no obvious material form. Are they linked, and if so, how?

The unexplained

Descartes said that the two were entirely different, meeting and interacting somehow through a small gland in the middle of the brain – the pineal gland. Today most people studying this issue disagree with Descartes, arguing that the mind and the brain are one and the same, and there is a lot of evidence to show that the brain does indeed directly generate the mind – and that if you damage the brain the mind also suffers. But we still don't know exactly how the electrical firing of a network of nerve cells translates into a thought, or vice versa.

MIND AND BODY

As far as you are aware, your mind controls only actions that you are conscious of, such as moving your hand or saying a word. After all, you

The brain–mind connection
Descartes expounded the theory that muscular action was a result of the eye relaying an image to the pineal gland, which triggered movement – hence his belief that the mind was located in the pineal gland.

don't start thinking differently, or experiencing an emotion, if your kidneys start to produce more urine, for example, do you?

In fact your mind and your body interact at many levels. Hormones released by your body can affect your brain and in turn your mind, making you angry or excited, sad or relaxed. Meanwhile your mind can affect your body – if you are depressed your immune system functions differently, and just thinking about something can trigger the release of adrenaline or other hormones.

Mind over matter

Normally, bodily processes such as blood flow to the skin or the rate at which your heart beats are not under your conscious control, so your mind has no influence on them. But we are now beginning to understand what Eastern mystics have long known: that with proper training these processes can be consciously controlled. Almost anyone can learn to reduce blood flow to specific areas, speed or slow their heartbeat, or even block out pain.

Highest order
Many unconscious processes are governed by the brainstem, whereas the nerve signals required for movement are generated in the cerebellum. The 'higher' brain functions such as language, logic and awareness of self are processed in the cerebrum.

Cerebrum

Pineal gland

Brainstem

Cerebellum

The pineal gland – one of a kind
Because it was the only structure not duplicated on both sides of the brain, Descartes believed that the pineal gland was the site of mind–brain interaction. Later, New Age thinkers called it the 'Third Eye'. The pineal gland is known to produce melatonin and helps to regulate your sleep–wakefulness cycle.

Every thought, emotion, sensation and movement is under the direct control of the brain, itself a collection of some 100 billion nerve cells.

Mind–brain relations

Using the latest scanning technology, scientists are beginning to discover which parts of the brain seem to be related to which parts of the mind (see pages 18–19).

Mind models

Thinking is a complicated business – on pages 20–21 we look at models of mental processes that seek to explain how it works.

Animal instincts

Part mental, part physical, emotions are created and controlled by the ancient parts of the brain that were the earliest to evolve. See pages 22–23 for more on the limbic system.

Sleepy head

What happens to your mind when you are asleep? What are dreams? Turn to pages 24–25 for some of the answers.

Brain soup

Neurotransmitters, hormones and other substances are constantly sloshing around in your head. How do these chemicals affect your mind – and can your mind affect them? See pages 26–27 to find out.

Mapping the mind

By studying victims of accidents and illness, and more recently through advanced scanning techniques, we have gained exciting insights into how specific areas of the brain are linked to specific mental processes and functions.

THE GREAT JIGSAW PUZZLE

Ordinarily your mind works as a whole – a single unit. For example, when you're listening to someone you're simultaneously processing visual and auditory information about them, understanding their words, and combining this new information with memories and knowledge already in your head. These different components fit together smoothly and seamlessly, so that you experience a single process.

Components and clues

We know from the evidence of medical cases that damage to specific parts of the brain can damage specific parts of this process. If your visual cortex was damaged, for example, you would hear, recognise and understand the person, but not see them. So your experience would be made up of different components. Using evidence from brain-damaged patients and from brain scans relating brain activity to specific tasks, we can now link some mental components to areas of the brain.

It would be misleading to claim too much knowledge, however. Mental processes are almost never entirely confined to one area – indeed some processes, such as memory, seem to be distributed all over the brain. Meanwhile, how the different components of consciousness bind together to give a single experience remains unsolved, as does the biggest mysteries of all: the location of the conscious awareness of self.

Sensation
Every part of the body can be pinpointed on a particular part of the cortex called the sensory strip (coloured purple, above). If that part of your body is touched, the corresponding part of your sensory strip is activated so you become consciously aware of the sensation.

Movement
Next to the sensory strip is its motor equivalent (coloured yellow). Activation of part of this area of the cortex corresponds to movement of the matching part of the body.

Visual information
reaches conscious awareness when the visual cortex at the back of the brain is activated.

Sound and smell have their own areas of the cortex: they are picked up by and processed in the auditory and olfactory areas respectively.

LOBES OF THE BRAIN
Each hemisphere of the cerebrum is divided into four lobes.

The parietal lobe
receives sensory information from the body.

The occipital lobe
receives and processes visual information.

The frontal lobe
is responsible for voluntary movements.

The temporal lobe is where auditory information is processed.

Language abilities
relate to several areas of the cortex, including Broca's area in the lower frontal lobe, and Wernicke's area in the temporal lobe (named after the scientists who discovered them).

THE CEREBRUM

Sensory perception, mental activities and abilities such as memory and intelligence, and voluntary muscle movement are functions of the cerebrum, seen in exploded view below right and left.

The cerebral cortex *is the outer layer of the cerebrum, responsible for all the brain's higher functions. Conscious awareness is mainly generated here.*

The thalamus — *the gateway to the brain — integrates all sensory inputs.*

The amygdala *processes emotional memories.*

THE LIMBIC SYSTEM

Emotions are mainly produced and regulated by the limbic system, although your conscious awareness of them depends on the cortex.

Forward planning, reasoning and other 'higher' mental faculties *such as creativity are mainly localised to the prefrontal cortex, the area immediately behind the forehead.*

The hippocampus *is involved in learning new memories.*

The hypothalamus *links the endocrine and nervous systems.*

The cerebellum *controls the movements of various groups of muscles, to ensure smooth movement.*

THE BRAIN STEM AND CEREBELLUM

Movements, posture, balance and unconscious functions such as heart rate are coordinated here.

The medulla — *part of the brainstem connecting the brain and spinal column.*

How sensations become conscious

All incoming sensory impulses, whether from the outside environment (through your eyes, for example) or from inside the body (such as a hunger message from your stomach), first travel to the thalamus, the 'gateway' to the brain. From here impulses branch out. Some go to lower brain structures where they might trigger unconscious responses, such as speeding up the rate of your breathing. Others go to the cortex, where they produce conscious sensations, so that you become aware of what you are sensing or feeling.

The working mind

What actually goes on in your head to produce a thought? The processes of thinking can be described from several angles: there is the underlying activity of the neurons; there is the way that different areas of the brain become activated by different inputs; and there is the way that corresponding mental components are called into play.

PATTERNS OF NEURONS

The conversion of the electrical activity of neurons (nerve cells) into thoughts and feelings seems to be concerned not so much with the firing of individual neurons as with the pattern of firing of a whole collection of neurons. A useful analogy is to imagine that each neuron is a dancer. When a group of dancers perform an intricate piece, the movements of each individual dancer are important, but not so much in themselves as in how they contribute to the dance as a whole and the overall effect that is produced. The principal dancers in *Swan Lake* could perform on their own, but the effect would be very different from that produced by the whole *corps de ballet*. In a similar way, individual neurons firing on their own produce an effect, but a particular thought equates to the pattern produced by a whole group of neurons firing together.

KEEPING IN STEP

For the group of dancers to perform a dance together, they need to follow an underlying rhythm. Nerve cells are the same. Their electrical activity takes the form of an oscillation between being negatively and positively charged, and they must oscillate in time with one another if they are to create meaningful patterns. This is why your brain generates a characteristic rhythm of electrical activity – the so-called brain waves that speed up or slow down to reflect your level of arousal or consciousness.

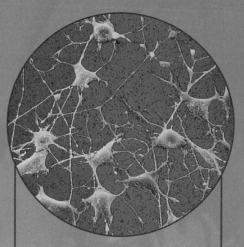

TINY DANCERS

Just as each dancer's movements contribute to the overall effect of the ballet, the firing of individual neurons in the brain contributes to a firing pattern of a group of neurons that equates to a particular mental process or thought. Each neuron has a thick axon which carries impulses away from the neuron. The branching dendrites (above) receive information from other neurons.

Dyslexia, Parkinson's, epilepsy and some mental illnesses may be caused by different parts of the brain being slightly out of step with one another.

Perception and recognition

The branch of psychology known as cognitive psychology explores how the mind works by setting people mental tasks then observing how they tackle them. This evidence is used to build models that describe the mental steps involved in thinking. One of the simplest models describes the process of seeing and recognising an object.

When you look at an object – let's say a chair – nervous impulses from the retina trigger neurons in your visual cortex to fire in a pattern that corresponds to your perception of the visual properties of a chair (it has a back, four legs, and so on). The pattern they create relates to another firing pattern among a group of neurons in the language part of the brain, which corresponds to the word 'chair'. It also links to a memory held in a particular firing pattern of neurons in the cortex which is your knowledge of what a chair is and what it is for – for sitting on. Collectively, these different but linked patterns convert the raw visual input – your eyes seeing a chair – to the conscious awareness that you are looking at a chair.

Perception is multi-faceted but essentially it involves the action and inter-reaction of one or more of the senses on the cortex in the brain.

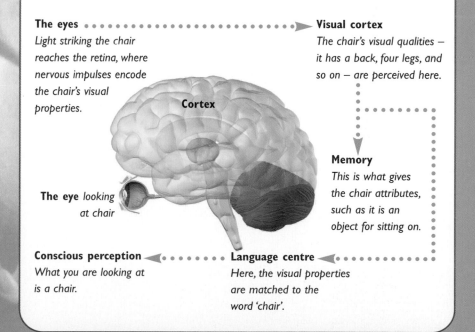

The eyes
Light striking the chair reaches the retina, where nervous impulses encode the chair's visual properties.

Visual cortex
The chair's visual qualities – it has a back, four legs, and so on – are perceived here.

Cortex

The eye *looking at chair*

Memory
This is what gives the chair attributes, such as it is an object for sitting on.

Conscious perception
What you are looking at is a chair.

Language centre
Here, the visual properties are matched to the word 'chair'.

The emotional mind

A human isn't a machine – we have feelings which affect how we operate and think. This partly reflects our evolution as animals, because emotions are produced and controlled by one of the oldest parts of the brain. Human emotions are also shaped by psychology.

RECIPE FOR EMOTION

There are two main factors that combine to produce the subjective experience you know as an emotion – the physical and the psychological.

The physical side of emotion is produced by a combination of neurology in the firing of nerve cells and physiology in the action of neurotransmitters and hormones and the effects that they have on the body. It is these physiological processes that produce what are known as the visceral sensations of emotion – dry mouth, sweaty palms, racing heart, unsettled stomach, and so on.

The psychological aspects of emotion include the effect of context – for instance, a rollercoaster ride produces fear, but because of the context this emotion becomes pleasurable – as well as the influence of 'higher' mental processes such as learning, memory and self-image. These influences are particularly important in more complex emotions, such as guilt or shame.

NEUROPHYSIOLOGY OF EMOTION

Emotions are closely associated with the set of structures deep within the brain, collectively known as the limbic system. Versions of the limbic system can be seen in the brains of creatures such as the crocodile which are ancient in evolutionary terms, proving that it's been around for a very long time. The limbic system is closely connected both to the cortex and to the parts of the brain that produce visceral sensations.

Ready for action

A part of the limbic system called the amygdala makes an initial assessment of incoming information from the senses and triggers the relevant emotion. Depending on this assessment, the limbic system then activates glands in the brain and the nervous system to produce a physiological response, preparing the body for action, such as running away from something scary, for example. Different types of emotion produce different patterns of physiological response.

PSYCHOLOGY OF EMOTION

Experiments show that the physiological signs of emotion can be duplicated using drugs, but this does not produce the subjective experience of emotion. Your mind combines input from knowledge, memory and context to determine what sort of emotion you feel in a situation and how strongly. This processing takes place in the cortex which, if necessary, can override the amygdala. Once the brain has determined the type and strength of emotion, the limbic system signals the temporal lobe in the cortex. Activity here corresponds to the subjective experience of emotion – in other words, to how you feel.

Experience over emotion

If you suddenly came across a person in a dark room you believed empty, this might trigger your amygdala to produce a fear response. It would prompt your heart and breathing to speed up, and glands in your brain to produce adrenaline to get your muscles ready for action. If the person was someone you knew, however, your cortex would use memory to recognise the person and override your amygdala – and the fear would subside.

Evolutionary benefits of emotion

Why do we feel emotions at all? Wouldn't life be simpler without them? Emotions evolved because they help to keep us alive. They probably developed from primitive instincts that make animals run away from predators and try to mate with members of the opposite sex. As we became more intelligent and self-aware, we still needed to be able to react quickly to predators or potential mates. More complex emotions, such as guilt and shame, probably evolved to make us more successful as social animals: people who don't experience such emotions are called sociopaths because they don't adapt to society – and ultimately they suffer for it.

Different roles for left and right

New research shows that it is the left hemisphere of the brain that processes the emotional meaning of language – it decides which emotion is triggered by a statement according to the content of the statement. However, it is the right hemisphere that processes the way things are said – that is, it decides the tone of voice in which a statement is made, which in turn influences the emotion triggered in the listener.

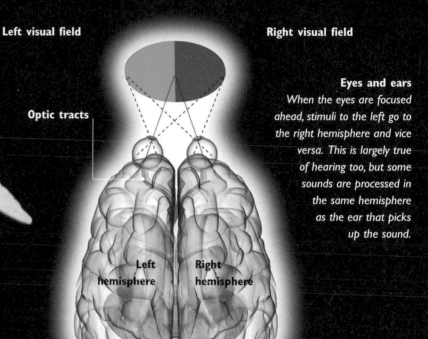

Left visual field

Right visual field

Optic tracts

Eyes and ears
When the eyes are focused ahead, stimuli to the left go to the right hemisphere and vice versa. This is largely true of hearing too, but some sounds are processed in the same hemisphere as the ear that picks up the sound.

Left hemisphere

Right hemisphere

Cerebellum

The importance of context

Experiments strongly suggest that there is an element of context to emotion: if we are expecting to laugh or be sad, our faces tend to adopt a classic expression, making it more likely that we will go on to experience the expected emotion.

The sleeping mind

*Sleep and dreaming are among psychology's most enduring
mysteries, posing questions about the nature of consciousness.
What happens when you go to sleep? If you're not conscious,
are you still really you? And what is the purpose of dreams?*

**You spend the equivalent
of about 120 days asleep
every year – that's about
a third of your life.**

THE ARCHITECTURE OF SLEEP

By monitoring the brain waves and eye movements of
volunteer sleepers, researchers have built up a picture
of how sleep is structured into stages, known as 'sleep
architecture'. When you first fall asleep you enter stage 1 of
non-rapid eye movement (NREM) sleep. This is light sleep,
from which you are easily woken. After around 7 minutes
you drop into stage 2 sleep and over the next 10–25
minutes you reach stage 3 and then stage 4, deep sleep.
During stage 4 sleep most brain activity slows right down
and only the brainstem – the part of the brain that
controls basic functions such as breathing – continues to
operate normally. In other words your 'mind' shuts down,
and you temporarily disappear – at least in terms of your
personality, knowledge, memories and the other things
that truly make you who you are. It can take up to 15
minutes for a person to be fully aroused from deep sleep.

Our sleep needs and quality change over a lifetime,
with babies needing up to 17 hours sleep a day, much
of which is stage 3 or 4, or REM sleep. By the age of 60,
6 hours of shallow sleep a night is the norm.

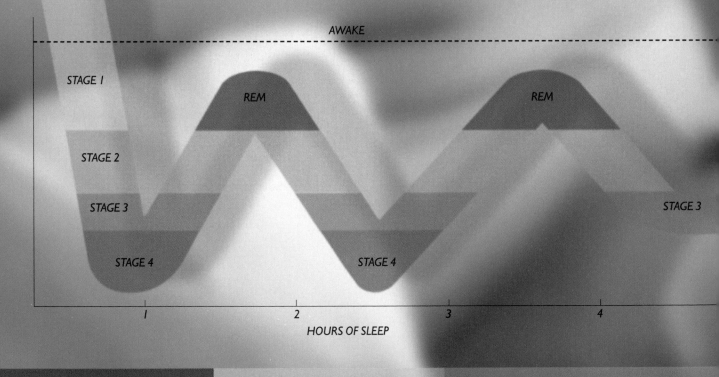

AWAKE

STAGE 1

REM

REM

STAGE 2

STAGE 3

STAGE 3

STAGE 4

STAGE 4

1   2   3   4

HOURS OF SLEEP

SLEEP CYCLE

*Adults generally pass through the five phases
of sleep every 90 minutes or so, although
the time spent in each phase changes over
the course of the night and over the lifespan.
When you first drop off you spend more
time in deep sleep and only a couple of
minutes dreaming in REM sleep, but by the
morning your REM phases may be up to
30 minutes long.*

STAGE 1

Stage 1 NREM
*This stage is only slightly removed from
wakefulness – researchers term it transitional
– and if the phone rings or your baby cries
you are instantly awake again. It lasts only
a few minutes. Brain activity slows and is
characterised by theta brain waves.*

STAGE 2

Stage 2 NREM
*Stage 2 represents the onset of true sleep.
Short bursts – lasting a second or two – of
brain activity known as sleep spindles
interrupt the still slowing brain activity. Brain
waves are still classed as theta waves, but as
this stage progresses these are gradually
replaced by large, slow, delta brain waves.*

Welcome to Dreamland

After a period of deep sleep your brainstem sends out arousal signals and prods your cerebral cortex back into consciousness. Your mind reappears, but not into the waking world. Instead, you are now entering the fifth phase of sleep – rapid eye movement (REM) sleep, when dreams take place. During REM sleep your consciousness is insulated from the information coming in from your senses. Instead it operates within a dream world created inside your brain. Your consciousness is not totally cut off from your senses, however – if a telephone rings, for instance, the sound may be incorporated into your dream.

Sleep paralysis

During REM sleep, your mind is totally cut off from your voluntary muscles (except for the eye muscles), so that you cannot act out your dreams – you may have experienced a feeling of being unable to move if, for example, something scary in a dream makes you try to run away. In some people this paralysis carries over into the waking state, and they find it impossible to move for a few minutes when they wake.

Sleeptalking and sleepwalking occur in stage 4 of non-REM sleep and because this sleep is so deep, sleepwalkers are unlikely to remember the episode.

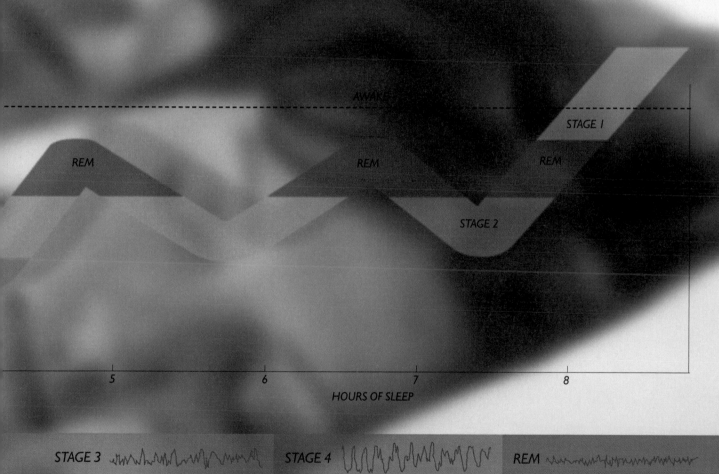

AWAKE

REM   REM   REM

STAGE 1

STAGE 2

5   6   7   8

HOURS OF SLEEP

STAGE 3   *STAGE 4*   *REM*

Stage 3 NREM
Stages 3 and 4 NREM are referred to as slow-wave sleep. When delta brain waves represent 20 per cent of total brain activity, the sleeper has reached stage 3 NREM sleep; stage 4 begins at 50 per cent.

Stage 4 NREM
The night's first episode of stage 4 NREM sleep is likely to last from 20 to 40 minutes during which the sleeper's heart rate, blood pressure and breathing rate are at their lowest. Stages 3 and 4 sleep usually only occur in the first couple of 90-minute sleep cycles each night.

REM sleep
Also called active sleep, REM sleep is associated with heightened brain activity during which dreams occur. Brain waves at this time are small and fast, and the visual and motor neurons in the brain fire as quickly as they do when you are awake. Longer periods of REM sleep towards morning are the norm, regardless of bedtime.

The chemical mind

Nothing makes the link between mind and body clearer than how the body's natural chemicals can influence or alter mood. The nerve cells that generate your mind are constantly bathed in a soup of chemicals, and as the composition of the soup changes, so does the state of mind.

MIND, MOOD AND MOVEMENT

Neurotransmitters are chemicals that carry messages between nerve cells. Since communication between nerve cells is what creates your mind, neurotransmitters are essential to consciousness. Normally the levels of neurotransmitters in different parts of the brain are carefully regulated, but imbalances can arise for a number of reasons – genetic factors, disease, the effects of diet and toxins, and so forth – with consequences for your mind.

- Serotonin This is the main neurotransmitter used for communication by the nerve cells that create and regulate mood; it also influences those that regulate arousal levels. Serotonin levels in the brain can be affected by diet – for instance, eating a high carbohydrate meal can boost levels in the brain, improving mood but reducing arousal levels (that is, making you sleepier). Longer-term serotonin imbalance, which can be an inherited trait or can be brought on by drug abuse, can cause depression. It is commonly treated using anti-depressant drugs, which attempt to restore the serotonin balance.

- Dopamine This is the main neurotransmitter used by nerve cells that control movement. Low dopamine levels caused by Parkinson's disease interfere with the conscious control of movement making it difficult for sufferers to coordinate their movements or move their facial muscles to display emotion. A form of dopamine has been used as a drug treatment for Parkinson's, but its side effects – depression and psychosis – illustrate the wide-ranging effects of neurotransmitters on the mind.

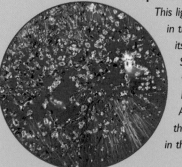

Depression and serotonin

This light micrograph of serotonin in the human brain clearly shows its crystalline structure. Serotonin is a powerful vasoconstrictor and assists in blood clotting and metabolism. An imbalance in its levels in the brain is a major factor in the development of depression.

HORMONAL INFLUENCES

Hormones are chemical messengers that affect cells and organs throughout the body, including the brain and therefore the mind. They can influence everything from your basic drives up to your highest mental functions. Here are a few examples:

 Cholecystokinin *is released in response to the arrival of food in your stomach and affects the hunger-control centres of your brain, which in turn generate the conscious sensation of having satisfied your hunger.*

 Melatonin *is generated by the pineal gland and affects the brainstem, which in turn signals the rest of the brain to wind down its activities, making you sleepy.*

 Testosterone and oxytocin *are sex hormones that increase sexual desire, which in turn affects most aspects of your thinking, from perception to judgement.*

 Oestrogen *is a sex hormone that also helps to regulate higher mental functions like intelligence and memory. For instance, the hippocampus, a brain structure involved in forming memories, is rich in oestrogen receptors. Falling levels during and after the menopause can slightly impair a woman's memory and learning.*

 Adrenaline *gets your body ready for action, while also preparing your mind. It increases concentration, helping you to focus on features of the environment that are important and react more quickly to them.*

Altered states of consciousness

We have all experienced two states of consciousness – ordinary waking consciousness and the consciousness of dreaming during REM sleep – but there are others. Psychoactive drugs, for example, can artificially alter consciousness to change perceptions, thinking, mood, coordination and level of mental arousal.

They do this by interfering with the balance of neurotransmitters or directly altering the patterns of neural activity in the brain. Meditation or dance can be used to reach a different level of consciousness. A general anaesthetic will also dispel consciousness.

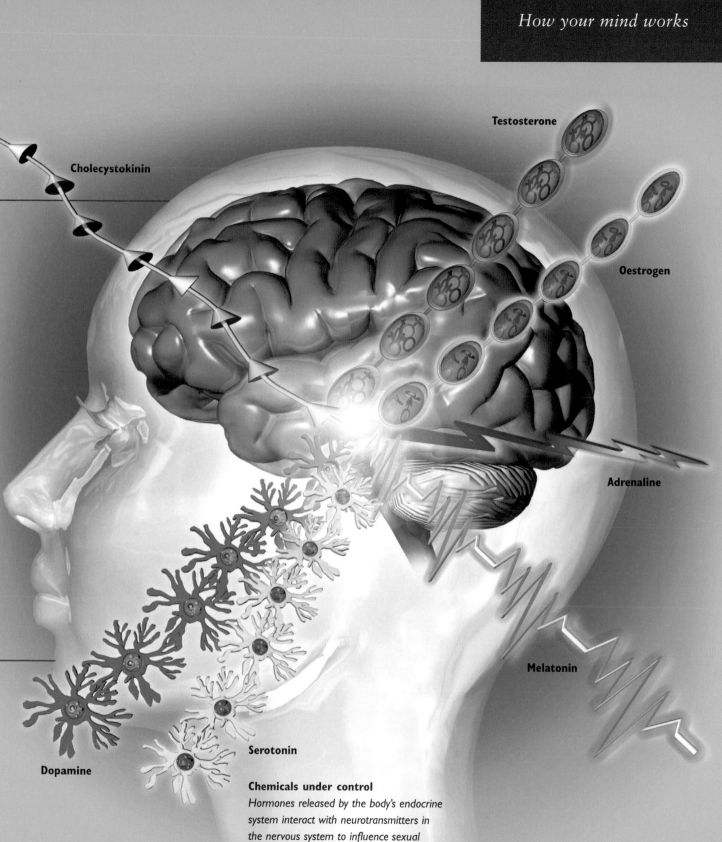

Testosterone

Cholecystokinin

Oestrogen

Adrenaline

Melatonin

Serotonin

Dopamine

Chemicals under control

Hormones released by the body's endocrine system interact with neurotransmitters in the nervous system to influence sexual development and desire, digestion, blood pressure, growth and metabolism, in addition to stress levels and emotions. The nervous system itself can inhibit or stimulate the release of hormones.

Memory and the mind

Memory is a powerful mental tool that has been central to human success and lies at the heart of every individual's personality. It consists of several different systems that work together to help us form, store and retrieve memories.

There are two main memory systems – short (working) and long-term memory. A constant river of information arrives in your brain and is held in a sensory register, where your attention selects only the most important or noticeable bits for consideration in short-term, or working, memory. Information in your working memory can be used immediately or, again depending on its importance or notability, passed on to your long-term memory (LTM). Here it can be stored for later retrieval.

SHORT-TERM WORKING MEMORY

Your working memory has a limited capacity. Taking in new information pushes out old information in a process known as interference. You also lose bits of information over time in a process known as decay.

According to psychologist A.D. Baddeley's model of working memory, it has three parts: the visuo-spatial sketch pad (VSSP), the phonological loop (PL) and the central executive. The PL is used to rehearse information stored in working memory so that it doesn't decay.

LONG-TERM MEMORY

Most of the information that comes into your working memory is only temporarily useful or notable, but some items are consciously or unconsciously processed for longer-term storage. To be stored in LTM, information has to be encoded in some way. The simplest way is rehearsal, but it takes a lot of rehearsal to encode something so that it will last, and so rehearsal is called a shallow encoding method.

For more effective encoding you need to take advantage of the true nature of LTM. LTMs are not stored as discrete packets of information but as complex networks of association. For instance, if you remember meeting a friend at the cinema your association network might include the location, the film, the fact that you were late, what your friend was wearing, your conversation and so on.

Deep encoding involves drawing connections between new information and other memories or knowledge, to build up a denser web of connections. The more strands in your web, the easier it is to retrieve the memory.

In theory, the human brain has the ability to store more memories than there are atoms in the universe. In practice, your short-term working memory can only store seven pieces of information at a time.

Background image
A light micrograph of neurons in the brain. Neurons receive information from many sensory sources, consider it, then fire off a response. Some of this information is immediately discarded, other pieces are stored for later use.

Mnemonics

Mnemonics are devices that improve your ability to retrieve memories by making deep encoding easier. They work by consciously building up the web of connections that make up a memory, and in particular by making connections between the information to be recalled and other information that is easy for you to recall.

A classic mnemonic device is to remember a list of items by associating it with your memory of a well-known route. For instance, you might associate each item on the list with a landmark on your journey to work. Because you are so familiar with your daily commute, it is easy to remember the landmarks, and along with them the items you have associated with them. Other mnemonic devices, include:
- Remembering initial letters (ROYGBIV), or making up a sentence (Richard of York gave battle in vain) – the order of the colours of the rainbow.
- Drawing a mental picture.
- Using rhyme.
- Associating with existing memories.

Information *from the senses or imagination constantly enters the brain.*

You hold the information in a **sensory register,** *while . . .*

. . . you give it your **attention** *and* **filter** *out the most important or noticeable bits for consideration in working memory.*

Memory model
This model of how memory works divides information into that which is for immediate use and that which you decide might be useful later, so encode and send to your long-term memory. Cues or prompts may be necessary to trigger retrieval from long-term memory.

Working memory *of limited capacity (about 7 items) and duration, about 30 seconds.*

Visuo-spatial sketch pad *(VSSP) stores mental images.*

Phonological loop *stores verbal information: numbers, words, or phonemes.*

Central executive *brings the contents of the VSSP and PL to your conscious awareness.*

Attention filter *decides what it will be useful to remember and sends it for . . .*

Encoding *– drawing connections between new information and other memories or knowledge. The web of connections passes into long-term memory.*

Retrieval *happens quickly and with little effort most of the time, with hints or prompts helping to trigger recall. Other times, it takes longer. After struggling all day to remember a name, for example, it may suddenly pop into your head.*

Long-term memory *stores anthing that needs to be remembered for more than 30 seconds. Some long-term memories last a lifetime, others for only an hour or so.*

Implicit memory *includes learned abilities such as riding a bicycle as well as things you don't consciously know – a face you have seen before when you haven't been introduced to the person, for example.*

Explicit memory *includes information you can consciously recall, such as your mother's name or what you had for dinner last night.*

Personality

What makes you, you? What makes you different, but at the same time similar to lots of other people? Your personality is unique, but you share traits with your family, friends and lovers. Where do these aspects of personality come from?

There are more than 20,000 words for describing personality in the English language.

Your personality is your psychological structure, the unique combination of characteristics, patterns of thinking, feeling and behaviour, that makes you who you are. The building blocks of this structure are the same for everyone, but the way they're put together is different for each individual. Personality is one of the most complex and debated areas of psychology, because theories of personality have to explain so much – what the building blocks of personality are, where they come from, how they fit together, how much control we have over them and whether hereditary or environmental factors have the greater influence. Theories abound, but none has yet been developed to explain all the aspects of human personality.

THE FIVE MAIN TRAITS

One of the most important theories of personality is the 'trait theory'. This asserts that, just as you can describe an object in terms of a number of basic dimensions such as height, width, density, colour and so on, so you can describe someone's personality according to a number of basic trait dimensions. A useful analogy can be made with colour. There are many different colours, but they are all part of a single spectrum – they vary along one dimension (wavelength, in the case of colour).

Exhaustive study using questionnaires known as personality inventories has revealed five major personality dimensions, or traits (see below). Obviously there are

THE FIVE MAIN PERSONALITY DIMENSIONS

Agreeableness–antagonism
At one end of this dimension are people who are good-natured, trusting, cooperative, modest and altruistic, while at the other end are people who are selfish, bad-tempered, arrogant, suspicious, demanding, unsympathetic and anti-social.

Conscientiousness–irresponsibility
This dimension ranges from responsible, orderly, hard-working, neat and dependable people on the one hand, to reckless, impulsive, irresponsible and aimless characters at the other extreme.

many more ways of describing personality than this, but almost all the other types of trait you can think of boil down to variations along these five dimensions.

WHERE DOES PERSONALITY COME FROM?

Your personality is the result of a combination of factors. Firstly, your genes and instincts (the products of genetic inheritance and evolution) are responsible for the raw material of your personality. This element of personality is sometimes called 'temperament', and is independent of what happens to you after you are born – in other words, your temperament would be broadly the same wherever and whenever you grew up.

Secondly, your personality reflects the culture and society you come from, the way you were brought up and the influence of your family and friends, and the media. Finally, your own personal experiences and choices, the knowledge you acquire, and the effects of random and unpredictable events in life, influence how your personality is shaped and how it continues to develop.

DO YOU HAVE FREE WILL?

Several theories claim that your personality and therefore your desires, thoughts, feelings, intentions, motivations and so on, are more or less entirely determined by factors outside your control. Although it may seem to you that you decide what to say and do, where to go or how to respond to a situation – in other words, that you have free will – this is, in fact, an illusion because all of these decisions are the product of the interplay of other forces: your upbringing, your training and your genes. You may choose to disagree with this and insist that you do have free will, but the counter argument would be that this is because you were brought up to believe in it, or you have made a conscious choice to do so!

Emotional stability–instability
Sometimes known as neuroticism, this dimension describes how carefree or anxious, relaxed or tense, even-tempered or volatile, hard to upset or unstable someone is.

Extraversion–introversion
This dimension describes how outward or inward looking you are, and covers a huge number of related characteristics – cheerful vs broody, talkative vs taciturn, sociable vs reclusive, assertive vs non-assertive, loud vs quiet, and so on.

Openness–close-mindedness
This dimension refers to how open someone is to new experiences, information and feelings, and how well they deal with ambiguity and shades of grey, as opposed to liking things to be familiar, simple, clear-cut and unchallenging.

31

Intelligence

The defining characteristic of the human mind is its intelligence, which has created the world's great art, literature, music, architecture and technology. Yet there is little agreement over what intelligence is or where we get it from.

WHAT IS INTELLIGENCE?

Intelligence is defined as the ability of an individual to adapt to an environment – in other words, the ability to analyse the environment and work out what to do accordingly. Intelligence is not the same as knowledge, learning or ability, although it can improve the application of all three.

Raw mental power

The competing theories of what constitutes intelligence (see below) are partly based on tests that show that some people are good at some types of questions and other people at other types. But statistical tests show that in fact there seems to be a common factor that applies across all types of intelligence test – in other words, that someone who is good at a verbal test is also more likely to be good at a mathematical test. This common factor has been called G, for 'general intelligence'. G is a measure of someone's raw mental power.

A useful analogy is with rally cars. Different cars might have different characteristics, wheel and tyre types, which mean that some cars do better on dirt tracks while others get better times on snow or ice. The different handling characteristics, tyre types and so on are like a person's abilities with different types of problem – for example, mathematical versus practical problems. One factor that will boost the performance of all the cars, whatever their differences, is a more powerful engine. G is the equivalent of engine power. A person with a higher level of G is more likely to be successful whatever they attempt.

Piecing it together
A construction worker needs both concrete and abstract intelligence, or analytical and creative, depending on the model. Excellent spatial skills are also important.

The good doctor
Doctors need characteristics from all the subsets of intelligence, whatever the model. Certainly they fit the crystallised/fluid model well, acquiring significant amounts of raw data then using it and adding to it over the course of a career.

Types of intelligence

There are several theories of what constitutes intelligence, with many psychologists believing that it breaks down into several subtypes. There are three common current models.

Abstract
Concrete
Social

Analytical
Practical
Creative

Crystallised
Fluid

A theory of three
This asserts that the three elements to intelligence are: abstract – the ability to work with symbols; concrete – the ability to work with objects; and social – the ability to relate to people.

Another threesome
In this model intelligence is made up of analytical, creative and practical intelligence, where practical intelligence is the same as common sense or 'street smart'.

Only two facets
In this theory intelligence is either crystallised, which is a person's acquired knowledge, or fluid, which represents their ability to use this knowledge.

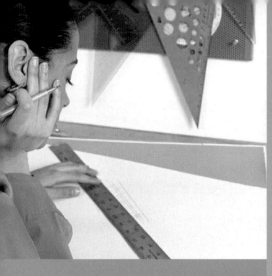

EMOTIONAL INTELLIGENCE

For many years research on intelligence focused on the importance of the G factor, but more recently people have begun to realise that some subtypes of intelligence are at least as important. One of these subtypes is emotional intelligence (EI). A bit like social intelligence, your EI is about your ability to perceive, understand, empathise with, react appropriately to, manage and alter your own and other people's emotions, impulses, feelings and concerns.

People with high levels of EI are more likely to be self-aware, confident, balanced and fulfilled, and are also better at dealing with people. They make good salespeople, managers, team workers and leaders, as well as doing well in caring professions and other 'people jobs'. A few tests of EI have even been devised so that people can measure their 'EQ'.

Figuring it out
According to the first theory (see box, below left) skill in mathematics is due to an individual's abstract intelligence; the second theory roots it in analytical intelligence. A further theory (not shown) has half a dozen subsets, one of which is logical-mathematical intelligence – scientists, surveyors and navigators would all fit into this group.

Teaching and learning
Teachers need high levels of social and emotional intelligence to nurture their students towards their full potential. Linguistic intelligence, a trait that they share with writers and storytellers, is also an asset in this profession.

IQ TESTS

Intelligence is usually measured with tests that give a score called an Intelligence Quotient (IQ), and are therefore known as IQ tests. When the tests were devised, the scoring system was set so that an IQ of 100 was the average score. Although your score on an IQ test is a good indicator of past and future success in life, the tests aren't very good at measuring people's abilities in fine detail – their common sense as opposed to their ability to solve abstract problems.

NORMAL IQ SCORES

Whatever the population, graphs plotting IQ scores follow the same shape: nearly 70 per cent of people score between 85 and 115 and 90 per cent between 70 and 130; only 0.1 per cent of people score less than 55 or more than 145.

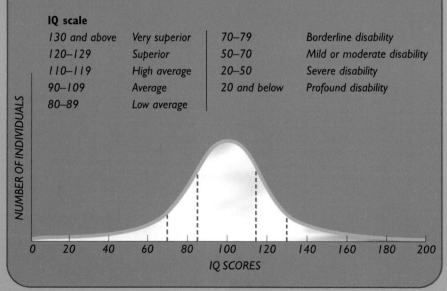

IQ scale

130 and above	Very superior	70–79	Borderline disability
120–129	Superior	50–70	Mild or moderate disability
110–119	High average	20–50	Severe disability
90–109	Average	20 and below	Profound disability
80–89	Low average		

Nature versus nurture

Was your fate mapped out in your genes from the moment you were conceived? Or did you come into the world a blank slate, ready for environment and experience to define every feature of your mind? Are you the product of nature or nurture?

THE ONGOING QUESTION

To what degree are your characteristics and personality the result of your genes or the result of your environment? Did you inherit your intellectual abilities from your parents, or were they determined by your schooling? If a man is aggressive and violent, is it because he carries genes for such behaviour or because he was physically abused as a child? Questions like these are as old as science and remain at the centre of modern research into genetics, behaviour and psychology.

Traditionally there were two schools of thought on the nature–nurture debate. One argued that most of our behaviours and characteristics were innate, the other that almost everything was learned. Not surprisingly, the truth lies somewhere in a complex mixture of the two.

Making your own environment

The picture is complicated because genetics and the environment are not entirely independent of one another. Many environmental factors are subtly influenced by genes, in a process called genetic–environmental covariance.

Take musical ability, for example. To some extent this is determined genetically, and is something that you inherit from your parents. But without training – an environmental influence – you are unlikely to develop this innate ability. There are three ways, however, that your musical genes could influence your environment:

- **Passively** If your parents had musical genes to pass on to you, they are likely to have been musical themselves, and would provide a musical environment at home that would enhance your musical inclinations.
- **Evocatively** Genes can evoke particular responses from people through the characteristics they help to create. So, for instance, because your genes gave you musical talent you might be selected for a musical scholarship.
- **Actively** People seek out environments that fit with their genetically inherited characteristics. Because of your musical inclinations, you might join the school orchestra, making your environment even more musical.

Genes are not enough

Conversely, environment can affect the way a person's genes are expressed. Someone might have inherited the genes to be tall, but through not getting the right nutrition during crucial growth periods end up shorter than their potential. The relative impacts of genetic and environmental influences are impossible to determine separately, because they almost never work independently of one another.

Genes or environment?
A musical child may inherit musical genes from one or both parents, but unless the child is raised in an atmosphere where music is played and appreciated and latent talent encouraged, those genes may not find expression.

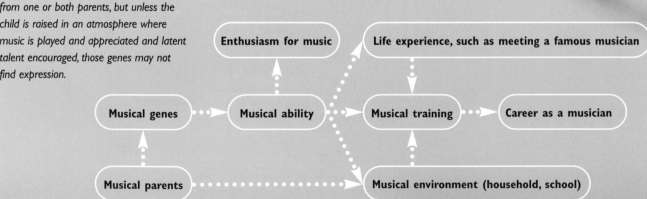

Socialisation helps
Nursery school can be a time when children start to iron out some of the differences in their genetic disposition to language and learning. Social interaction with their peers teaches valuable life skills such as turn taking and negotiation, as well as providing a safe environment in which to start practising creative, spatial and analytical skills.

WHAT DETERMINES HOW INTELLIGENT YOU ARE?

Studies of identical twins separated at birth show that their IQs end up being very similar, which suggests that your IQ is mostly determined by your genes, and therefore inherited from your parents. According to such studies, up to 75 per cent of the variation in people's IQs is the result of genetic influences. Looked at another way, upbringing, environment, schooling and so forth account for between 40 and 25 per cent of the difference between different people's IQs. But since environmental and genetic factors interact, such figures might not give the whole story.

THE LANGUAGE INSTINCT

Apart from simple physical reflex actions, almost none of our behaviour or characteristics seem to be purely instinctive, but some of them depend, nonetheless, on abilities that are 'hard-wired' into our brains. The best example of this is language. Language is something that you learn from other people while you are growing up, but your ability to learn language is hard-wired into your brain. This set of structures in the brain is called the Language Acquisition Device (LAD). During your early childhood, your LAD enables you to pick up any language simply by hearing it and interacting with people who speak it. So although language is learned, your ability to learn it is innate.

Basic instincts
Humans are probably the animals with the fewest instincts. As babies we demonstrate some well-known instinctive behaviours, such as the startle or the rooting reflex, but we lose these as we age. By adulthood only a few instincts remain – we duck if something comes towards us, blink if something touches our eyes and yawn if someone else is yawning.

Governed by the helix?
Your genetic inheritance – present in the DNA that came from your parents – largely determines your potential and the various ways you could turn out. However, your upbringing and environmental influences determine what happens to that potential.

Male and female minds

Men are from Mars and women are from Venus has become a cliché, but is there any truth behind it? What are the real differences between male and female minds, and how much do they owe to biological differences between the genders?

VIVE LA DIFFERENCE!

There are a host of biological, psychological and socio-cultural differences between men and women, but their extent is the subject of much debate.

- **Biological differences** The differences in sex chromosomes in men and women lead to the formation of different sexual organs, body types and levels of sex hormones. Men have slightly larger brains, but certain areas of the female brain contain more nerve cells than the same areas in the male brain. What this might mean in terms of mental functions is not clear.

- **Emotional differences** Women are supposedly more emotionally sensitive and empathetic than men. However, being more 'emotional' is not necessarily the same as being more 'emotionally intelligent'.

- **Intellectual differences** Although, on average, both genders get equal scores on IQ tests, tests that measure more specific mental abilities do seem to show some minor differences between the genders. Women are, on average, better at multi-tasking – more able to cope with several mental tasks at once, such as talking whilst making something with their hands. Men, on average, are better at forming mental

Men's brains are, on average, bigger than women's brains, but only in proportion with their greater overall body size. Brain size is not believed to relate to intelligence.

WHERE DOES MALE GENDER COME FROM?

A host of influences, internal and external, determines our behaviour. The process of internalisation teaches boys – and girls – to behave appropriately for their gender.

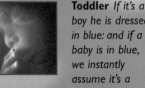

Fetus *Around the 6th week of pregnancy a gene on the Y chromosome activates, causing the formation of testes, the production of testerone and the development of a male body.*

Toddler *If it's a boy he is dressed in blue: and if a baby is in blue, we instantly assume it's a boy. We reinforce stereotypes by buying boys construction sets, cars and trucks.*

Puberty *High testosterone levels make men more 'masculine' in terms of physiology and behaviour. High testosterone levels make young male monkeys 'play rough'; with less testosterone they are more like young females.*

Adult *Models of gender behaviour come from family, friends (for example, the 'don't be such a cissy' school) and the media (more boys want to be like David Beckham than Michael Jackson, for example).*

Background image
A DNA autoradiogram consists of four rows of irregularly spaced bands which represent the positioning of the base pairs of chromosomes on a DNA molecule. This banding makes up an individual's unique genetic code.

representations of space and objects in space, which makes them better at things like map reading and navigation.

- **Socio-cultural differences** Most cultures have well-defined roles that each gender is expected to follow. These are partly the result of physical realities such as pregnancy and childcare which still have a major impact on women's lifestyles.

THE ORIGINS OF GENDER DIFFERENCES

Like any other aspect of the mind, psychological differences between men and women come from two sources. One is biological, the other environmental – in this case, the social and cultural environment.

- **Biological sources** The root difference between the sexes is the presence or absence of a Y chromosome since it a gene on the Y chromosome, known as Sex-determining Region Y (SRY), that prompts the formation of testes. In the absence of the Y chromosome and its SRY, a fetus follows the 'default' body plan, in which ovaries develop.

- **Social and cultural sources** As they grow up, children watch role models to learn how to behave. These models include their parents, friends and the media. Internalisation is the process whereby children absorb these role models and make them part of their personalities. But gender stereotypes may owe a lot to biology. For example, 'it's a woman's job to be maternal' is partly the result of physical realities, such as pregnancy.

WHERE DOES FEMALE GENDER COME FROM?

Female characteristics, like male ones, are a result of an interplay of genetics – the female body plan and hormones – and the influence of family, friends and the media.

Fetus *In the absence of a Y chromosome, ovaries develop and pump out female sex hormones, guiding the development of female body structures.*

Toddler *We can reinforce gender stereotypes as babies grow into children. For example, we still tend to dress girls in pink and give them dolls and teasets.*

Puberty *High oestrogen levels at puberty initiate the menstrual cycle, which in turn determines whether a woman becomes a mother, further defining her role in life.*

Adult *Female gender stereotypes may be partly affected by biology: do more women stay at home to bring up children because working while pregnant or bringing up children can be such hard work?*

A day in the life of the mind

The many influences that have combined to make you who you are find their expression through even the most mundane of day-to-day activities, as you bring into play widely differing mental abilities and attributes to meet the diverse challenges of everyday life.

Over the course of a day your mind goes through many changes – changes in your level of consciousness, changes in mood, changes in state of mind and attention. Throughout the day, however, you maintain a single thread of consciousness, as the many different elements and processes that make up your mind – many of which you are not even aware of – combine to produce a single internal 'narrative'. That narrative is you.

8:30 Drivin' along in your automobile

The rush-hour traffic is bumper to bumper, and in the cars on either side of you the tense faces of the drivers make it easy for you to infer their states of mind, using your 'theory of mind' abilities. Your own reaction to the traffic is determined by your personality – and since you sit at the emotionally stable end of the neuroticism dimension, and don't often have to travel at this time, you are relatively unaffected by the rush-hour stress. You listen to a lively news programme, disagreeing with the opinions of the politician involved. You recall clearly that he said the opposite several months ago because it was the day you were made redundant, and everything about that day is 'chunked' together in your long-term memory.

09:00 Medical matters

Losing your job provoked a major depression, for which your doctor prescribed medication to alter the balance of chemicals in your brain. Although you developed mild insomnia as a result, you persevered and after some weeks started to feel better, and developed a more positive attitude to your future. After some months, the doctor lowered the dosage and, since the depression didn't recur, the dosage continued to reduce until the antidepressants were phased out. At your appointment today, the doctor confirms that you no longer need them at all.

12:00 Teacher training

Your re-evaluation of your life's goals prompted you to pursue an ambition that had been sidetracked – training to become a teacher. After months of reading to get yourself up to speed with your first degree subject, you started college. The lectures are challenging, but you are enjoying the stimulation and you increasingly realise that you are glad to have left your former career behind. Your abilities at reasoning and calculating are at least the equal of your younger fellow students and you find their company invigorating.

23:00 And so to bed

You are so busy these days that you hit the pillow ready to fall asleep and the nights of insomnia seem a world away. Tucked up in bed you gradually begin to shift down through the levels of consciousness to deep sleep. Your brainstem coordinates the shutdown of higher mental functions – you lose awareness of your surroundings as the input from your senses is no longer routed to your conscious mind, your muscles are cut off from conscious control, and the underlying oscillation frequency of your neurons drops to the slow delta wave pattern. As consciousness disappears, so do you, not to reappear again until your mind reactivates and starts dreaming for the first time tonight, about 90 minutes after you first dropped off to sleep.

19:00 Weekend visitors

As luck would have it your brother and his family are visiting for the weekend, and your niece is just the age of the group of students you will face in the classroom on your first school placement which starts on Monday. She is interested in your course materials and you have a lively debate on a subject that she is currently finding difficult. As you explain logically what's involved, it's clear that you have got through to her, and you feel a little more confident about stepping into class next week.

2

Keeping your mind healthy

A LIFETIME OF MENTAL HEALTH

Our minds shape everything we do, and everything that happens to us has an impact on the mind. The success of our relationship to the world around us, over the course of a lifetime, is key to mental health and happiness.

 43 *Understanding the potential threats to the mind at various life stages is a good first step toward keeping it healthy.*

 46 *Through studies of the brain when engaged in various activities, scientists are getting closer to understanding how an individual's mind works.*

 48 *Humans are emotional beings: understanding your emotions and empathising with those of others helps to ensure everyone's needs are met.*

 50 *Parents have an enormous influence on their children's emotional wellbeing, as each child's individual personality gradually unfolds.*

 53 *Strategies to preserve mental ability and agility can help to prevent skills declining through infrequent use and increasing age.*

The healthy mind

Mental health is not static: there are no precise definitions of what constitutes good mental health and individuals' mental states have to be seen in the context of the society in which they live and work. Age too plays a part in mental health.

What constitutes mental health during the adult years? A widely used standard of mental health is the 'absence' of a defined mental disorder. Although this standard has its limitations, it remains useful as a starting point. Among its limitations, this definition excludes adults with mental disorders who function well in between episodes of illness. These people often consider themselves to be 'mentally healthy' in spite of a history of mental problems and the risk of recurrence.

Defining mental health by the absence of mental disorder does not convey a full picture of mental 'health'. An assortment of positive personal traits or characteristics have been seen to contribute to a healthy mental state: self-esteem, optimism and resilience. These and related traits are seen as important sources of personal strength, which people need to weather the storms of stressful life events.

Mental health and mental illness are not polar opposites, but may be thought of as points on a continuum.

CHANGING DEFINITIONS

Definitions of mental health are dictated by social norms and as such have changed throughout history. It was only in the 1970s that homosexuality, for example, was no longer recognised as a disease in the major Western classifications of psychiatric disorder.

The current British mental health legislation for compulsory hospital detention specifically excludes sexual orientation, as well as alcohol and drug problems and most categories of learning disability and personality disorder, but this is a legal framework that is subject to change. It would be possible to draw up mental health legislation that defines 'mental disorder' in such a way that it covers almost anyone!

Stigma

Stigmatisation of people with mental disorders has persisted throughout history. Today, perceptions of those with mental illness vary with diagnosis: the public is more likely to think of schizophrenia as a mental illness than depression, for example.

All this is quite apart from the controversy that psychiatric diagnoses have often courted. The anti-psychiatry movement of the late 1950s and 1960s, proposed that there was no such thing as mental illness, and people's problems were being defined medically as a means of social control. We now know much more about mental illnesses, and their biological reality is on a much firmer footing.

A world apart
Cultural values and norms play an enormous part in our evaluation of mental health. What may be normal, say, for a London teenager, may be very far from normal for a middle-aged Japanese businessman.

A HEALTHY PERSONALITY

Mental health and mental illness are dynamic, ever-changing phenomena. At any given moment, a person's mental status reflects the sum total of that individual's genetic inheritance and life experiences. The brain interacts and responds continuously – both in function and in its very structure – to multiple influences, across every stage of life.

Mental health and mental illness are also the products of various personality traits and behaviour patterns. These underpin an individual's ability to handle psychological and social adversity, and stressful life events. Such traits are thought to have either positive or negative effects on mental health during adulthood. They include:

- **Self-esteem** This refers to a set of beliefs about your own worth, competence, and abilities to relate to others. It is defined as having the confidence to cope with problems, either independently or by obtaining help from others.
- **Neuroticism** This refers to psychological and emotional responses that focus on the dangerous, harmful or defeating aspects of a situation.
- **Avoidance** This describes the predisposition to withdraw from new situations and to avoid personal challenges.
- **Impulsivity** This is associated with poor control of emotions, especially anger, novelty seeking and difficulty delaying gratification.
- **Sociopathy** This refers to dishonest, hurtful, unfaithful or dangerous conduct for personal gain. It is described as antisocial, and often characerised by a tendency to break laws and rules.

CULTURAL NORMS

The various traits and behavioural patterns that epitomise mental health do not, of course, exist in a vacuum: they develop in a social context. This gives a clue as to how we can approach the idea of normality or health. It is that which is considered normal or healthy in a particular social or cultural group. In other words, if your ideas and feelings are socially and culturally congruent, you can be said to be normal or healthy. There is no absolute normality or absolute health – both are defined in terms of their context. Having said that, it is possible to recognise desirable characteristics that can promote a sense of happiness or wellbeing more often than not, within the correct cultural and social context.

48 per cent of adults will suffer from a mental health problem at some time in their lives.

ACROSS THE LIFESPAN

Psychiatric disorders occur at different times in the lifespan. No-one really knows the reason for this, or indeed any of the age-related timings of mental illness. It may be that pre-existing vulnerability can show itself at different stages of our development. It is also the case that many stressful life events occur during adulthood – such as divorce, economic hardship, work overload – which can trigger mental problems.

Severe or repeated trauma in childhood may have long-lasting effects on psychological development, affecting adult behaviour patterns and response to stress. Perhaps the most widely documented evidence of such enduring effects has been shown in young adults who experienced severe sexual or physical abuse in childhood. These individuals experience a greatly increased risk of mental health problems thoughout their adult life.

The development of schizophrenia may stem from a vulnerability caused by brain injury at or around birth, or it may be part of a family condition. It is unusual, however, for a child to develop the symptoms of a serious mental illness such as schizophrenia, which peaks during the late teens and early 20s in men, and in the mid to late 20s in women.

Anxiety disorders are the most common mental disorders in adults, affecting twice as many women as men – although increasingly children are being diagnosed with anxiety disorders. Mood disorders such as depression and bipolar disorder, on the other hand, tend to occur generally later in life, from the age of 30 onwards, peaking perhaps during the 40s and 50s. For example, almost half the women who become depressed during their lives do so at around the time of menopause.

Finally, there are conditions that are more associated with later life. Dementia is perhaps the best known example. The majority of people who develop Alzheimer's and other forms of dementia do so after the age of about 70. Again, although dementia is not rare, we do not know precisely how common it is in the community, since there are many stages of dementia. Many symptoms are atrributed to normal ageing; minor symptoms of loss of memory are very common and usually benign.

LIFE'S POTENTIAL MAJOR STRESS POINTS

There are some key stressors over the course of a lifetime that can impact on mental health. Being aware of potential dangers can help to prevent them.

SCHOOLCHILDREN

A recent study carried out by City University, London, found stress among the young to be 'worryingly high'. Bullying is one of the most common problems among children – more than 20,000 called ChildLine about bullying between April 2000 and March 2001, far more than for any other issue.

STUDENTS

Exams are a big worry for most young people. Between April 2000 and March 2001 ChildLine spoke to nearly 1000 schoolchildren and students: most felt panic-stricken, overburdened and over-whelmed, as if their whole life was in the balance. It is important that students are given help to cope with the pressures, to prevent illness or serious depression.

ADULTS

A survey in 2000 revealed that 44 per cent of people in the UK found moving house to be their most stressful life event. There are many pitfalls: fear of a sale falling through can stretch buyers' price limits, while sellers may drop prices to prevent sale collapse. Anxiety over surveys, contracts and the move itself are also stressful.

IN MIDDLE-AGE

Depression is twice as common in women as it is in men. This may be linked to low oestrogen levels, which could explain the increased risk of depression during the menopause.

SENIORS

Some people experience depression for the first time quite late in life. Retirement can cause feelings of grief or loss of purpose, before readjustment takes place.

Understanding your mind

All mind processes are brain processes, but although we know a great deal about how the cells in the brain work, we are far less clear on how these basic processes give rise to thoughts and consciousness.

WATCHING THE BRAIN IN ACTION

Modern techniques for imaging the brain involve tracking the process of chemicals and blood flow in different regions of the brain. This has allowed us to watch the brain as it performs activities: we can watch the brain's reaction to music, speech, patterns, memories and touch. We can watch the brain experiencing pleasure. We can even examine the brain experiencing hallucinations. Imaging techniques can also distinguish between a 'normal' brain and the brain of someone with mental problems.

Imaging techniques rely on computers which produce stunning pictures. It is easy to be convinced that we are seeing the mind itself in action. However, these images are really computer-generated statistical representations of hundreds of thousands, even millions, of tiny points of data that are recorded indirectly from the working brain. We are, in essence, seeing a depiction of what may be going on, but are not necessarily witnessing 'reality'.

THE RATIONAL MIND

For centuries man has questioned the nature of the mind and how we acquire knowledge. Ancient thinkers believed that human knowledge came into the mind as divine revelation – a gift of insight from God. Gradually philosophers concluded that the brain itself was the seat of the 'rational' mind. In the 19th century, a new era of philosophical thinking – now known as the Enlightenment – swept away older spiritual views of the mind in favour of 'reason'. Coinciding with the coming of the Industrial Revolution, this fostered a more 'scientific' and mechanical view of the brain and mind.

One of the most serious and influential approaches to the mind was made in the work of Sigmund Freud (1856–1939). His ideas of the workings of the mind were derived from the mechanical principles that were current at the time. However, his ideas of the conscious and unconscious mind, together with the components of ego (self), id (animal) and super-ego (conscience) proved an almost incalculable influence, to the extent that the notions have become part of everyday life. But as with many everyday notions, they throw up problems under analysis. It is not easy, for example, to decide exactly what we mean by the term 'unconscious'. In addition, it is not easy to interpret Freud.

More recent psychoanalysis has focussed on how our sense of self is constructed by our interactions – with others and the environment.

MEASURING THE MIND

Most people enjoy doing the personality questionnaires that are published in magazines or on the Internet. Such questionnaires can 'examine' your attitudes towards your partner, your emotional intelligence, your assertiveness, your willingness to be part of a team, your spirituality and so on.

Brain waves change frequency during the different stages of sleep.

Exercise creates the same brain waves as meditation or chanting.

The brain at rest and play
During different activities our brains produce electrical waves of varying frequencies. High frequency beta waves are linked to day-to-day alertness, while low frequency alpha waves are linked to relaxation. Theta waves are very low frequency and are connected with imaginative imagery.

Most of these questionnaires are harmless enough, as long as they are not taken too seriously. We are not 'fixed' in space or time, and we are constantly changing. This is one of the reasons that no single system of analysis is able to capture your unique individuality. Each system can give potentially interesting insights only if it is treated lightly. At their very best they can supply information that confirms what you probably already know about yourself. It is unlikely that they will reveal something particularly new. However, the benefit of having different ways of looking at yourself is that you can begin to identify certain traits and characteristics that you may not have been aware of, or that you have not wanted to acknowledge. This can help some people to understand and appreciate themselves as a 'whole' individual.

Questionnaires can play an important part, more formally, in psychiatric or psychological evaluation, but only in a supporting role. They are not used as a diagnostic tool.

PERSONALITY: STRENGTHS AND WEAKNESSES

Personality is viewed as a many faceted aspect of the self, and is the way in which the self interacts with the world. There are many tests and methods available for discovering your personality type. Among these measurements of personality, none is sufficiently comprehensive to supplant all the others.

One model views personality as a mixture of temperament and character. Temperament is what we are born with, and involves functions such as dependence on reward, avoidance of harm and the seeking of novelty. These behaviours are loosely related to major chemical systems within the brain, such as dopamine for reward dependence, scrotonin for seeking novelty and noradrenaline for avoiding harm.

Character facets include the ability to co-operate, levels of persistence, self-transcendence and self-determination. They are learned during childhood and adolescence and are expressions of how we are able to interact with others, to

commit to a task and to see ourselves in the wider context of society and the world.

Other models of personality which highlight particular personality strengths and weaknesses have found popularity in industry and self-help settings. These can be useful in evaluating suitability for careers but, again, they should be placed in the appropriate context. The result of a personality questionnaire cannot give a full picture of an individual.

PERSONALITY DISORDERS

The personality is composed of a whole range of traits that adapt the individual to the environment. For example, if we show no sense of suspiciousness, we could fall into traps, either set by others or in the environment. In a social context we should have the ability to sustain a conversation – to involve and interest another person.

If an individual trait becomes so magnified as to dominate the picture, then it is possible to talk about a disorder. Personality disorders are the exaggerations of personality traits that in their correct proportion are normal. For example, most people would accept that imagination is good. People with a highly developed imagination can be very creative as writers, artists and scientists. If, however, their imaginary world becomes more important to them than their real world and relationships, if they become isolated, suspicious and entirely incorporated into their own world, then this highly developed imagination tips over into the realms of a personality disorder, in this case perhaps a schizoid personality disorder.

Music frequencies can mimic brain waves, and activate the whole brain.

Positive emotions such as love generate low frequency brain waves.

Understanding your emotions

Human beings think emotionally: 'feeling' is our predominant state of mind. Having a high emotional intelligence, being secure in your sense of self, and understanding the feelings of others can be a key factor in long-term mental health.

Emotion relates to a pattern of feelings we experience when faced with a particular object, situation or person. It also relates to the outward expression of those feelings.

Human beings do not primarily experience the world and other people in terms of abstract ideas, but through their feelings. Emotions can be said to be the way a person assesses the significance of external stimuli, so as to prepare the body for an appropriate reponse.

Emotions are often experienced as bodily sensations. We are all aware of our bodily responses to anger, fear or happiness. These are often involuntary – for example, it can be difficult to experience fear without feeling butterflies in the stomach.

COMMUNICATION

Our emotions are among the most potent means by which we can convey what we are feeling. Humans have two means of communicating emotion; through facial movements and speech. There are thought to be six basic facial expressions: anger, happiness, fear, suprise, disgust, and sadness. These are recognised across cultures with a high degree of reliability. Our facial expressions can also convey a wide range of subtle emotions, such as irritability.

When using speech to convey our emotions, if we are verbally skilled and confident expressing our feelings we will be able to express more of our emotional needs, and have a better chance of fulfilling them.

UNDERSTANDING OTHERS

When we feel uncomfortable with a person's behaviour, our emotions alert us. If we learn to trust our emotions and feel confident in expressing ourselves, we can let the person know we feel uncomfortable as soon as we are aware of our feeling. This will help to set boundaries which are necessary to protect physical and mental health.

If emotions like love, anger and fear were just bodily functions comparable to hunger and thirst, it would be unreasonable to judge whether someone's emotional response is justified, and whether we blame them or praise them for their emotions. It seems that one of the main reasons why emotions are important is that we consider people's emotions as a reflection of their character.

EMOTIONAL NEEDS

All humans have basic emotional needs. These needs can be expressed as feelings, for example, all people need to feel:
• secure and unafraid;
• effective and competent;
• accepted and respected by parents and significant others;
• a sense of worth and feeling 'ok'.
While all humans share these needs, each differs in the strength of the need. When these needs go unmet, however, people become frustrated. This is especially true for children, who act out their frustration in various ways which are typically seen

I know how you feel
Children learn in the preschool years that they are not the only people who feel happy or sad, and can sympathise with their friends in bad times and share their joy in good times.

as misbehaviour. The better we can identify their needs and satisfy them, the fewer the behavioural problems.

EMOTIONAL INTELLIGENCE

In order to interact efficiently with people we must not only be able to work out what they are thinking or what their emotions are, but, fundamentally, must know the same about ourselves. Some people are not able to put their feelings into words. Either they do not recognise them or cannot describe how they feel.

From early childhood, we learn how to understand the feelings of others. We learn to use empathy, which is an ability to identify with someone else's feelings (to put yourself in their place), and so understand what they must be going through. Sympathy is when we feel their emotions as well. As we grow older, the action of sympathy is modified so that we do not necessarily feel the emotions of another person, but can, for instance, feel pity for them. Compassion consists neither of empathy nor sympathy, but is a recognition of someone else's emotion or struggle and a sense of solidarity with it.

Someone who is able to empathise, sympathise and feel compassion, and verbalise feelings accurately and with integrity, is someone who has a high emotional intelligence. Such a person need not be intellectual or academic.

To begin with, there is no validated, reproducible measure of emotional intelligence. It is possible, however, to examine your responses to questions such as those in the box. This may allow a person to identify particular gaps or shortcomings in their interactions – maybe they need to listen more, or be more tactful.

TEST YOUR EQ

Choose your reactions to the following situations, to monitor your EQ.

You are job hunting and have applied for several but have not even been shortlisted. The newspaper with job vacancies arrives. Do you:
a] Consider another line of work.
b] Put the paper on one side and see how you feel tomorrow.
c] Revisit your CV to try to identify why you have not been shortlisted.
d] Look for appropriate vacancies that interest you, and keep trying.
Answer: d shows a positive outlook.

You are running late for an appointment, the traffic is heavy and you are still many miles away. Your car engine suddenly stops and you cannot restart it. Do you:
a] Panic and, though you know nothing about it, stare at the engine trying to see what might be wrong.
b] Call a breakdown organisation, ask for speedy assistance, and settle down to wait.
c] Ask some passersby to help you move your car to a safer position, then make your way on foot.
d] Call the people you are meeting and tell them that you cannot come because your mother is ill.
Answer: b shows pragmatism.

You are drinking with a friend when someone accidentally jostles him and spills his drink. Your friend leaps up with his fists clenched. Do you:
a] Hold him in his seat, it's no big deal – you can get another drink.
b] Try to resume your conversation from before the incident took place.
c] Join him and get ready to fight.

d] Tell him that you get annoyed when it happens, but you have done it yourself and it was an accident.
Answer: d shows even-handedness.

You are arguing with your teenage child who shouts some deeply wounding remarks. Do you:
a] Throw your child out.
b] Ask your child to apologise.
c] Walk away.
d] Take a break for half an hour then resume the discussion.
Answer: d, because you both need time for the anger to subside.

You are at a party with colleagues whom you know slightly. They know each other well and you feel left out. Do you:
a] Make for the drinks counter and stay there for as long as possible.
b] Stand, hoping that someone will come up and make conversation.
c] Go home.
d] Circulate the room and join in the conversation as well.
Answer: d shows maturity.

You are in charge of organising a meeting, but forget to book a room. Everybody turns up, but the meeting room is in use. Do you:
a] Try to pretend that it was the group using the room who made the mistake about the booking.
b] Admit that you forgot to book the room and find another venue.
c] Panic and run away.
d] Ask each member of the meeting, personally, for forgiveness.
Answer: b, we all make mistakes.

Getting a good start

One of the greatest gifts parents can offer their children is a stable, affectionate and secure base from which to learn about the world and their place in it. The value of a loving childhood to adult mental health can be enormous.

An expectant mother is in a position to give her baby the very best start in life. One of the best ways to achieve this is through a healthy lifestyle. The link between smoking, drinking alcohol or taking drugs, and problems with a baby's growth and development in the womb has been well established. The most obvious result of this is low birth weight. Evidence suggests that babies with low birth weight are at higher risk of problems later on.

Although this may be true of the population as a whole, it does not necessarily apply in individual cases. Many children who have gone on to achieve great things intellectually and in other areas, have been of low birth weight, born to mothers who smoked, drank or both and were older than 35. For an individual, it is not possible to predict the outcome. Nevertheless, given the findings in the population overall, the best advice to a mother-to-be is not to smoke or drink alcohol.

In order to give their babies every possible advantage, expectant mothers are also advised to eat a balanced diet and to take vitamin supplements; in particular vitamin B_{12} and folic acid which are important for the developing brain of the fetus.

PARENTING

There can be few life experiences more fraught with difficulty and anxiety than being a parent. Everyone has an opinion on how it should be done. Parents are often blamed, and more often blame themselves, if things turn out wrongly or badly for a child.

There is a sense of what can constitute bad parenting. Inconsistency of approach, rejection, physical and verbal abuse, and inattention to basic physical needs are all potentially detrimental to the baby. But there are babies who have withstood some or all of these things to develop well and successfully.

It is far less easy to define what constitutes 'good' parenting. Perhaps the psychiatrist and therapist Donald Winnicott, took the best view of this when he introduced the concept of

New sensations
At birth babies can hear high-pitched noises, and may be calmed by lower tones. They can locate sounds in front of them. By 20 weeks babies begin to recognise familiar voices.

the 'good enough parent'. He saw parents as supplying a spectrum of abilities and skills to their task and suggested that there was a wide range of what was 'good enough' to foster the development of the child. In other words, the parent needs to be 'good enough' to get the child off to a good start.

The most important things in child care are love, consistency, a tension-free home, showing by example, sensible expectations and confident parents. It is all too easy to believe that child care is a complex science, when in fact it's completely natural.

Babyhood and bonding

Attachment theory is one of the most popular ways of examining a baby's development. The theory was designed to explain bonding, the process by which young animals become attached to their parents through physical touch.

Maternal deprivation – a lack of physical affection and nurturing – can lead to significant behavioural problems in adulthood, including poor parent–child relationships, however the need for 'mothering' is probably less gender specific than originally believed. What seems to matter most is that a baby has an affectionate nurturing environment in which to grow and learn.

During babyhood, the brain adapts and assimilates new information at a greater volume and speed than at any other time in their lives. The environment represents a constant stimulation, and although this can sometime be overwhelming, it is important to maintain the stimuli.

To a newborn baby, objects flit in and out of existence when he or she needs them. For example, a breast or

---

UNDER-10s

Can a child be too young to read?

In 1955 an organisation was started in the USA which became the Institute for the Achievement of Human Potential. Their research suggested that very young children should be taught to read, in order to release their 'genius' potential. Today, such extreme approaches to child development are not advised. Young children should not be forced into reading too early; this can have a detrimental effect on the child. Reading should be seen as an enjoyable activity, not a task. One of the main ways in which you can encourage children to read is by sharing books and reading aloud to them. They will learn to talk about the story and the pictures, join in the parts they know, and eventually recognise the words on the page.

There is no age too early to start reading 'to' your child: reading is a skill we acquire in a social context. If your child is late starting reading, remember, each child learns at a different pace and you can't hurry them. However once a child is ready to learn, nothing can hold them back!

---

bottle 'miraculously' appears, and as far as the baby is concerned, is created in response to hunger.

By about 18 months, babies can understand that not only do objects exist outside of them, but that objects exist all the time and that they do not depend on the baby to be produced. This is a critical stage in the development of mind. It has been suggested that up until this time a baby's life is a 'looking glass life', where nothing makes sense because there is no sense.

Intelligence – and there are many controversial differences in what 'intelligence' is – does not seem to be something which is fixed for life when you are born. The child whose

developmental milestones, including learning, are persistently delayed, is unlikely ever to shine academically. But it is also true that a child who is developmentally advanced but who receives little or no stimulation is equally unlikely to shine. The majority of children, by definition, are neither greatly advanced nor greatly delayed, and it is for them that the influence of the environment can be greatest.

Interested parents who spend time with their babies, nurturing, playing and providing stimulation are more likely to produce children who will reach their full potential, regardless of 'baseline' intelligence. An unstimulated baby may not shine.

TODDLERS AND PRE-SCHOOL CHILDREN

A child is learning all the time. One of the largest and most complex tasks is to learn language, but children do it very successfully, almost effortlessly. Apart from intellectual skills, toddlers and pre-school children develop social skills at this stage of life.

Toddlers need to learn how to interact with others, how to be sensitive to their feelings and needs, and how to share things. Going to playgroups or nurseries can be of significant help in socialisation. Acquiring social skills can be more important than academic skills during these years. It can take a long time to catch up on unlearned social skills, but intellectual skills are rather easier to develop.

EARLY SCHOOL YEARS

In the early school years, learning and socialisation continue apace. A child who is able to learn well has increased confidence, which will help further learning. Although there is no place for a high pressure learning environment, parents can do a great deal to help a child with reading and numeracy. Playing simple counting games, and spending time with books and reading and talking about stories are all helpful.

In the case of reading, the goal is not simply to achieve the ability to decode words, but also to understand the meaning of language. The pictures in children's reading books are as important as the text.

SCHOOL CHILDREN

Childhood is marked by dramatic changes in physical, mental, and social-emotional skills and capacities.

As children grow, their abilities to form close relationships become highly dependent on their social skills. These include the ability to interpret and understand other children's non-verbal cues such as body language and voice pitch.

Children whose social skills develop well use eye contact, often mention the other child's name, and may use touch to get attention. In contrast, children who lack such skills tend to be rejected by other children. They are often withdrawn, do not listen well and find it difficult to join in group activities. They may exhibit conduct disorder, such as fighting, dominating, or being spiteful. Social skills improve with opportunities to mix with others.

DEVELOPMENTAL PROBLEMS IN TEENAGERS

The developmental tasks of adolescence are identity formation and separation from the family. Adolescents start to look outside the family for role models and possible identities and try them out.

A shoulder to cry on
Adolescence can be a time of anxiety and emotional turmoil. Parents can support their teenager through difficult periods with love, security, consistency and continuity of care.

Adolescence is also the time when any anxieties left over from the toddler stage may resurface. Adolescence is the period during which we learn that we can be safe in the world without the need for constant protection.

In relation to developmental problems, it is important to assess whether any anxieties an adolescent is expressing are developmental or traumatic, because a large part of normal adolescent behaviour is about limit testing, defying authority figures and exploring sexuality; aggressive impulses are normal. However, in a traumatised adolescent, acting up can be a defence against anxiety – a cry for help. About one in five teenagers pass through a prolonged phase of emotional difficulties in which anxiety and depression are common.

Maintaining mental fitness

Like any instrument or skill, the unused mind will lose its powers. Throughout our lifetime we should endeavour to surround ourselves with a rich amount of stimuli to maintain our mental health – variety and challenge are rejuvenating.

USING YOUR MIND

Over the past 25 years major studies on ageing have found that mental decline is not inevitable as we get older: some dementias are avoidable. So why do many elderly people experience mental decline as they age?

The same advice that we follow to achieve physical fitness, applies to mental fitness: 'use it or lose it'. Just as you build muscular strength by physical exercise, your brain is strengthened through mental exercise. The decline in mental abilities, such as memory loss, sluggish thinking, and blocks in problem-solving are not inevitable if the brain remains challenged.

DIFFERENCES IN THINKING

Although we start to lose brain cells from our mid-twenties onwards, the vast majority are still in place and working as well as they ever did when we are in our eighties and nineties. However, at that age we may be slower physically. Reaction times and reflexes will almost certainly have started to slow.

Older people think differently in many respects. They take longer to arrive at a judgement. It is usually a more balanced judgement, based on a wider examination of data than a younger person possesses. This has been examined in many studies and, in the past it was known as wisdom.

LIFELONG LEARNING

If you live in front of the television, you are not using your brain. Instead you need to consistently challenge your brain so it will age healthfully.

Regular intellectual exercise has been shown to provide a strong antidote to Alzheimer's and other forms of senile dementia. If you start long before you reach old age its onset perhaps may be prevented. Scientists recommend brain exercises from the age of 30 onwards as a way of building lifelong mental health.

Researchers have found that studying and spending a long time in education can also protect people from the worst effects of Alzheimer's in old age. This capacity for learning persists throughout life, many older people take up classes in subjects in which they have had no previous academic training. Passion and interest also keep the brain fit.

Challenge and newness

A vital component of brain health is challenge. In terms of successful ageing it is not enough to continue the same activities, year after year. The brain needs new challenges if it is to remain a healthy, functioning organ. The brain at first responds to a new challenge, but decreases its growth when the newness wears off. If you have been working on the same kind of crossword puzzles year after year, try advancing to more complicated puzzles or introduce a game that will challenge different skills that are lying dormant.

Mind games
Throughout life we need to keep our minds active. It has been shown that exercising our mental skills and maintaining a stimulating environment reduces the effects of ageing.

Use it or lose it

Regularly taking part in activities which require high levels of mental activity will help to maintain cognitive functioning in later life. To create a mentally fit lifestyle it is important, especially when you are older, to add interest to your daily routine, and to use your brain actively throughout the day.

1 Games

Playing bridge or chess stimulates the brain enormously. Bridge players must use working memory, show intitiative, sort cards and keep many items in sequence, while chess players plan ahead and use logic and strategy. These mental challenges involve the brain's frontal lobe — studies have shown that this also stimulates the production of white blood cells, thereby improving the immune system.

2 Hobbies

Hobbies can be a lifeline of mental fitness and almost any hobby will do. The important thing is that you enjoy it and that it interests you. Ideally, there should be a mental component. For example, collecting stamps for the sake of filling pages in your album presumably has little mental benefit. But collecting stamps with a theme, or doing some research about the stamp or the scene that it depicts will be mentally stimulating.

3 Hand–eye coordination

Hobbies like bowls, which help to maintain hand-and-eye coordination, are excellent for brain health. Studies have even shown bingo to keep the mind agile. In tests for memory and mental speed, bingo players were faster and more accurate than non-players, due to their ability to check numbers quickly and their rapid hand-eye coordination.

5 Gardening

Many purely physical activities fail to reduce the risk of mental decline, but gardening — which involves both mental and physical effort — has been found to be very beneficial.

4 Exercise and movement

Exercise brings oxygen to the brain. As we age it is important to get oxygen to the hippocampus: this part of the brain deals with recent memory and visual spatial processing. Dancing is the physical activity that requires the most mental effort, and recent studies have shown its dramatic effect in preventing mental degeneration.

54

10 Learning
Learning a foreign language is perhaps one of the more radical forms of intellectual stimulation. But it doesn't matter what you decide to do, as long as it's something that excites you, engages your interest and challenges your intellect.

9 Word games
Games that involve word play, such as Scrabble, are great for the brain. You could try making up your own word games, such as taking a sentence from a magazine or newspaper, and constructing another sentence using the same words. Or whenever you meet someone, come up with at least two words beginning with the same letter as their name. You could also try learning five new words every day, and using the words in a sentence.

Elderly people who engage in pursuits such as dancing or playing chess are 75 per cent less likely to develop Alzheimer's.

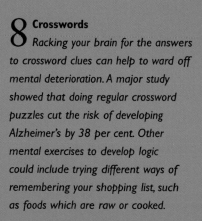

6 Reading
Reading a book develops many thought processes and helps to stimulate the imagination. As additional mental exercise to stretch your verbal abilities, whenever you come to the end of a chapter, imagine that you have to summarise it as briefly as possible. You could then do the same for the whole book when you finish it.

7 Visuospatial ability
Visuospatial awareness is the ability to make quick and accurate estimates of areas, distances and volumes – the general proportions of things and their distribution in space. These abilities are used when you pack a car boot, for example, or in quickly estimating how many people are on your left and right when you first walk into a room.

8 Crosswords
Racking your brain for the answers to crossword clues can help to ward off mental deterioration. A major study showed that doing regular crossword puzzles cut the risk of developing Alzheimer's by 38 per cent. Other mental exercises to develop logic could include trying different ways of remembering your shopping list, such as foods which are raw or cooked.

LIFESTYLE AND MENTAL HEALTH

Good mental health and a positive attitude to life are largely matters of luck or fortune, but lifestyle factors are also important and these are under an individual's control. Eating well, avoiding potentially harmful substances, exercising regularly, and perhaps above all getting enough sleep and learning to relax are within everyone's grasp.

 57 *Knowing which foods feed the physical needs of the brain is an ideal way to start planning mind-healthy meals and snacks.*

 62 *The old adage 'a healthy body in a healthy mind' has been proven true: exercise has many positive benefits for mental health.*

 66 *One of the most effective ways to handle the stresses of everyday life is to be able to switch off from them through relaxation.*

 68 *Sleep restores both mind and body – getting a good night's sleep and establishing a healthy sleep routine is a priority.*

 70 *Making the most of opportunities that present themselves, and accepting not-so-good as well as good results, is the key to having no regrets.*

Eating for a healthy mind

Certain foods are better than others for lifting mood healthily and conversely some foods and drinks can depress mood. Getting the balance right is not difficult, as long as a few simple guidelines are followed.

Studies are gradually providing evidence to support the theory that the foods we eat can affect the chemical composition of the brain. Your diet can affect your mood, alertness and physical performance.

THE SCIENCE

Chemical messengers in the brain, called neurotransmitters, carry information between nerve cells. In theory, certain nutrients in foods are precursors to neurotransmitters and the amount in the diet will affect the quantity of neurotransmitters that the body produces. In practice, this is much more complex because foods contain many nutrients that interact together, and these interactions affect the production of neurotransmitters. Precursor nutrients are found in the following foods.

Protein

During digestion, protein foods are broken down into amino acids. One amino acid, called tyrosine, increases the production of the neurotransmitters noradrenaline, dopamine and adrenaline, which increase energy levels as well as alertness. This means that eating protein foods rich in tyrosine, such as fish, chicken, pork, beef, lamb, tofu, pulses and eggs will give an energy boost. Also, trials using tyrosine supplementation against depression have shown encouraging results in lifting mood.

Carbohydrates

These stimulate the release of the hormone insulin. Insulin rapidly removes amino acids from the bloodstream, apart from one amino acid called tryptophan. Tryptophan is converted into a neurotransmitter called serotonin in the brain. Serotonin has been shown to reduce pain, depress appetite and make you feel relaxed and less stressed. In large doses, it can induce sleep. Rich sources of tryptophan include turkey, bananas, milk, bread and cheese.

A study published in Britain looked at the effects of lowering levels of tryptophan in volunteers, some of whom had a family history of depression. The results showed that depleting tryptophan levels caused mood depression in half of the subjects who had an immediate relative with depression. In addition, subjects showed impairment in their ability to recall and recognise words that they had learned during the period that tryptophan was depleted.

Caffeine

Taken in small doses, caffeine can be an effective anti-depressant and research has shown it can boost mood. Furthermore, studies have shown that this effect can be produced without having to increase the dosage each day. Higher doses may have adverse effects.

Studies have also shown that caffeine can benefit performance as well as help to sustain attention during the post-lunch dip and after prolonged work. Some research has suggested that among regular consumers of caffeine, abstinence can even have negative effects such as lowered alertness, muddle-headedness and impaired

psychomotor performance. These effects can be rapidly reversed by the equivalent of the caffeine content in a strong cup of tea (60mg) although additional doses during the morning do not appear to give further benefit.

Selenium

According to scientists from the Department of Psychology at the University of Wales in Swansea, a deficiency in selenium (an essential trace element found in cereal grains, meat and fish) may be associated with increased anxiety, depression and fatigue. The current average adult intake of selenium for women and men is thought to be around 43 micrograms (mcg) per day. This compares unfavourably with the government's recommended daily intake of 75mcg for men and 60mcg per day for women.

Selenium is found in varying concentrations in soils throughout the world. While levels are high in North American soil, they are comparatively low in Britain and Europe. Due to a decrease in imports of selenium-rich, high-protein wheat

flour from the USA and Canada, and an increase in the acquisition of locally produced wheat, daily selenium intake among the British population fell dramatically from 60mcg in 1978 to around 43mcg by the 1990s. The Food Standards Agency noted that there has been a decrease in bread consumption over the past 10 years, which is also believed to be a cause of the reduced intake of selenium. Finally, the low bio-availability (the amount that the body is able to use) of this mineral in soils due to acid rain and excessive use of artificial fertilisers, has also affected selenium intake.

A study published in *Biological Psychiatry* in 1991 was designed with the aim of examining the impact of selenium on mood. The 50 subjects who took part were either given a daily placebo or a 100-mcg selenium supplement over a five-week period. They were asked to monitor their feelings and moods, together with the foods they had eaten, so the researchers could estimate their overall daily intake of selenium. The results showed that the lower

the level of selenium in the diet, the more the subjects reported feelings of anxiety, depression and fatigue. The results also showed that these feelings subsided following the addition of selenium supplements to the diet.

Another study published in 1996 in *Biological Psychiatry* showed that of 11 healthy men given a selenium-rich or selenium-poor diet for 99 days, those who had a low selenium status initially experienced more depressed moods.

But beware about overdosing. In 1991, the Department of Health reviewed the daily amounts of minerals necessary for an average adult. This review found that excessive doses of selenium – over 3.2 milligrams (3200 mcg) per day, or more than 40 times the RDI for men – are toxic and can lead to neurological abnormalities, hair loss, and, in severe cases, paralysis.

Eggs

Eggs contain a vitamin called choline. Choline is a precursor to the brain neurotransmitter called acetylcholine. A lack of choline may

Selenium content of selected foods

To ensure adequate amounts of naturally occurring selenium without supplementation, include seafoods, meats, whole grains and Brazil nuts in the diet. The recommended daily requirement for selenium for adult men is 75mcg and for women 60mcg – estimates suggest that most people do not get this amount daily and may therefore be deficient.

	PORTION (g)	SELENIUM (mcg)
Brazil nuts	20 (6 whole nuts)	50.8
Kidney	10	14.6
Prawns, boiled	60 (large handful)	13.8
Spaghetti, wholemeal, cooked	220 (large plate)	13.2
White rice, boiled	180 (large bowl)	9
Crab meat	10	8.4
Lamb chop, grilled	70 (1 chop)	2.8

cause poor concentration and memory impairment. People with Alzheimer's disease have been shown to have low levels of acetylcholine.

Omega 3 fatty acids

Some types of polyunsaturated fats contain omega 3 fatty acids and recent studies suggest that these may have a positive effect on depression and behavioural problems. A study in Massachusetts in 2000, found that areas with a high consumption of omega 3 fatty acids were associated with decreased rates of depression. They also found that individuals with major depression had marked depletions of omega 3 fatty acids.

Omega 3 fatty acids also have an important role to play in behaviour. A study by researchers in the UK published in the *British Journal of Psychiatry* in 2002 looked at the influence of supplementary vitamins, minerals and essential fatty acids on the anti-social behaviour of young adult prisoners. Their study was conducted on the theory that offenders tend to consume diets deficient in essential nutrients, which may adversely affect their behaviour.

The study was a double-blind, placebo-controlled, randomised trial involving 231 young adult prisoners. Their disciplinary offences were studied before and after nutritional supplementation. Compared to those taking placebos, subjects receiving supplements committed an average of 26.3 per cent fewer offences. Compared to pre-supplementation, offenders who took essential fatty acids for at least two weeks, showed an average reduction of 35.1 per cent. This suggests that some types of 'good' fats may have a role far beyond keeping our hearts healthy.

Fish oils for brain health
Oily fish contain fatty acids, which have been shown to be beneficial for mental health. Some children with ADHD have lowered blood levels of these fatty acids.

Good sources of omega 3 fats include oily fish, vegetables and lean red meat. Intake can be increased by eating one to two servings of oily fish such as salmon, trout, mackerel, sardines or tuna a week. Other sources include flaxseeds and flaxseed oils. Flaxseed oil comes in an edible form and is high in unsaturated fat. Flaxseeds are available from health food shops and can be sprinkled on salads or cooked vegetables or combined with flour to make breads and pancakes.

THE B VITAMIN GROUP

• **Folate** Clinical studies have shown that patients with diagnosed depression have a significantly low amount of folate, a vitamin in the B group, in their blood. One study published in Scandinavia in 1989 found that the lower the folate, the more severe the depression. A study in 1991 showed that folic acid supplementation significantly improved clinical and social recovery in depressed patients. Good sources of folate include green leafy vegetables, fruits, fortified breads and cereals.

• **Thiamin** Some studies have shown that depressed patients are slightly deficient in thiamin (vitamin B_1). A study in 1997 looked at thiamin supplementation and its effects on mood among 120 female college students. Students were either given

59

THE IMPORTANCE OF BREAKFAST

For one reason or another, many people, including school children, skip breakfast. Some people feel they don't have time to sit down in the morning to eat a nutritious breakfast. Some, especially children, are not physically capable of eating breakfast when they first wake up.

Studies suggest that children who don't eat breakfast at home suffer short-term hunger during morning schoolwork and this has a negative impact on their memory and attention span. Other research has suggested that hungry children are less likely to behave well at school. One study has shown that children who were given a glucose drink were more attentive and showed fewer signs of frustration in tasks.

Several studies have found that children's attendance at school improves when they are provided with breakfast. In the USA, those who took part in a school breakfast programme were less likely to be absent or late compared with non-participants. A study in the UK compared school test scores between 335 pupils from low-income backgrounds who took part in a school breakfast programme for three months and 688 non-participating children from similar backgrounds. The results showed that participants scored better in school tests of language, maths and reading. All told, eating breakfast is very good advice indeed.

A MIND-HEALTHY START

1 Wholegrain cereal provides a range of essential nutrients, including protein, which is vital for healthy muscles; carbohydrates, the ideal energy source in the morning; fibre, which keeps the digestive system healthy; and vitamins and minerals, which can aid the production of certain neurotransmitters in the brain.

2 Cereal alternatives include wacky waffles which may be just the thing to tempt children into eating breakfast. Try adding fresh fruits and jams for extra flavour, or alternatively you could try frozen yoghurt. Carbohydrates are a great source of energy, which could be just what children need in the morning.

BREAKFAST SELECTION
To add variety, try a different breakfast each day. Here are some suggestions:
- Yoghurt topped with fruit.
- Wholewheat toast topped with low fat spread or marmalade.
- Wholegrain cereal topped with dried fruit.
- Boiled egg and toast.
- Toasted muffin with peanut butter and chopped banana.
- Bagel with cream cheese.

1   **2**

Chocolate contains phenylethylamine, a stimulant which is said to create the same reaction in the body as the feeling of falling in love.

a supplement containing 50mg of thiamin or a placebo. After two months, those taking thiamin more than doubled their previous psychological test scores on clear-headedness and mood while students taking the placebo showed no change. The group taking thiamin also increased their speed in a reaction-time test, while the placebo group remained unchanged. Good sources of thiamin include whole-grain cereals, bread, yeast extracts, pork, nuts, and pulses.

• Pyridoxine Pyridoxine (vitamin B_6) is important in the nervous system and a deficiency has been shown to cause poor memory and concentration. Low mood has often been associated with pre-menstrual syndrome (PMS) and a recent review of studies examining the effect of vitamin B_6 supplements and PMS has shown that doses of up to 100mg a day are likely to relieve symptoms such as depression. Doses of higher than 200mg a day, however, may cause nerve damage. Rich food sources of pyridoxine include meat, wholegrain and fortified cereal products, bananas, nuts and pulses.

COMFORT EATING

During periods of stress some people eat compulsively. While the effects of stress differ from individual to individual, it does seem to induce some people to change their eating patterns and food choices. Some studies have shown that some adults experience appetite loss while stressed and hence under-eat, while others over-indulge, particularly on high fat, high sugar foods. This is known as stress induced eating (SID).

Chocolate craving and PMS

Food cravings, notably for chocolate, are commonly reported among women in the pre-menstrual phase. Whether this is related to psychological or pharmacological factors is uncertain.

Chocolate contains a number of active compounds, such as theobromine, phenylethylamine, magnesium, caffeine and anandamides, but some researchers believe these are unlikely to account for any of the beneficial effects reported after eating chocolate. There is evidence to suggest that the desire for chocolate increases during the pre-menstrual phase, when levels of plasma magnesium are low, but it is unlikely that eating chocolate is an attempt to increase magnesium intake. A bar of chocolate contains only 50mg of magnesium and studies of magnesium supplementation show that over 1000mg are needed to improve symptoms of PMS.

People probably crave chocolate because eating it stimulates endorphin release. Endorphins occur naturally in the brain and act to block the sensation of pain, giving people a natural 'high'.

Exercising for a healthy mind

Exercise has enormous benefits for the mind, in lifting mood and alleviating depression. It aids sleep, which in itself is often a cause or symptom of poor mental health, and contributes to improved self-esteem.

EXERCISE AND MENTAL HEALTH

Exercise is known to have a beneficial effect on mood and much research has been conducted in order to establish whether exercise can be used therapeutically to alleviate depression. The results suggest that regular exercise is an effective way to lift mood, and its effects can be felt instantly, unlike medication. People who suffer from anxiety also improve when they exercise regularly. The physiological benefits for the body are well documented and the good news is that everyone can benefit. Choose something that can easily fit into your daily routine.

Increasing energy levels

It is now recognised that exercising increases the body's energy levels. It is not true that exercise makes you tired and drains you. Exercise actually gives you extra energy and increases your well being. But it does seem contradictory to say that you gain energy as a result of expending it through exercise. To make sense of this we need to understand how exercise affects brain chemistry. With increased oxygen the brain becomes more alert and works more efficiently. Oxygen is transported to the brain in the blood, so the greater the blood flow to the brain, the more oxygen it receives. The flow of blood to the brain increases during exercise as your heartbeat increases and your brain cells absorb more oxygen. As a result, you feel more energetic.

Circle of health
Exercise improves blood flow to all parts of the body, including the brain, so that you feel energised and alert. It also alleviates stress, a major cause of mental health problems.

Better brain chemicals

But it isn't just the flow of oxygen that is elevated during and after exercise. Research also indicates that the production of neurotransmitters (brain chemicals) is increased. Neurotransmitters are important for the adequate communication between nerve cells and contribute to a range of bodily functions.

One such neurotransmitter, serotonin, for example, influences sleeping and waking cycles, libido, appetite and mood. Reduced serotonin levels have been linked to depression. Regular exercise and the subsequent increase in physical fitness that results can raise serotonin levels in the brain leading to improved mood and feelings of well being. Some research indicates that it is the rise in body temperature brought about by exercise that influences the neurotransmitters. Exercise also increases the production of the neurotransmitters dopamine and noradrenaline, which are also needed to combat depression. In someone who is not depressed dopamine and noradrenaline increase alertness and perk us up. Physical activity is also known to 'burn up' stress chemicals, such as adrenaline, bringing about a more relaxed state of mind.

Natural high

Prolonged, continuous activity also stimulates the production and release of those feel-good chemicals, the endorphins, resulting in that 'happy feeling' associated with exercise, often referred to as 'the runner's high'. This feeling of euphoria is why so many people feel invigorated and enthusiastic after exercise. Endorphins are natural painkillers

(20–30 times more powerful than morphine) that occur in the brain. They have been called the 'morphine within', because they are constructed of a substance similar to morphine. They act by binding to the brain's pain receptors, which blocks the sensation of pain. It is thought that this release of endorphins is part of the 'fight or flight' response. The body recognises that it is pushing harder than usual, but cannot distinguish whether or not there is any actual danger. As well as having pain-relieving properties, endorphins regulate blood pressure and body temperature. They also enhance the immune system, help to improve memory and have even been proved to have anti-ageing effects.

Undeniable benefits

Clearly there are massive benefits to be had from exercising in terms of improved mood and feelings of well being. By following an exercise programme on a regular basis, the body will produce a greater level of neurotransmitters and endorphins. Active people benefit from a natural high while staying in good physical shape. They also have more energy as a result of the increased oxygen supply available to the brain.

It is reasonable to assume therefore that people who exercise regularly are likely to experience greater satisfaction with life and be better

able to cope with life's challenges. Working out on a regular basis protects against obesity, heart disease and cancer and it also boosts the emotional and mental outlook on life. People who work out regularly tend to have higher self-esteem and fewer physical and mental health problems. Indeed, the effect of exercising, in terms of how it alters brain chemistry, is so beneficial that recent research suggests that it may be just as effective in treating mild to moderate depression as medication.

Clinical depression and exercise

Many studies have found that exercise significantly relieves physical and emotional symptoms in clinically depressed people. Those who suffer from anxiety have also been shown to improve when they exercise regularly. American research into

A word of caution

TALKING POINT

Some people may exercise excessively as they find the 'high' they get from endorphins addictive. Their workouts become fixes, and even injuries or illnesses will not discourage them because they are relentlessly searching for endorphin-induced mood elevations to mask the pain of everyday living. However, while this is something to be aware of, the benefits of exercise far outweigh the possible dangers and this should not discourage someone from taking up exercise.

Researchers suggest that we should laugh at least 15 times a day to help to alleviate stress.

fatal heart attacks indicates that depression, lack of exercise and physical health are closely linked. On average, depressed people only exercise about half as much as people who aren't depressed. Clearly exercise and depression influence each other – a sedentary lifestyle increases the risk of depression, and depression increases the likelihood of a sedentary lifestyle. Exercise boosts energy, which people with depression commonly lack. It would seem then that using exercise in a preventative way to ward off depression not only makes us feel better in the short term, but is essential for maintaining our long-term health.

WHICH EXERCISE IS BEST FOR MENTAL HEALTH?

No real evidence suggests that any one kind of exercise is best for promoting mental health. Most studies have looked at running and other aerobic activities, such as swimming and cycling. What seems to be key is the intensity of the exercise undertaken, rather than the type. Research indicates that the most effective way to achieve alterations in brain chemistry and high levels of endorphins is through aerobic exercise lasting at least thirty minutes at 50–75 per cent of the maximum heart rate. (Maximum heart rate can be calculated by subtracting your age from 220.)

The Walk-Run Programme

If you are new to running it is best to begin with a walk-run programme. For example, you could run for one minute at a comfortable pace (you should be able to hold a conversation) and then walk for two minutes as briskly as you are able to recover. If you repeat this pattern 10 times you will have completed 30 minutes of aerobic activity. When you find you can manage this easily you can gradually increase the length of time that you run. It is also advisable to walk for 10 minutes before starting and to cool off for 10 minutes with a stroll when you have finished. When you are first starting, follow the programme three times a week. Then, when you feel more fit build up to five times a week. This is a gentle and structured way to start an exercise programme. It can prevent you from doing too much straight away. It is always best to consult a doctor before embarking on any new exercise programme.

Exercising to reduce depression

Some studies have looked at the effects of low-intensity aerobic exercise such as walking and weight training, and have found that these types of exercise are effective. If you are depressed, for example, just taking a brisk walk three times a week may help you recover faster, and reduce the severity of the depression. Something as simple as walking the dog can help ward off the blues in the first place.

The most important thing is to get out there and do something and, preferably, make it something you enjoy – you'll be far more likely to stick with it. Laughter increases endorphin production too, so having a good laugh while you exercise will help stack the odds in your favour. There are social benefits to exercise that can help improve mood too. Joining a club or meeting friends to walk or workout will also lift the spirits. Having someone to exercise with is more motivating too for many people. It has also been shown that you are more likely to experience an endorphin high if the

positive health tips

Five ways to get more exercise

- Keep experimenting with different types of exercise until you find something you really enjoy – then you won't be able to wait to get out there.

- Find a training buddy and have fun – it is more motivating for most people to have company.

- Set yourself positive and realistic goals – focus on what you want not what you don't want and you will be more likely to succeed.

- Think back to how good you felt last time you exercised and get back into that feeling – this will encourage you to get out there again.

- Walk to work, use the stairs, carry your shopping, do the garden and clean the house yourself. All these activities will help to make you fit.

exercise you do is one that is familiar to you and your body. Think of exercise that you used to enjoy as a child. Once again, if exercise has some meaning for you, you are far more likely to be motivated.

Motivation

It is vitally important that you set positive, realistic goals for yourself. Try and shift your focus on to how you want to be, rather than thinking about what you don't want. Think about the healthy person that you want to be and start to act as if you are that person already – this will make it easier to make healthier choices for yourself. Finally, make sure you exercise because you want to, because of what you get out of it, not because you think you should. Don't be afraid to keep trying out different types of exercise until you find something that you really enjoy, something that makes you feel more alive. Then you really will be exercising for a healthy mind.

EATING AND EXERCISE

It is important to eat before you exercise, especially in the mornings. If there is insufficient energy available from carbohydrate sources the body begins to break down muscle tissue to fuel exercise. Clearly this is counter-productive and undesirable as you would hope to develop your muscles through exercise not cannibalise them! Eating around an hour before exercise is a good time – choose foods low on the GI (glycaemic index – see list) as these will give you a sustained source of energy during the session.

During the session and in the following hour, it is important to replenish energy stores as quickly as

LOW GI FOODS	HIGH GI FOODS
Before you exercise fill up on foods that will release energy slowly during your workout to keep you going.	*During and after your session, you should choose high GI foods, to replenish your energy stores.*
Porridge	Bananas
Pasta	Raisins
Oats	Muesli bar
Oatmeal biscuits	High glucose isotonic sports drinks
Noodles	Kiwi fruit
Beans	Figs, dried
Yoghurt	Pineapple
Apples, apricots, plums, peaches	Watermelon

possible. Choose high GI foods as these enter the body at a much quicker rate, causing a rise in blood sugar. At rest, this wouldn't be considered beneficial but it is a good strategy during and immediately after exercise, as the sugar will be used instantly as fuel. Eat high GI foods little and often during a long exercise session to prevent a drop in blood sugar. It takes around 45 minutes for sugar levels to rise, so if you wait until you feel tired it will be too late.

Learning to relax

Modern life can be stressful with hectic schedules and a tendency to over-commit. Taking time out for ourselves and learning effective relaxation techniques can go a long way toward restoring mental equilibrium.

Some stress is necessary to help drive you each day. It helps you to focus on your goals, to concentrate and to deal with problems. But too much stress or constant stress is harmful.

The fight-or-flight response

Stressful situations cause your body to release stress hormones, such as adrenaline, into your bloodstream to enable you to cope. This release of adrenaline is called the 'fight-or-flight' response. The right amount at the right time is useful. But this response causes problems if too much adrenaline is released or if it is released at the wrong times.

The physical symptoms of too much stress include dry mouth, sweating, light-headedness or feeling faint. However, the mental symptoms can be just as unnerving – feeling anxious or panicky, experiencing difficulty in concentrating and sleeping poorly. All of these in time may lead to depression.

BENEFITS OF RELAXATION

If you can learn to relax you will feel calmer. A calm mind is much better able to cope with stress. You will find it easier to concentrate, to focus and be in touch with others and with what is going on round you.

You will have a clearer idea of what you want to do and how to do it. You will be more efficient, and get more satisfaction out of doing and achieving. You will sleep better and wake up refreshed. You will be a better partner, a more tolerant or 'fun' parent, an appreciated friend.

If you are physically relaxed your body will function better. You may have noticed headaches or backache or stiffness of your joints when you are tense. These are due to tightening of your muscles. You may have felt so tired as to be literally physically drained. When you relax your

Easing tensions away
Time spent relaxing in a leisurely bath is not time wasted: it helps to relax the mind and ease painful or stiff muscles. The effect is even better with the ambient lighting of several sweet-smelling candles.

RELAXATION DURING PREGNANCY

Doctors and midwives have long known about the value of relaxation in pregnancy. Women who have learned relaxation techniques often experience a less painful labour and need fewer painkilling drugs. Research suggests that in women with a history of premature labour the use of relaxation tapes results in longer pregnancies and larger babies when compared to women who don't use relaxation therapy.

muscles relax too, so that tension disappears, your body moves effortlessly, and you feel energised.

Relaxation helps to beat stress

It isn't difficult to see that if your mind and body are relaxed you will function better. Your brain will work more effectively: solutions to problems that seemed so evasive when you were tense become quite apparent when you are relaxed. Perhaps you have noticed how much easier it is to complete a crossword puzzle when you are relaxed compared with when you are tense. Reading a book is more pleasurable when you are relaxed because you concentrate so much better and find that you don't have to keep re-reading passages. But, more importantly, when you are relaxed you interact with other people much more easily, with obvious benefits at work, at home and in your social life. Day-to-day problems become easier to address and deal with when you are relaxed. Relaxation literally helps you to beat stress.

SIMPLE WAYS TO RELAX

Yoga or meditation can be effective ways to relax, but are not necessary. Some people like to relax in a warm bath: you will feel the stress and tension leaving you. An alternative is to read a good book for half an hour. Just make sure that the book is not a real page turner, which could have the opposite effect!

Exercise can be relaxing

Walking the dog, walking with a friend or on your own and thinking over pleasant memories or anticipating an upcoming holiday can all be relaxing for some people. For others, physical exercise is the route to relaxation. Aerobic exercise (when the heart rate is raised for at least several minutes) can release endorphins, or 'happy hormones', in the body. Many people find techniques such as massage, aromatherapy, yoga, meditation and self-hypnosis helpful.

All these methods have one thing in common: they give you the opportunity to allocate a special time in the day exclusively for you. Creating your own space, both in terms of place and time, when you can concentrate on yourself, is the key to relaxation. We all need time for ourselves. Think of it as 'quality time' devoted to you – a time to think, to meditate, to take stock. Of course, the pressures of everyday life may make it difficult for you to find this special time, and this creates a vicious circle of stress, no relief, then more stress.

If you feel stressed it's important to try to create a calm environment in which to live. Use colours that you find soothing, soft background music and scented candles, and try to avoid clutter. Pets can be very relaxing too. In fact, some homes for the elderly encourage visitors to bring along dogs or cats for the residents to stroke.

Pet therapy
Several studies have shown that simply owning a pet can reduce depression, loneliness, anger and stress. A dog also has to be walked, with owners benefiting from the relaxing effects of the exercise.

A good night's sleep

When you go to sleep, your body goes to work, consolidating the day's learning into memory and improving your ability to absorb and remember everday skills. A good night's sleep is re-energising and helps you to prepare for the next day.

WHY SLEEP IS IMPORTANT

We all know that sleep is important for a healthy body and mind but we do not really understand how sleep produces its benefits. Insufficient good-quality sleep results in tiredness, poor concentration, irritability and a reduced attention span. This can have disastrous effects at work, in relationships, when driving, or during leisure pursuits.

Chronic (long-term) lack of sleep affects the body's immune and repair systems so that there is a greater likelihood of infections and illness. There is also a vicious cycle in which lack of sleep makes you 'over-tired'. This makes you tense, making it even more difficult for you to get to sleep.

Recognising a problem

The most obvious consequence of poor sleep at night is sleepiness the following day. However, sometimes people feel sleepy without being aware of having slept badly the previous night. Often, the cause is snoring and sleep apnoea.

Plain snoring disturbs the sleep of a spouse or partner rather than the individual responsible and practical measures can be taken to alleviate the disturbance. But if snoring is also accompanied by apnoea, this will cause daytime sleepiness and may lead to mental problems.

Apnoea is a condition in which the airways repeatedly block and breathing stops for half a minute or so throughout the night; to clear the blockage the person wakes up, though too briefly to remember doing so. Breathing aids are available to prevent apnoea.

Narcolepsy is a rare condition in which a person switches from full wakefulness to dreaming sleep during the day, even whilst engaged in activities. It usually starts in childhood, often accompanied by cataplexy, a condition of sudden weakness or paralysis.

AGE-RELATED SLEEP NEEDS

Sleep needs change through life. The older you are, the less total sleep you need. From infancy to adulthood, sleep decreases by more than half.

Newborn babies need about 16–17 hours sleep. This is taken throughout the day and night. Between the age of six to nine months babies need approximately 14 hours sleep. By the age of one to three years this drops to an average of 13 hours sleep.

Children between the ages of three to nine need approximately 11 hours sleep; this drops to an average of 10 hours between the ages of 10 to 13. Teenagers need about nine hours sleep to function normally.

Sleep experts recommend that adults should obtain at least seven to eight hours sleep a night. Many older people aged between 60 and 80 spend only six hours a day sleeping.

FINDING THE RIGHT AMOUNT OF SLEEP FOR YOU

Lie-ins, especially if they are long, can cause rebound tiredness. Quality of sleep reduces after your mind and body have had what they need, and you may not wake up refreshed after a lie-in. Good-quality sleep depends on keeping regular hours – going to bed and getting up at more or less the same time each day.

Although the average duration of sleep for an adult is about seven or eight hours some people need as little as four. Most people need at least five hours of so-called 'core' sleep. The amount you need is the amount that leaves you feeling refreshed each day. If you regularly get less than six hours a night sleep, the chances are you're building up a 'sleep debt' and may be compromising your health.

What causes poor sleep?

By far the commonest reasons are stress, anxiety, worry and depression. Further causes may be:

- **Psychological** – for example, grief and anger.
- **Physical** – including pain (such as arthritis), breathing problems (such as smoking-related lung damage), heart disease, stomach problems (such as acid reflux) and restless leg syndrome.
- **Lifestyle-related** – especially a poor bedtime routine; too much caffeine, alcohol or tobacco late in the day; too little exercise during the day; too much vigorous exercise just before bedtime; doing shift work or suffering from jet leg.
- **Age-related** – sleep tends to become more fitful, which is why so many older people have daytime naps.
- **Drug-related** – both prescribed (such as beta-blockers) and illicit.
- **Environmental** – trying to sleep in a bedroom that is too cold or hot, not dark enough or too noisy (for example, with a snoring partner or in a house on a busy road).

QUALITY SLEEP HABITS

Your body has an internal clock, which sets such body rhythms as temperature, hormone levels and stress chemical levels (such as adrenaline). Your body clock is very accurate and takes a long time to re-set. This explains why shift workers suffer from insomnia and this is also a major component of jet lag. So, for good-quality sleep, you need to develop good sleep habits.

A healthy sleep routine
Aim for a bedtime that is more or less the same time each evening. Aim to get up at the same time each day. Try to avoid naps during the day

Cut out the stimulants
Avoid stimulants, especially caffeine (which is present in coffee, tea, many fizzy drinks and most chocolate), alcohol and nicotine in the late afternoon or evening.

Gradually wind down
Have a warm non-alcoholic caffeine-free drink followed by a warm bath, ensure that your bedroom is pleasantly warm, read a book that is not too exciting and listen to soothing music for about 15 to 30 minutes – and you should feel ready to go to sleep.

Take regular exercise
Try to have regular exercise most days, but avoid vigorous exercise just before you go to bed.

Don't fight it
If you are having difficulty going to sleep, or if you wake in the night and can't get back to sleep, don't toss and turn. The more you fight sleeplessness the more awake you become. It is better to turn on the light, read your book for 15 minutes, listen to relaxing music and then close your eyes again. Try hiding the clock to avoid 'clock watching'.

If in spite of following the steps above you find that, night after night, you are unable to sleep consult your doctor. This is especially important if you feel anxious or depressed. You will be asked questions to see if stress or depression are preventing you from sleeping. There may be a discussion about suitable prescribed medication. If depression is clearly the cause, you may be asked to consider talking therapy or anti-depressant tablets or a combination of both. If you are tense and anxious or you have got into the habit of expecting not to sleep, a short course of sleeping tablets may be helpful so don't worry too much if tablets are prescribed. Provided they are taken exactly as your doctor prescribes, they won't be addictive and they won't cause any long-term harm.

Living life to the full

People tend to get out of life what they put in: the people who seem to do most have most energy, more interests, a wider circle of friends and acquaintances and a generally more positive attitude to life.

Many young adults seem able to 'burn the candle at both ends'. While this may not be physically wise, they may derive mental benefits from being open to new ideas, never refusing an invitation, wining, dining, dancing, embarking on a challenging career, and forming relationships.

Age undoubtedly brings social and financial responsibilities, but it is important not to lose zest and enthusiasm for life, simply because you now have a career ladder to climb, bills and mortgage to pay and children to nurture and care for.

TAKING A BREAK

A break from the normal routine can bring great feelings of wellbeing and, if you can combine a break from routine with stunning scenery, good food, culture, sea, sun or snow, so much the better. Travel broadens the mind, but if travel is not an option, it is still important to take a break from the daily commute and normal working-week routine.

The increasing 24/7 culture can make co-ordinating family breaks difficult. Although a few schools approve short breaks for children during term time, family holidays generally tend to be restricted to school holidays and, depending on where parents work, there may be competition for these prime holiday slots. The mental – and physical – benefits of time away for all the family, however, make forward planning well worthwhile.

Family holidays and extended get-togethers can be a source of stress, however. High expectations and closer proximity can cause minor disagreements to surface. If your family get-togethers do tend to become tense, it might be better to avoid them for a time.

Some couples happily fit into a 'my family one year, yours the next' routine over important festivities such as Christmas and New Year. For others, they can an annual source of stress. However, if you want to opt out, it can be easier than you might think. Talk to other family members: they may be getting tired of tradition, too. Alternatively, booking a few days away over the holiday might help to avoid causing offence over breaking with routine.

BEING OPEN TO CHANGE

The problem for many of us is how easy it is to slip into habits that do not do our mental health much good and may actively harm it. Resistance to change or simply lack of interest can mean that many life-enhancing opportunities are not taken advantage of. If you feel that your mental abilities are stagnating, try some of the following:

- Do something cultural that you have never done before, such as going to an opera or ballet, art exhibition, or even a rock concert if

Shock of the new?
Being receptive to new ideas and pastimes broadens the mind, and may introduce you to life-enhancing new experiences and a new group of friends.

you missed out in your youth. Keep an open mind: it you really don't like it you don't have to go again, but you may enjoy yourself.

- Play a sport that you have not played before, or not played since your teens. Local clubs and fitness centres often have 'come along to see if you like it' weekends.
- Take a different kind of holiday: walking, riding, painting, sailing, foodie, yoga.
- Watch some live sport, preferably something you've not seen before, or at least for some years. If it is out of doors, so much the better.
- Do you have a skill that you could pass on to children? Many primary schools welcome locals who can coach sports, teach chess, help children with gardening and cooking, and so on. People who help in this way derive great mental benefits from being around and sharing ideas with young people.
- Join or set up a reading circle, an informal group of people who get together regularly to discuss what they have read. This encourages reading, gives a focus to it, and sharpens perhaps jaded critical faculties.
- Learn a language or a new skill, perhaps something you have always wanted to do, but never felt there was time for.

RELATIONSHIPS

There is nothing more life-enhancing than a good relationship, but stress, frustration or resentment in a relationship can result in depression and anxiety. Relationships are not static and some people find change itself stressful. Nor do relationships make themselves: individuals do have to work at them. It is also important

for parents not to neglect their relationship with each other in the over-riding demands of raising a family. Refreshing breaks together can cement a strong relationship.

Ending a relationship

While good relationships are important, you owe it to yourself to walk away from a relationship that is not supportive and nurturing. The harm to self-esteem and self-worth of a confrontational or abusive relationship is immense. Although ending a relationship can be difficult at any time, it is especially so after some years and if there are children involved. It is easier if it is a mutual decision; it is also easier if you have supportive friends and family.

Getting away
A different sort of holiday, perhaps based round a hobby or interest, can be a relaxing way to recharge your batteries.

GOING FOR IT

Most people do not regret what they do as much as what they don't do. It is not uncommon for people to feel as if it is too late to fulfil some of their life aims, but this is usually not the case. Although life-changing decisions can be difficult, they often turn out to be right. Changing careers, returning to education, ending a relationship, moving house and travelling are not decisions to take lightly, but talk to friends and family about their choices to help you to reach the right decision for you.

SUPPORT NETWORKS

Although they are a vital part of life for many people, a great number of us will never need to join a formal support group to help us to resolve a particular problem or a particularly difficult life choice or stage (see page 86). That does not mean, however, that we do not need a support network. Traditionally, the extended family was the support network, perhaps along with the church. These days it is more likely to be a group of friends or colleagues to whom we can turn when life seems difficult. The ability to discuss daily events and laugh about them, helps to keep things in perspective. We are less likely to brood over particular issues or worry about perceived slights. In this way social networks are valuable for alleviating stress.

Young mothers
Get together with other new mothers for regular walks. Not only are you getting some fresh air and exercise, you can also share the strains and stresses — as well as celebrating the joys — of motherhood. Mother and baby groups also provide the opportunity to chat and socialise with other mothers.

Work wise
In many settings, work colleagues are the ideal support network: they understand immediately the pressures inherent in any organisation. Some people set aside regular lunch dates simply to catch up, share gossip, unburden themselves over the latest deadline or target or celebrate a success.

Having faith
Religion has been a great support for many individuals, and while we are becoming an increasingly secularised society, those who do seek support from a religious figure or institution often benefit from it. It is often not necessary to belong to a specific faith to seek guidance from one of its ministers.

IMPROVING MENTAL HEALTH

Understanding the positives and negatives of emotions and pressures such as anger and stress, and learning how to cope with or overcome them, goes a long way towards promoting mental health.

 74 *Lifestyle measures that promote physical health, such as eating well and exercising regularly, have a positive effect on mental health too.*

 76 *Stress energises and motivates, but too much will do harm. Simple self-help measures may be all that are needed to keep stress levels down.*

 78 *Poor self-esteem is at the heart of many mental health states, but there is a lot that individuals can do to enhance their self-esteem.*

 80 *While anger in certain circumstances is an understandable reaction, too much anger is counter-productive and needs to be controlled.*

 82 *Assertive people manage to strike a healthy balance between looking out for others while being sure their own needs are met.*

 84 *The ability to react positively when your spirits are low can make the difference between an odd bad day and a serious depression.*

 86 *There are times when self-help is not enough. Knowing when and how to seek support can be vital to good mental health.*

Maintaining mental health

Good mental health depends on avoiding behaviours and situations that may have a harmful effect and on positively seeking enhancing and beneficial behaviours, states of mind and outlook.

PREVENTING EMOTIONAL PROBLEMS

To have emotional problems from time to time is part of the price we pay for having complex and adaptive brains. As such, a life free from any emotional problems is as unlikely as a life free from stress. However, some people can be more vulnerable than others to developing mental problems. This can be due to poor environment or severe adverse life events. In addition to social factors, psychological factors such as personality, level of general anxiety or persistent low self-esteem, can also mean that some people will be more vulnerable than others to mental health problems.

People at high risk include children who live in poverty or who show learning and behavioural difficulties. Members of families experiencing separation, divorce and bereavement are also at high risk of emotional problems. The unemployed and long-term carers of people with disabilities that make them dependent for most of their activities of daily living are especially at risk. Finally, being pregnant can increase the risk of depression, as can having young children and little social support. Women – particularly – who lose a parent before the age of about 11 are more vulnerable than others to later depression. Emotional problems can be prevented to some extent, at least in part, by support for first time parents, widely available nursery education, close working with schools, training in social and problem-solving skills. Respite care for carers and the involvement of different agencies in a coordinated fashion can be important in preventing emotional problems.

ALCOHOL AND OTHER DRUGS

Although few, if any, countries have in place a 'War on Alcohol' in the same way that they have a 'War on Drugs', the fact remains that alcohol is responsible for severe emotional and physical problems. You do not need to be dependent or an alcoholic to suffer the adverse effects of alcohol. Alcohol is a depressant drug and, although many people try to use it as a kind of self-medication for anxiety, depression or sleeplessness, it is seldom effective even in the short term, and almost never in the long term. Alcohol use can lead to

The World Health Organization found in 1996 that married women with children had a higher risk for depression than single women, married women without children or men regardless of status.

domestic and workplace conflict, family breakdown and loss of work. Alcohol can cause direct damage to the cells of the brain and crosses the placenta to affect a developing baby. In an extreme form, fetal alcohol syndrome, accompanied by severe learning disabilities, may be found.

Recognising problem drinking before it gets out of hand can be vital in preventing emotional problems and maintaining mental health.

The dangers of illicit drugs, such as heroin, amphetamines, cocaine, and so on, are well recognised. However, the effects of commonly used, everyday drugs such as caffeine and nicotine are often overlooked.

DIET

Diet is central to mental health (see page 57). A balanced diet will also keep you physically healthy. Sugary foods, which release large amounts of sugar into the bloodstream quickly can sometimes have a brief mood-lifting effect. However, rapid fluctuations in glucose level can result in increased anxiety, sluggishness, listlessness and even mild forms of depression.

Foods with a low glycaemic index, that release their sugar more slowly over a longer period, are less likely to cause fluctuations in blood glucose level that can trigger mood problems. Such foods include vegetables, many fruits, oatmeal and some bran-based cereals, although corn flakes and other common breakfast cereals actually have a high glycaemic index.

EXERCISE

There is mounting evidence that exercise has a positive effect on mental health. Although research studies are difficult to perform in this area, the general results are positive and suggest not only that exercise may prevent mental disorders such as anxiety and panic over the long term, but may help to treat the conditions if they develop.

SUPPORT

Even the most reclusive or shy person needs human contact. We are not by nature solitary animals, and complete solitude can have an adverse effect on mental health. Experiments with volunteers who were deprived of all sensory stimulation resulted in some bizarre symptoms, including delusions and hallucinations. People who are able to develop and maintain a social network often show lower levels of anxiety and depression. When they do become depressed or anxious, they find their available support beneficial in maintaining their treatment.

Support is not a one-way street. Helping and supporting others, friends, family or acting as a volunteer, can give a sense of purpose and improve self worth, both critical in the maintenance of mental health. Although it is not good constantly to compare yourself with others, encountering others and seeing that they, too, have their own problems, can help you to see your own problems in perspective, perhaps allowing you to maintain a positive outlook.

Maintenance of a sense of perspective is also essential to good mental health. You could try, for example, to envisage how a current difficult situation might look in ten years' time. How does what is happening to you look in the context

Giving and receiving
Although they are dealing with problems which callers find overwhelming, volunteers tend not to become depressed: their training teaches them to listen and be objective, and in return they derive strength and purpose from the work.

of what is happening in the world in general? If you can count your own blessings and good fortune now and previously in your life, perhaps what you are experiencing now can be seen in a different perspective.

The sense of perspective, and the maintenance of a positive outlook, can be supported by particular activities such as yoga, tai-chi and meditation. Several psychological studies have indicated that people who meditate regularly have lower levels of stress and lower blood pressure, than those of the same age and sex who do not meditate.

Coping with stress

Stress is an inescapable part of life. What is important is to be able to manage stress – an ability that varies from individual to individual – and to recognise when levels are rising beyond what you can cope with.

THE STRESS QUESTIONNAIRE

To find out if you are suffering from stress, respond to these statements.

		Y	N
1	I sleep for 6 hours or more at least 4 nights a week.	☐	☐
2	My weight is about right for my height.	☐	☐
3	I have been smoking more than usual lately.	☐	☐
4	I need an alcoholic drink when I return from work and/or to help me sleep.	☐	☐
5	I feel anxious every day before going to work, but OK at weekends and on holiday.	☐	☐
6	I have no influence or control over my workload or the way I do my work.	☐	☐
7	I feel emotionally drained most of the time.	☐	☐
8	I get little or no recognition for my efforts.	☐	☐
9	I have at least one close friend with whom I can discuss personal matters.	☐	☐
10	I have to neglect my family and friends because of work.	☐	☐
11	I spend two hours or more each day travelling to work.	☐	☐
12	I have enough income to meet my basic needs.	☐	☐
13	I regularly do something just for fun.	☐	☐
14	I have hobbies that I enjoy.	☐	☐
15	I regularly give and receive affection.	☐	☐
16	I give more than I ever get in return.	☐	☐
17	It seems as if I never see my house in daylight.	☐	☐
18	I do not have enough time or resources to do my job.	☐	☐
19	If I am angry about something, I just let it out.	☐	☐
20	My job offers me little intellectual satisfaction.	☐	☐

For questions 3, 4, 5, 6, 7, 8, 10, 11, 16, 17, 18, 20, score 1 for 'Yes', 0 for 'No'.
For questions 1, 2, 9, 12, 13, 14, 15, 19, score 0 for 'Yes', 1 for 'No'.

A score of 11 or more means that you may be very highly stressed.
A score of 7–10, means you need to make sure that things do not get any worse.
A score of 4–6 means that things are OK, but don't get complacent.
A score of 0–3 shows that you have got the balance right – for now.

Stress is not an illness. There is no psychiatric diagnosis of 'stress'; no criteria that must be met to decide if 'stress' is present; and no recognised or reproducible way of deciding its severity. Only post-traumatic stress disorder (PTSD) is an official psychiatric diagnosis, and even that is controversial. In Japan, *karoshi* (death from overwork) is becoming more widely recognised as a real, though difficult to prove, condition. The concept of stress was first seen in 1956. Stress was described as the way the body responds to demands: firstly, by preparing for action; secondly to withstand ongoing stress; and finally collapsing in exhaustion from intolerable long-term stress.

From these beginnings, we have today reached a point where it is not going too far to say we have a 'stress industry'. People go to law to seek compensation for work stress – and the Courts and Employment Tribunals are responding. Stress-related symptoms and 'burnout' account for millions of pounds in payments and lost work each year.

RECOGNISING STRESS

Stress is a subjective, individual matter. Three different people could find the same situation stressful, unproblematic, or boring. It all depends on how individuals see the demands, and how they cope.

The nature of the stress matters. Variety is the spice of life, and its lack can be stressful. A repetitive, routine job can be more stressful than a varied one, at least in the short term.

Perhaps most importantly of all, people need a degree of control over their lives to feel happy. If they feel little or no control, and that nothing they think matters or influences the direction of events, people become stressed and resentful. The amount that someone is paid at work is not the only, or even the main, consideration in stress, but a fair reward is a sign of appreciation and undoubtedly helps.

HANDLING STRESS

Prevention is better, and easier, than cure. So it is important to recognise the signs of stress before they become entrenched. It is a good idea to perform a 'stress audit' from time to time, either once or twice a year or if your situation changes, for example by changing your job. The questionnaire opposite can provide a framework for doing this, but the important thing is to maintain the balance between work and leisure in your life.

If you think you are experiencing stress talk to your GP, who can give you advice and medication if needed.

Balance work and leisure

To move away from a position of perceived powerlessness or being undervalued at work may be excellent advice, but like much commonsense advice, it is easier said than done. And changing jobs in itself can be stressful. If you are not able to modify your work, or make it more interesting and varied, try making some changes in your life outside work.

- Revive old interests or hobbies, or start new ones.
- Spend more quality time with family and friends.
- Learn a new skill or start taking classes.
- Work at maintaining a positive mental outlook.

Learn to relax

Relaxation is a skill just like any other and needs to be learned. Meditation, even if very simple or rudimentary, has been shown to improve mental and physical health. There are many forms of meditation: try them out till you find one that suits you. Yoga is very beneficial, too, and you don't have to be able to twist your limbs into the lotus position to enjoy a yoga class.

Cut the caffeine

Too much caffeine increases the symptoms of anxiety and can interfere with sleep. You may be surprised at how much better you feel if you significantly cut down, or cut out altogether, your caffeine consumption for two weeks. If you drink lots of coffee or cola, you may suffer from headaches or cravings for a week or so after quitting, but such symptoms will soon pass.

Eat smart

Foods that contain lots of sugar that is released quickly (that is, foods with a high glycaemic index, such as sweets and pastries) are effective as short-term mood boosters. The effect is short lived, though, and a rebound dip in mood is common.

Fluctuations in sugar level can have an adverse effect on mood, as well as playing havoc with a balanced diet. Stress-busting foods have a low glycaemic index – they are converted to sugar slowly by the body. They include wholegrain bread, vegetables, beans, buckwheat and oatmeal. Also, as people under long-term stress seem to be more prone to infection, it may be worth taking supplements such as zinc and vitamin C to help boost immunity.

SPECIAL TIME
Make regular time and space for yourself. Women, in particular, can neglect themselves in this respect, but doing something for yourself relieves stress.

STRESS-RELIEVING FOODS
Vitamin B (especially B$_3$, B$_5$ and B$_6$), selenium, omega-3 fatty acids and taurine can all ease symptoms of stress. Fruit, fish and nuts – especially almonds and brazil nuts – are rich in some or all of these,

CALMING TEAS
As well as being refreshing, herbal teas such as camomile and mint exert a calming effect on many people.

Improving your self-esteem

Low self-esteem can trigger a chain reaction which can be mentally and physically debilitating. There are some simple strategies for improving self-esteem, however, which other people have found useful and effective.

Unlike animals, human beings have 'self awareness'. This means that we have the ability to define who we are and then decide if we like that identity or not. This judgement of ourselves determines our self-esteem: if we reject parts of our identity we can cause ourselves enormous pain and psychological damage.

How do we get low self-esteem?

People who regularly focus on the aspects of themselves they don't like are gradually chipping away at their own self-esteem. Everyone has a critical inner voice, but people with low self-esteem tend to have a more vicious and vocal critic. This inner critic blames you for things that go wrong, compares you to others (and finds you wanting) and sets impossible standards for perfection.

This critic tells you how you should be living, keeps a list of your failures, and convinces you that other people are bored or disappointed by you.

Does low self-esteem matter?

In the same way that you would protect a physical wound, people with low self-esteem start to avoid anything that might aggravate the pain of self-rejection in any way. They take fewer social, academic or career risks. They make it more difficult for themselves to meet people or push hard for something where they might not succeed.

Most people feel frustrated with their lives due to lack of self-esteem. It renders many people incapable not only of achieving, but even setting objectives because it deprives them of motivation.

HOW DOES POOR SELF-ESTEEM AFFECT YOU?

It gives you a poor self-image and makes you feel unworthy. You don't like or appreciate yourself. You feel inferior. This makes it difficult for you to relate to other people. If you don't like yourself it is hard to like others, or to imagine them liking you. This leads to problems in relationships both at home and at work. It can also lead to long-term unhappiness, even depression. This may trigger problem behaviour such as over-reliance on alcohol or drugs.

IS SELF-ESTEEM VANITY?

People who have self-esteem love themselves, but that doesn't mean that they are in love with themselves or are vain. It means that they appreciate themselves, have a respect for themselves and know their own worth. And because we tend to think of others as we think of ourselves, if you love yourself and appreciate yourself, you will love others and appreciate them too.

IMPROVING YOUR SELF-ESTEEM THROUGH THERAPY

The first step is to acknowledge that low self-esteem is a problem. There are now several different kinds of talking therapies available: these include counselling, psychotherapy, cognitive therapy, behaviour therapy and hypnotherapy. The basis of many therapies is that you learn to appreciate yourself and reduce your inner critical voice.

Neurolinguistic programming, or NLP, is one such therapy. You might be asked to visualise yourself through the eyes of someone who appreciates you. This could be your mother, your partner or a good

5 Steps to building your self-esteem

Low self-esteem can be a vicious downward spiral: the sooner you can break the circle, the better.

1 Learn to relax. This takes time and practice, but if you can learn to switch off at will, you will begin to feel better about yourself.

2 In a relaxed state of mind, think objectively about your good points. Focus on the characteristics your family and friends love and value in you.

3 Recall moments in your life when you felt good about yourself, when you felt in control. Re-experience those feelings.

4 With all your good points and positive feelings about yourself in mind, visualise yourself facing difficult situations.

5 If this doesn't seem to work talk to your GP about your suitability for some form of talking therapy.

BRINGING ON BACK THE GOOD TIMES

Recalling times when you felt good about yourself and your place in the world, and recapturing the feelings of elation, can help to improve fragile self-esteem.

'On my wedding day I felt my husband's unconditional love and the support of my whole family.'

'The day I took part in and completed the London marathon, I felt an overwhelming sense of physical achievement and an unbelievable mental high.'

'When I first held my baby in my arms, I understood what it means to be at peace with the world.'

friend. You will be asked to feel what that person feels when they look at you, to feel their admiration for you, to feel their respect for you and, most important of all, to feel their love for you. In this way you learn to appreciate all your good points, and learn to love all aspects of yourself. It may take several sessions with slightly different approaches each time, but such a technique can work very well.

Cognitive therapy enables you to understand why you don't feel good about yourself. It helps you to focus on the individual aspects of your emotions and behaviour so that you can learn to change them. Again, you learn to understand and appreciate your good points and either to

accept or work on your bad ones, whilst at the same time you learn to love yourself, 'warts and all'.

Many people have a list of 'shoulds', which dictate how they should live their life. Therapy can show people how to reverse this type of internal self-talk. It can also help unravel the thought habits which interpret reality in an unrealistic way.

BUILDING SELF-ESTEEM ON YOUR OWN

Although not so easy, you can build good self-esteem on your own. There are many books and tapes designed to help with this. Many start off by teaching you how to relax deeply. This state of mind enables you to focus more easily on yourself.

One technique is to recall a situation in your life when you felt really good – concentrate on the positive emotions. Then think about a current situation where you feel nervous or anxious. Now experience that situation with the strong positive feelings in your mind. This can help show you that you can feel good and confident in difficult situations – and you can be in control.

It is important to take your time to build self-esteem – it doesn't happen overnight. Do not feel discouraged if you do not feel as confident on a particular day: our moods change often affecting the way we feel. As you make small steps each day, you will be rewarded with a greater sense of calm and confidence.

Anger management

It is perfectly normal to feel angry sometimes, but if anger is inappropriate or out of proportion it can cause problems – and not just for people on the receiving end of bad temper, but for the physical health of the angry individual too.

WHAT IS ANGER?

Anger, along with fear, disgust, relief, shame, joy, surprise and sadness, is one of our primary or core emotions. It may also be an important part of our survival instinct.

We get angry as a result of undesirable events caused by another person or situation. It is a temporary state that varies in intensity from irritation to intense fury and rage. Anger is not in itself necessarily a bad thing and it can be an appropriate and healthy response to a situation. However, anger has often been seen in moral terms as a passion that should be controlled.

Anger and everyday living

Anger occurs in different settings and for different reasons in different people. Some people are more prone to anger than others. We all know of people who are quick-tempered, who have a short fuse. It is likely that an inability to articulate underlying feelings or emotions (or even an inability to describe emotions at all – alexithymia) may be reflected in ready anger. The usual social inhibitions that encourage people to keep their temper under control often dissolve under the influence of alcohol or other drugs.

People who may be excessively shy, anxious or uncomfortable in social situations may respond to their feelings of discomfort by losing their temper easily, often with the most trivial of triggers. For some kinds of personality, perceived abandonment or lack of a caring attitude may precipitate anger. In others, the appearance of not getting that to which they feel entitled may produce considerable anger.

Propensity to anger is often a stable characteristic. Children who display high levels of anger continue to do so at the same level into adulthood. This may be because of an in-built tendency, but it may be because they learnt early that being angry gets them what they want.

Anger and mental disorders

Anger is a feature of psychiatric disorders and is an important risk factor for violence among people with mental disorders. Although the majority of psychiatric patients are not dangerous in any way, violence in psychiatric hospitals is a problem.

Anger is, not surprisingly, strongly associated with danger to others. It is probably the most important emotion that differentiates aggressive from non-aggressive people.

Anger is also closely related to depression. Depression may represent an unhealthy turning inwards of angry or aggressive feelings. People who find it difficult to talk about how they feel about a trauma they experienced in the past, often turn the anger inwards. This is expressing anger in an unhealthy way.

Between 65 and 80 per cent of assault patients in accident and emergency are intoxicated at the time of the injury.

What happens when we get angry

Emotional anger is accompanied by physiological arousal. The heart rate and blood pressure increase. Hormones including adrenaline and steroids are produced, readying the body for physical action. Blood is diverted from non-essential parts of the body, such as the gut, to the muscles of the limbs. The muscles need more oxygen and so breathing quickens and we become aware of a heartbeat. 'Butterflies' can be felt in the stomach as blood is diverted. The palms sweat, pupils dilate and awareness of surroundings becomes more intense.

This stress response accompanies each episode of anger. If recurrent anger is unmanaged, the constant flood of stress chemicals can lead to long-term health problems such as digestive complaints, high blood pressure, heart attack and stroke.

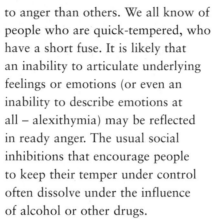

How should I deal with an angry person?

When confronted with an angry person, it is essential not to escalate the problem by counter-attacking. Allowing the situation to cool down, or using pleasurable distractions, may divert the anger harmlessly. Offering an angry person a punch bag to pummel may actually escalate their sense of anger rather than reduce it.

ASK THE EXPERT

TIPS TO CONTROL ANGER

Anger management is about recognising potential flashpoints and learning to deal with them. These strategies may help.

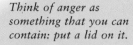

Think of anger as something that you can contain: put a lid on it.

Consider whether your anger is due to the effects of alcohol or caffeine – and take remedial action if it is.

Adopt a positive outlook by moving forwards rather than dwelling on the past: don't feel shackled by your past.

Try to see things in perspective and ask yourself if this incident is really worth all the aggravation of losing your temper.

Accept that some things are frustrating, but nobody's fault.

Keep a sense of humour in tense situations: negotiate with words not fists.

MANAGING ANGER

Motivation is crucial, as modifying behaviour can be a difficult process. Once learnt, well-managed anger is a useful emotion that can help you to make positive changes in your life.

To modify severe anger, it is important to recognise the triggers of anger. For example, if someone becomes intensely angry at everyday incidents while driving (so-called 'road rage') some form of re-education in driving skills may be helpful. Someone who readily becomes 'fighting drunk' should avoid alcohol or at least reduce consumption. Exposure to the trigger may sometimes be counter-productive, as it may cause brooding about the perceived injury or insult resulting in more, not less, anger.

Children should be taught how to express anger properly – so it is important to lead by example. Teach practical problem-solving skills and the difference between aggression and appropriately expressed anger.

The following ideas can help you to express anger in healthy ways:
- If you feel out of control, walk away from the situation temporarily until you cool down.
- Recognise and accept the emotion as normal and part of life.
- Try to pinpoint the exact reasons why you feel angry.
- Once you have identified the problem, consider coming up with different strategies on how to remedy the situation.
- Do something physical, such as going for a run or playing sport.

Anger management training

Anger management classes or training may take place in a group setting or on a one-to-one basis. The therapist tries to see the client's point of view and understand the nature of their anger, and will help to analyse what behaviour in others makes them feel angry. This understanding may make the actions of others seem less deliberately harmful to the client. Sessions will usually include some education about what anger is, and how it arises and affects you. Clients will be helped to change their approach to confrontations from a punishing, angry state of mind to a more negotiating or forgiving one. If their anger occurs when drinking or using drugs, they may need help to address that aspect of their life.

Assertiveness training

Parents steer their children to 'stand up for themselves', but by adulthood many people have lost this skill. But expressing your needs in a non-threatening manner can spell the difference between contentment and frustration.

WHAT IS ASSERTIVENESS?

In a civilised society, we should all have the right to form our own opinions and, providing we are not harming others, decide how we want to live our lives. We have a right to express ourselves, to say no, and to confess we do not understand.

Being assertive means attempting to achieve our legitimate and reasonable wants without resorting to aggression. The key words are 'legitimate' and 'reasonable'. What you want must be legitimate. If you do not have the authority or the right to ask for something, then asking for it is not being assertive, but aggressive. Even if something is legitimately yours for the asking, if it is not reasonable, then asking for it is also aggressiveness.

Children are taught to stand up for themselves. As long as this does not involve verbal or physical aggression, this will form a healthy basis for assertiveness. They are taught how to express their thoughts and desires clearly, while maintaining a dialogue of communication with others.

As an adult, you should be able to express yourself after considering your response. You should be able to ask for help without being made to feel humiliated or incompetent. Everyone also has the right to change his or her mind.

COMPROMISE AND NEGOTIATION

One cannot consider rights without responsibilities, however. Increasingly, and properly, we all have to account for our actions in some way. In a civilised society this means that we assert our own interests and needs, but not necessarily at the expense of others, or, particularly, at the expense of the rights of others.

This means that everyday life is a matter of compromise. To be able to negotiate compromise without becoming a doormat is at the core of assertiveness. Of course, sometimes – as in any negotiation – you will not get everything that you want.

BODY LANGUAGE

As humans, we say more to each other without using words than we do by means of speech. Body language and posture give away what we are really thinking.

Assertive body language involves steady and direct (but not staring) eye contact, posture that is erect and well-balanced, and hand gestures that have relaxed motions – the body appears open, not defensive.

EVERYDAY ASSERTIVE BEHAVIOUR

Every day we are faced with situations that can be annoying and frustrating. Instead of bottling up your feelings or exploding in anger, try the assertive approach and calmly make your voice heard.

DON'T STAND FOR IT
If someone pushes in front of you in the supermarket queue, point out that others are waiting too.

FOOD FOR THOUGHT
You see a hair that is not one of yours on your plate at a restaurant. Don't demand to see the chef and threaten to sue the restaurant for unhygienic practices. Instead, simply point it out to the waiter and ask for a fresh portion.

BAD TIMING
A work colleague stops by for a chat and a cup of tea, not realising that you have a deadline and they are interrupting you. The assertive response is to tactfully ask if you could get together later – at lunch or for afternoon coffee perhaps – as you need to finish the piece of work.

PRINCIPLES OF ASSERTIVENESS

- Accept your right to get what is legitimately and reasonably yours. Recognise that some people do not like others to be assertive.
- Practise being assertive on the first occasion of undesirable behaviour from others. Difficult situations can creep up because the first or second instance of the behaviour may seem insignificant.
- In any difficult interpersonal situation, make sure you are clear about what you want to happen. Decide what you can achieve immediately and what you will tackle later.
- Put yourself in the other person's shoes. What do they want and can you help them achieve it? Why are they behaving in a difficult way?
- Think carefully about what you will say. Always ask yourself: 'Will this improve the situation – will it help me and both of us to work effectively towards what we want?'

- In particularly difficult situations mentally rehearse the words you will say. Perhaps seek advice from a trusted friend or colleague.
- At the beginning of almost any situation offer praise. Try to make the atmosphere unthreatening; you want the person to listen to you.
- Keep your voice and expression neutral and keep the volume down.
- Listen – people interpret your listening as a sign of respect.
- State clearly what you want the other person to do. Be direct, not blunt. If you beat around the bush people worry and expect the worst.
- Check the facts – ask people directly whether or not something happened. Don't rely on hearsay.
- Never turn your criticism of someone's work or behaviour into a personal criticism or insult.
- When people become angry and insulting, strive to stay calm. Be aware of your anger and control it.
- Practise being persistent. Some people escalate their aggressive or manipulative behaviour when faced with assertive people. Do not give in to threats or attempts to make you feel guilty – this shows that aggressive behaviour works.
- Ask for the person's help. Explain how their demand or behaviour affects you and others.
- Being assertive sometimes means finding a compromise. This may mean moving from an extreme position to a middle one.
- Respond positively to other people's assertive behaviour. Show this by saying 'Thank you for being honest' or 'I am glad you told me'.

ASSERTIVENESS TRAINING

If your approach to a difficult conflict situation is either passive or aggressive, you will not often get the outcome you want. Assertiveness training aims to teach specific assertiveness techniques, including understanding what you want and need, and conveying it clearly in your body language and words.

MECHANICAL BREAKDOWN
A fault on your car re-appears soon after being repaired. Don't lose your temper with the garage: phone them to say you are returning the car and expect them to fix it as soon as possible.

RESISTING PRESSURE
At work someone asks for your help on a report, but you have an urgent project to finish. Politely explain that you are too busy at the moment but can help when you have finished your own work.

NOT STITCHED UP
You find a fault on an item of clothing you have just bought. Resist thinking that it doesn't matter and you'll mend it yourself. Instead, return it to the shop and ask for a replacement or a refund.

Lifting your spirits

It is normal to feel down some of the time, it's a natural response to disappointment or trauma. Even persistent low spirits, however, can respond to simple self-help measures, designed to get you through a rough period.

Life is full of ups and downs and everybody gets dissatisfied from time to time. To suffer from occasional low spirits or thoughts of having taken a wrong direction in life is common and perfectly normal.

We cannot be happy all of the time. If something bad happens to you – if you suffer bereavement, go through the breakdown of a marriage, lose your job, or fail to be appointed after an interview – it is perfectly normal to be disappointed or sad. If you were not sad, then the loss was not all that great anyway, or you were reacting abnormally.

One of the problems in psychiatry is that psychiatrists use words such as 'depression' that are also in frequent everyday usage. For example, after a particularly trying day someone may say, 'I feel so depressed'. What they mean is that they feel low-spirited, dissatisfied or unhappy. They are probably not trying to convey a feeling that they suffer from a clinical depression or a depressive illness.

There is a spectrum ranging from normal mood, through pronounced and persistent 'uncommon' unhappiness, through to clinical depression which ranges from mild to severe, and in the latter there is a distinct risk of suicide.

Another problem is that when someone is caught in low spirits, they tend to be confronted with advice, such as 'cheer up … pull yourself together … everything will be okay', and so on. Although this is often a way in which friends and family help each other, if depression has taken hold, such an approach is counterproductive. It can make the person feel worse. They feel as if they are trapped in a deep hole and cannot get out of it. However, before that happens – if someone is simply feeling 'blue' or down – there are several things that can help.

SELF-HELP METHODS

If you are feeling down, the most important thing is to keep doing things to boost your mood and improve your outlook.

Low spirits often set off a chain of rumination or preoccupation with negative things. Being busy and keeping company with others, especially if they are friends who like and respect you, or at least amuse you, can be extremely beneficial. Low spirits are always worse for being concealed with dignity. Be open with people who you like and trust. Sharing your feelings can help, and you may find that other people experience similar thoughts.

Make the room in which you spend most of your time as bright and pleasant as you can, perhaps installing a natural light bulb, which may improve your mood, especially if you are someone who is affected when the nights draw in over winter. The reduction in the amount of available light can affect the levels of certain hormones in the body, causing a depressive effect in some people – the condition known as Seasonal Affective Disorder (SAD).

Avoid, if you can, melancholy or serious books, films and television programmes. Read a light-hearted book, or try watching comedies or more neutral subjects, such as wildlife documentaries, on television.

Some people find that focusing on spiritual thoughts and ideas can lead towards a greater sense of meaning in their daily life. You do not have to be a religious person to be aware of, and appreciate, the good things in your life right now, no matter how small. Generally speaking, when low spirits overcome you, take a short-term view of life – perhaps no further than teatime. But if you are a religious person, you may find reassurance in your faith and take solace from it.

Herbal mood lifter

Many people have been helped by St John's wort (*Hypericum perforatum*), which is available over the counter in many pharmacists, chemists and health food shops. Although St John's wort is a natural herbal remedy, it can have side effects including skin rashes and even

cataracts. St John's wort can also interact with other medications, including the contraceptive pill, so if you are planning to take St John's wort and are taking other medication, you must seek professional medical advice first.

Aromatherapy

Few things can have so profound an impact as specific smells and fragrances. Our sense of smell is tied directly to the part of the brain most involved with memory and emotion.

The pure essential oils used in aromatherapy have the ability to influence mood in a number of ways. Some oils can ease anxiety or depression, some lift mood, while others aid relaxation. You just need to add a few drops to a bath, a massage oil, or to water in an oil burner to enjoy their effects. As essential oils can be strong, most are not designed for use directly on the skin. Before experimenting with any new oil, find out if there are any warnings related to its use.

Beating the blues
Your attitude towards life has a bearing on how well you cope with everyday problems. These simple self-help measures can go some way towards maintaining an even keel.

BE AWARE OF THE WORLD AROUND YOU
Take refuge in the present and try not to think too much about the past or future. Live for the moment and take time to enjoy the little things – a sunny morning, the smell of freshly cut grass, a cosy fireside.

BE OPEN TO NOVELTY
See friends, take up new interests, or revive some old ones, and try to keep busy – this will stop you from dwelling on real or perceived problems. Try not to spend a lot of time alone or thinking about yourself.

BE FOODWISE
Take care over what you eat and drink, getting plenty of energy-giving foods such as wholegrains, and avoiding energy sappers such as sugar and salt. Pay particular attention to limiting your intake of caffeine and alcohol.

BE OPEN TO HELP
Recognise when things are getting on top of you and talk to someone when you need help: do not keep things bottled up inside. Remember that asking for timely help is a sign of strength, not of weakness.

Seeking support

Cynics would argue that support has become something of an industry, but it is a fact that previous generations had stronger, albeit more informal, support networks than we do today. Support is good, and timely support can be invaluable.

Past generations would perhaps be bemused by the concept of 'support' as we define it today. In an arguably more socially cohesive age, support was obtained from family, colleagues at work, friends or perhaps a community or religious leader. The family doctor could also be included in this list; but there was no support 'industry' comparable with that which we see today.

The most important social networks are still those supplied by family, friends and work colleagues. It is to those groups that we tend, quite rightly, to turn when in difficulty. As social animals, we need the support and company of others. Very few of us are comfortable with persistent solitude. Even monks, who spend much of their life in contemplation, live in communities.

Seeking support from social networks is completely appropriate and healthy. To need support is in no way weak or abnormal, we all need help from time to time to get through difficult periods.

WHEN IS EXTRA HELP REQUIRED?

When we experience problems it is usual for friends, family or colleagues to give advice, and offer understanding and support. Most people find that the simple act of someone else listening, can help to ease a worry or burden.

However, if a problem is too profound or intense, or feels too personal to share, it may be time to go beyond your normal network and seek professional help. A simple rule of thumb is that when the advice you get from your normal network does not strike a chord with you, or you are unable to talk to someone close to you about a problem, it is time to seek help elsewhere.

A drawback of the support you get from your normal social network is that, however close the friendship or family relationship, you generally have to be careful what you say, no matter how distraught you are. People who are in emotional trouble may not necessarily choose their words carefully and may appear more negative or critical than they really feel. Other people can be offended or disturbed by this, and the knowledge that this is possible may mean that the person in distress cannot freely air their concerns.

This self-censorship does not apply when you are talking to someone who is paid to listen to you. Counsellors and other therapists have been described as 'paid friends'. You are talking to someone who is in a position of being able to give you sympathetic and objective help without being judgmental or disturbed by what you say.

The website findsupport.co.uk aims to list all organisations in the UK that provide help, advice and support.

WHERE CAN I GO FOR HELP?

If you would like to see a counsellor you must always seek help from someone who is a member of a reputable professional organisation, medical or non-medical. This way you have the assurance that the person concerned will be sufficiently objective to offer you the most appropriate advice – and to tell you when they can not.

You can also receive significant support and input from books, radio and television. Talk shows and factual programmes about emotional problems are broadcast almost daily on radio and television. Many newspapers and magazines run columns where various experts (who give sensible, appropriate advice) deal with common problems. Such programmes and features can show people that they are not abnormal or alone. Just knowing that other people are suffering the same way can bring relief and encouragement.

Helplines

Many organisations now fund telephone helplines. These can provide a mine of practical and sensible information, especially about relevant local resources. In the United Kingdom, the National Health Service has set up a helpline, NHS Direct, where callers can speak to qualified staff about mental health problems. To some extent, NHS Direct fulfils a kind of gatekeeper function to the rest of the NHS, but callers can often receive advice over the phone. The Samaritans offer perhaps the best known telephone helpline. People in distress can call them at any time and receive a sympathetic hearing.

Where to go for help

Many organisations offer telephone support to individuals who are finding it hard to cope. Some of these, such as the Samaritans, will support across a variety of problems. Others are more focused.

Sex and relationships
Relate
Brook Advisory Centres
Sexwise
Lesbian and Gay Switchboard

Social, legal and financial
Citizens Advice Bureau
Women's Refuge
Shelterline

Children's problems
Childline
Anti-Bullying Campaign

Health
NHS Direct
Eating Disorders Association
National Autistic Society
Scope
Mencap

Addictions
National Drugs Helpline
Quitline
Drinkline
Alcoholics Anonymous
Al-ateen

Well run helplines recognise the value of simply listening to someone's problems. People who are seeking support are not necessarily seeking advice, but almost invariably they appreciate a sympathetic and empathic listener.

Many people today have access to the Internet, and there are seemingly almost unlimited resources for help and support there too. Websites offer information and support that varies in quality and value, it is therefore best to go to sites that are connected to hospitals, professional bodies and well-known support groups.

GETTING PRACTICAL SUPPORT

Support does not necessarily always need to be psychological. Practical support for particular areas of concern can be just as important. Financial counselling is one example. Many people have seemingly overwhelming financial difficulties. When confronted with such problems, their natural, but unwise, tendency is to try and ignore them, hoping that they will go away. They do not. Instead, it is important to adopt a practical approach to such problems, however difficult, and

it is here that professional support agencies such as the Citizens Advice Bureau can be extremely helpful.

Similarly, people who have relationship difficulties may obtain crucial practical support from organisations that began by offering guidance for troubled marriages but who have adapted to the changing times by covering relationships of every kind.

Groups such as Alcoholics Anonymous and the Alcohol Recovery Programme help those suffering from alcohol dependence. Relatives or carers of alcoholics can also gain support. Drug users and their relatives are helped by parallel organisations, and it certainly appears that there is a support organisation for every problem.

PRIVATE THERAPY

Always go to an established organisation or guild when looking for a therapist. They will talk to you to find out what your needs are and then select a therapist who may be suitable. This will not necessarily ensure the success of the therapy, but at least you will have an assurance that the person is qualified to offer the service advertised.

In the end, the success of therapy relies on a certain 'chemistry' between the client and therapist. If you do not feel comfortable with your therapist you may feel inhibited and lose the will to continue with your therapy. If you find this to be the case, do not hesitate to go back to the organisation and ask to see another therapist.

It is important to be aware of expectations you have when you see a therapist. A therapist will not magically 'solve all your problems'. They can however, help you to break down the major issues affecting you, and explore your thoughts and feelings from a different perspective to help you find a way forward.

Lifestyle coaching

Lifestyle coaching has become fashionable, although it remains fairly expensive. For some people having an outsider look at their personal and professional goals, and give them advice towards achieving them can be helpful.

MEDITATION

If you are seeking a more general solution to your turmoil, you may well find that learning to meditate can be very useful. People who meditate regularly often say that it has allowed them to regain a sense of perspective in their own lives.

Meditation is all about focussing the mind on something. It can be a single word, your own breathing, or a mental image. The mind can do this for a few seconds, but then it starts to think again. The challenge is to let these thoughts go and refocus. As the distracting thoughts arise, keep letting them go. Gradually they become less aggravating and you will feel freer and more at ease.

Many people are aware of nothing but their thoughts, worries and obsessions. Meditating a few minutes each day can help to make the mind clear, alert and relaxed.

RETREATS

Another way of obtaining such perspective is to go on a retreat. Few retreats are run by organisations with no religious affiliation, but the fact that you do not belong to the relevant religion need not stop you from attending. If you are on a retreat with a particular theme or philosophy, it may help to have some

Take time out
Many people find that their lives have become too stressful. Getting away from it all can provide some much needed tranquility and peace to put things into perspective.

When bereavement counselling can help

Most people experience common stages of grief. These do not occur in a particular order and they can be revisited many times, but experiencing them can help a person to complete the grieving process. Professional help can be required if someone finds they cannot move on from a particular stage of grief. The different stages of grief include:

- **Shock** This is usually the first response, most often described as numbness.
- **Disorganisation** The bereaved person may be unable to do the simplest things.
- **Denial** This is can be a defence against feeling too much pain at once.
- **Depression** This often emerges after denial, but becomes less intense with time.
- **Guilt** Can be about real or imagined situations, or for angry thoughts or feelings.
- **Anxiety** May feel like you are losing control of your feelings or general worry.
- **Aggression** Can range from irritability to intense anger with anyone.
- **Resolution** As emotions become calmer, an acceptance of death occurs..
- **Reintegration** Acceptance is put into practice, the bereaved starts to move on.

belief in it. However, most retreat centres offer non-denominational quiet sessions which anyone can attend. For many people the retreat has become an important refuge from the rough and tumble chaos of everyday life. It can provide valuable 'time out' in which to examine priorities and put issues into perspective. Most retreats are not expensive, and occur all year round in most countries.

BEREAVEMENT

Bereavement and grief are very complex and stressful issues. It is something that most of us will experience at some point in our lives. Everyone is different and people recover at different rates.

How you respond to a death will be very individual and personal. There are a number of common stages of grief (see box), these can be difficult to go through, but experiencing them can help a person to grieve fully.

Suppressing your grief will not make it go away. Friends and well wishers may seek to distract you from your grief because it is uncomfortable for them. It takes courage to grieve as it is often difficult and painful. You need to be encouraged to talk about your feelings with someone who will listen in a caring and confidential way.

Professional help

Many people need extra help, in the form of bereavement counselling or a support group. Seeking help is never a sign of weakness.

If you do need help, then reach out for it, visit your GP or contact a bereavement organisation. Many people have benefited from bereavement counselling and there are now hundreds of bereavement support groups all over the country. It is far better to address grief and anxiety during the beginning stages, rather than letting it manifest itself for months, or even years.

When should you ask for help?

You should ask for help if you are experiencing any of the following:

- If you are finding your grief hard to bear and you cannot handle the intense feelings or body sensations.
- If you feel that your emotions are not falling into place over time and you feel chronic tension, confusion, emptiness or exhaustion.
- If you have to keep active in order to feel anything.
- If you continue to have nightmares or poor sleep.
- If you are trying not to burden anyone with your feelings.
- If you have no person or group with whom to share your emotions and you feel the need to do so.
- If are find you are often clumsy and you are having accidents.
- If you continue to smoke or drink to excess or take drugs to cope since the event.
- If your work performance suffers.
- If your relationships seem to be suffering badly.

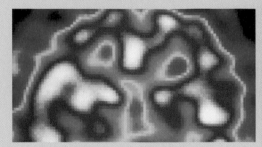

3

What happens
when things go wrong

Knowing what can go wrong

'Mental illness' is a catch-all term encompassing conditions ranging from depression to autism, from schizophrenia to alcoholism. Factors that can make individuals vulnerable to mental illness include age, inherited genetic predisposition and too much stress.

AGE-RELATED DISORDERS

Autism and Asperger's syndrome are both conditions that a child might be born with (that is, they are congenital) although symptoms often only become obvious when the child is a toddler; this is also the case with learning disabilities. Other disorders that emerge in childhood include attention deficit hyperactivity disorder (ADHD) and disorders to do with behaviour (frequently aggressive) and emotion (often linked with anxiety).

The majority of the most serious mental illnesses – especially manic depression (bipolar affective disorder, see page 139) and schizophrenia (page 152) – usually emerge during early adulthood. For such serious illnesses to occur during childhood is exceptional, and neither do they often first occur after the age of 40. Depression (page 142) can develop at any time from childhood onwards, but about

At any one time, at least one in every six adults in the UK has some form of mental disorder.

body disease. Senile dementia becomes more common as age advances, and the majority of people who survive into extreme old age have some structural evidence of senile dementia of the Alzheimer's type in their brain, even if they remain outwardly alert and with reasonable memory.

CHEMICAL IMBALANCE

Some mental conditions have an underlying chemical basis – they are the result of a physical imbalance of chemicals within the brain. Depression in particular is associated with reduced levels of the chemicals serotonin,

MORE COMMON

SYMPTOMS OF ANXIETY	SYMPTOMS OF DEPRESSION	EATING DISORDERS	OBSESSIVE COMPULSIVE DISORDER
14,000 PER 100,000 (1 IN 7)	12,000 PER 100,000 (1 IN 8)	3000 PER 100,000 (1 IN 33)	1200 PER 100,000 (1 IN 85)
About two-thirds of people suffering from anxiety also have symptoms of depression.	*This figure includes mild, moderate and severe (clinical) depression. Of this total, about three-quarters have symptoms of anxiety as well.*	*This includes anorexia nervosa, bulimia nervosa and compulsive overeating (see page 99).*	PHOBIA
			1200 PER 100,000 (1 IN 85)

half of all women who become depressed at some point in their lives do so at around the time of the menopause, when they are in their late 40s or early 50s.

Dementia in old age

In later life, senile dementia is the condition that gives rise to most concern. The commonest type of senile dementia is Alzheimer's disease (see page 135). This is a progressive dementia that occurs as a result of structural changes in the brain. Middle-aged people are sometimes affected, but the disease is more typically found among older people.

Vascular dementia, causing disorders of the circulation of blood within the brain, is also common, as is Lewy

noradrenaline and dopamine in the brain. The altered thought processing behind schizophrenia is believed to be due to abnormalities of dopamine metabolism within the brain. It is thought that some people have an inherited genetic predisposition towards a chemical imbalance that leads to mental illness. Unhappiness and stress can trigger this chemical imbalance, although it is not clear how this happens.

FAMILY INHERITANCE

Genetic inheritance may play a part in more than a few mental disorders. The genes children inherit from their parents can predispose them towards certain diseases and disorders. For example, the risk of developing schizophrenia is higher if a parent already has the condition.

Depression, a mood disorder, commonly runs within families. A family history of clinical depression indicates that members of that family are more prone to depression: in the jargon, they show 'genetic loading'. In addition to genetic inheritance there are also other factors at work here. Children observe parents and carers very closely and, to a large extent, imitate them. It is common for the children of parents who are depressed to be at a higher risk themselves of becoming depressed, partly because they have

LESS COMMON

DEMENTIA
1100 PER 100,000 (1 IN 90)
Over the age of 80, 1 in 5 people are affected by dementia.

SCHIZOPHRENIA
1000 PER 100,000
(1 IN 100)

learned that this is how adults behave and have, perhaps unconsciously, taken on board this style of coping.

TOO MUCH STRESS

Stress can cause mental illness. It can cause a tendency to worry too much or become angry, for example, to grow into a major problem. Stress allied to genetic predisposition to a particular mental disorder – be it a mood disorder such as depression or a psychotic illness like schizophrenia – can tip someone over into developing that mental disorder.

More common than you think

The prevalence rates above indicate the approximate number of cases of selected disorders in the UK at any given time. In total, it is estimated that at least one in four people will experience a mental disorder at some point in their lives. This does not include addiction to alcohol or nicotine, both of which are classified by psychiatrists as addictive disorders.

eating disorder

life events

congenital conditions

ageing

addictions

Stress can be specific or general

There is stress that is related to a specific event: bereavement or the break-up of a marriage, for example. There is stress brought on by a high-pressure, over-busy lifestyle. And there is stress brought on by social deprivation, in which poverty, unemployment and loneliness all feature heavily. Figures show that many forms of mental illness are more common wherever there is social deprivation on a large scale. A particularly vulnerable group as far as depression is concerned are mothers with children under 14 years old with partners who are not supportive or are absent entirely.

PROBLEMS WITH EATING

Eating disorders (see page 99) share some of the same characteristics as anxiety conditions and obsessive compulsive disorders. What brings them on is a complicated question with no straightforward answers, but they do seem to be a reaction to pressure produced by the high expectations set by modern society.

SUBSTANCE ABUSE AND ADDICTION

Substance addiction is in itself classified as a mental disorder (see page 96). In addition, addiction to alcohol and recreational/illicit drugs can interact with mental illness in different ways. Not only can substance addiction be profoundly mood-altering in the short term, but it can cause long-term unhappiness, often expressed as depression. The stress and unhappiness generated by an addiction affects not only the addict but also family and

What is the difference between psychosis and neurosis?

Although most psychiatrists are able to feel intuitively whether they are dealing with a psychosis or neurosis, the difference is rather more difficult to pin down in words. Broadly speaking, psychosis involves a disengagement from or loss of touch with reality. The person with psychosis does not generally realise this and suffers from a lack of insight into their own condition. That said, someone with a psychotic illness may still have a partial grasp of reality: having a psychotic illness is not necessarily all-pervasive, intruding into every aspect of the patient's actions or life. Neurosis, on the other hand, is never associated with a true loss of contact with reality, no matter how miserable or anxious the patient may become.

ASK THE EXPERT

friends. There is also increasing evidence that the use, especially the heavy use, of illicit drugs including cannabis (marijuana), can trigger schizophrenia.

PHYSICAL ILLNESS

Some mental disorders, notably dementia and delirium, arise from physical diseases affecting the brain. Apart from age-related dementia, there are also dementias related to HIV, syphilis or severe head injury, for example. Delirium (see page 102) can be alarming but is temporary. It can be brought on by fever, infection, alcoholic poisoning or withdrawal of a drug to which the patient is addicted.

The importance of good parenting
Of course there are many factors involved in mental illness other than parental neglect and abuse, but the importance of giving a child a happy, stable start in life with plenty of love and attention cannot be overstated.

Who's who – meet the mental health experts

The time is past when the recipients of mental health treatment had no say in its nature or delivery: consultation with patients is now established practice. The professionals involved in promoting mental health include the following.

PSYCHOLOGIST

Psychologists are not medical doctors, though they may have the title 'Dr' through having a PhD. A degree in psychology is followed by several years of postgraduate training for anyone who wishes to practise and specialise in one of the branches of psychology. Psychologists assess the function of the brain. A clinical psychologist also treats patients, usually through some form of cognitive behavioural therapy, although some psychologists are also trained in other forms of talking therapy. A developmental psychologist has a specialist interest in childhood mental disorders (see page 98). A psychologist cannot prescribe drugs.

THERAPISTS AND COUNSELLORS

Almost anyone can call themself a therapist. However, most of the mainstream therapies have reputable professional bodies to which therapists may belong. Anyone going to a therapist who is not a member of a professional organisation does so at their own risk.

- A **psychotherapist** is a term describing anyone who conducts talking treatments to a more complex level than a counsellor. A psychotherapist may be a psychiatrist, psychologist or other mental health professional. In practise, the title is often used by a therapist who is not a psychiatrist or a psychologist.
- A **psychoanalyst** specialises in the types of therapy developed by Sigmund Freud and his successors.
- A **counsellor** offers advice in a less structured setting than a psychotherapist. They may provide short-term help for a client trying to cope with a traumatic life-changing event such as bereavement or divorce. The training a counsellor receives may vary from a few weeks to several years.
- **Art and drama therapists** help patients to express feelings that would otherwise be difficult to articulate.
- **Alternative or complementary therapists** who may prove helpful to those with mental health concerns include hypnotherapists, aromatherapists, nutritional therapists, homeopaths, and others.

PSYCHIATRIST

All psychiatrists are medical doctors who have then chosen to specialise in psychiatry. To rise from training grade to consultant within psychiatry takes five to ten years. As medical doctors, psychiatrists can prescribe medication and electroconvulsive therapy, and may also conduct 'talking' therapies. Some have undergone special training in talking treatments to become 'consultant psychiatrists in psychotherapy'.

PSYCHIATRIC NURSE

Nurses with specific qualifications in mental health work play a vital role in mental health services. They work with GPs, psychiatrists, social workers and other health professionals. They can conduct many kinds of therapy, but they cannot prescribe medication, except in some areas and subject to very strict controls. As they become more senior and experienced, mental health nurses may specialise and take on their own caseload of patients.
- A **community psychiatric nurse** works as part of a community mental health team or is hospital based, and may or may not have counsellor training.

SOCIAL WORKER

Whether specialising in mental health work or not, these professionals play a vital part in the delivery of mental health services. It is difficult to underestimate the part that social stresses, such as problems with finance, accommodation or unemployment have on mental health. Social workers often act as therapists or counsellors, and are central to the process of compulsory admission to hospital under UK mental health legislation.

DISORDERS OF THE MIND

The more common mental disorders are divided by mental health professionals into groups of similar types. These divisions are generally along the following lines:
• Addictive disorders
• Childhood disorders
• Eating disorders
• Mood disorders
• Organic disorders
• Personality disorders
• Psychotic disorders
This section looks at the types of problem that fall within these groups; more detail and the diagnosis and treatment of specific disorders is given in the 'A to Z of Diseases and Disorders'. Of course, some mental health conditions could be placed equally well in several groups, and many patients have signs and symptoms that cannot be confined within one family of disorders.

Addictive disorders

An addiction is a compulsion to repeat the same behaviour again and again. There are two types of addiction: physical addiction to a drug of some kind, and psychological addiction to a behaviour rather than a drug.

PHYSICAL ADDICTION

Physical addiction occurs when the body is physically dependent on a drug: nicotine, alcohol, prescription or non-prescription drugs. When there is dependence, withdrawal of the drug causes physical symptoms such as trembling, sweating or vomiting. These withdrawal symptoms are alleviated if the drug is taken. Physical addiction to a substance is also known as a substance-related disorder.

Nicotine dependence

Smoking does not alter the general behaviour of a smoker, but in the long-term this compulsive habit is often lethal.

Alcohol dependence

Alcoholism is physical dependence on alcohol, such that sudden deprivation causes withdrawal symptoms. (For more information see page 134.)

Dependence on prescription or other drugs

Included within this category are:
• amphetamines;
• cannabis;
• cocaine;
• hallucinogens;
• inhalants, such as glue or a solvent;
• opium-derived drugs such as heroin, and opioid analgesics (painkillers) such as morphine;
• sedatives and antianxiety drugs such as the benzodiazepines (see page 119).
(For more information see page 144.)

Behaviours that indicate dependence

There are particular behaviour patterns that strongly suggest dependence. These apply to any substance addiction. To take alcohol as an example, for the dependent drinker the consumption of alcohol will be focused on the avoidance of withdrawal symptoms and will be largely independent of mood or setting. Drinking

Research indicates that the number of deaths associated with substance abuse in the UK each year are roughly as follows: Nicotine 120,000 Alcohol 35,000 Illegal drugs 1200

comes to dominate, and the thought of the next drink becomes a preoccupation, just as an obsession with the next 'hit' becomes dominant in a heroin or cocaine addict. The dependent drinker's alcohol tolerance may go up so that he or she may drink more and still be able to function. Increasing tolerance of higher and higher doses is a mark of addiction.

Withdrawal symptoms may be very minor at first. Later, however, they become severe, especially in the morning, when the dependent drinker craves alcohol in order to feel better. At the same time, the drinker becomes aware of the compulsion to drink. It becomes difficult, perhaps, to walk past a pub or off-licence without entering and buying a drink.

Many people with alcohol problems are able to stop drinking for reasonably short periods of time without too much difficulty. They find, though, that their dependence is rapidly reinstated if they start to drink again.

PSYCHOLOGICAL ADDICTION

Behavioural addictions are characterised by a poor ability to resist a particular compulsion or habitual activity. This becomes a problem when the compulsive behaviour is harmful in some way – to the person themself and/or to other people. The person may find the compulsion irresistible, but there is no physical dependence in the way that there is with substance abuse. Behaviours that fall into this category include:
- compulsive gambling;
- stealing, as with shoplifting;
- shopping, to the point of financial ruin;
- workaholism;
- some sexual behaviours, such as exhibitionism.

WHAT ARE THE TREATMENTS FOR ADDICTIVE DISORDERS?

Just as addictive disorders vary widely, so do treatments. Medical supervision of withdrawal symptoms, talking treatments, drug therapies and hypnotherapy all have their roles to play.

What is the outlook?

The outlook for conquering an addiction is good if the patient has appropriate support and is fully motivated. For there to be real hope of recovery, the addict must firmly believe that the problems associated with staying addicted are greater than the problems brought on by withdrawing from the drug or behaviour in question.

Do you have a problem with alcohol?

You can screen yourself for problem drinking by answering these questions. If you answer 'Yes' to any of the following, you may have a problem with alcohol. Think about how much you are drinking and consider how much it may be affecting you.

THE 'CAGE' QUESTIONNAIRE

C Have you ever felt you should CUT DOWN on your drinking?

A Have people ANNOYED you by criticising your drinking?

G Have you ever felt bad or GUILTY about your drinking?

E Have you ever had a drink first thing in the morning to steady your nerves or to get rid of a hangover – an EYE-OPENER?

Childhood mental disorders

Children can experience many of the same mental disorders as adults. In addition there are a number of disorders specifically linked with children; of these, some are lifelong, while others may diminish once adulthood has been reached.

DEVELOPMENTAL DISORDERS

- **Autism** (see page 138) A child with autism has great difficulty in communicating and forming relationships with others. About half of all autistic children talk very little or not at all.
- **Asperger's syndrome** (see page 137) Children with Asperger's syndrome also have problems with basic communication skills, but at a much milder level than those with autism.

DISORDERS SPECIFIC TO CHILDHOOD

- **Attention deficit hyperactivity disorder** (ADHD, see page 137) Hallmarks of this common disorder are poor levels of concentration, and overactivity to the point where social skills and progress at school are affected.
- **Conduct disorder** This is characterised by frequent antisocial behaviour such as aggression, destructiveness and deceitfulness. It may be associated with other disorders, such as ADHD.
- **Selective mutism** This is a persistent failure to speak in certain situations – at school, for example – when the child will speak normally in other situations.

In a world of his own
This four-year-old boy is autistic. The condition is three or four times more common in boys than in girls, though it tends to take a more severe form in many girls.

- **Tic disorders** These take the form of sudden, repetitive, involuntary movements. They usually disappear before adulthood. Tourette's syndrome (see page 155) is a major tic disorder that is a lifelong condition.

ADULT DISORDERS IN CHILDREN

Many disorders that are usually described in adults may occur in children too.

- **Anxiety disorders** (see page 100) These may show themselves as, say, refusal to go to school, withdrawal from friends, non-specific physical complaints, or bed-wetting. Special phobias come into this category too.
- **Post traumatic stress disorder** Sometimes this results in selective mutism in children.
- **Obsessive compulsive disorder** (OCD, see page 147) Children often develop mild obsessive compulsive behaviour – rituals that must be followed, such as shutting a door three times in succession rather than once. Sometimes symptoms are more serious.
- **Depression** (see pages 100 and 142) Children can become depressed and symptoms can resemble those experienced by adults, but sometimes they may differ. Depression in children can be linked to conduct disorder, anxiety, an eating disorder or substance abuse.
- **Substance misuse** (see page 96) Problems are most commonly alcohol, with illegal drugs coming a distant second until mid to late adolescence. The use of glue and other inhalants, however, is more a feature of childhood and early adolescence.
- **Eating disorders** (see page 99) These are not so common in childhood but dramatically increase in frequency in adolescence.
- **Psychotic disorders such as schizophrenia** (see page 105) These are very rare before the age of seven, with increasing incidence through adolescence.

LEARNING DISABILITIES

Learning disability may emerge in childhood (see page 145). It is graded from mild to profound, and is sometimes linked with developmental disorders such as autism, and other mental disorders.

Eating disorders

There have undoubtedly always been people with eating disorders, but it appears that today – in Western industrial societies at least – there are more people than ever before who are suffering from anorexia nervosa and associated conditions.

WHAT IS AN EATING DISORDER?

An eating disorder is an external sign of internal emotional or psychological distress. Sufferers eat, or don't eat, in an attempt to block out painful feelings. Anorexics and bulimics are attempting to assert some control over their lives by keeping rigid control over their weight. They have an obsessional attitude to eating and an over-riding preoccupation with diet and weight.

Binge eating – the hallmark of bulimia nervosa and compulsive overeating – is often sparked by unhappiness, loneliness or anger, resulting in an escalating compulsion to overeat. This is followed by guilt and self-loathing.

What are the main conditions in this category?

- **Anorexia nervosa** (see page 136) This disorder can be recognised by a refusal to maintain body weight at the minimally normal weight for the age and height of the patient. There is a terror of gaining weight or becoming fat, even though the patient is very underweight.
- **Bulimia nervosa** (see page 140) This disorder is characterised by recurrent episodes of binge eating followed by self-induced vomiting or other methods to prevent weight gain. Other methods include the use of drugs such as laxatives, enemas and diuretics, and fasting or excessive exercise.
- **Compulsive overeating** (see page 141) Binge eating disorders share some of the features of bulimia, but are not associated with the regular use of inappropriate behaviours to compensate for overeating.

Who is at risk?

People of both sexes and all ages can develop an eating disorder, but they are found most often in young women, from teenagers through to the late twenties.

Anorexia nervosa can kill; approximately one in three anorexics eventually die as a result of complications caused by their disorder.

When the mirror lies
Anorexia nervosa leads to a false, distorted self-image, in which the sufferer literally cannot see that she is too thin when looking at herself in a mirror. Instead she sees herself as being overweight and needing to continue to diet. Here, a counsellor is attempting to help a patient gain a true perspective of how she looks and her condition.

What are the causes?

There is no single cause. Genetic makeup and environment can each play a part. Families with high aspirations can put great pressure on a vulnerable family member who will resort to an abnormal eating behaviour as a way of dealing with such pressures. Role models in the media, too, can make it difficult for vulnerable girls to resist the temptation to drastically control their eating.

What are the treatments for eating disorders?

Someone with an eating disorder must be persuaded that it is in their best interests to adopt a normal and healthy pattern of eating. If this new behaviour is to be maintained, the psychological dysfunction that is causing the disturbed eating behaviour must be addressed, and the patient needs to be taught ways of managing the temptation to return to old eating habits.

Mood disorders

Disorders of anxiety and/or depression affect at least one person in three at some time during their lifetime. Both anxiety and depression are perfectly appropriate reactions to many situations, but they become a problem when they are out of proportion to their cause.

WHAT ARE MOOD DISORDERS?

The prevailing characteristic of a mood disorder is an exaggerated form of normal emotion, such as depression, cheerfulness or anxiety. The exaggeration is in the intensity of the mood, its duration and the fact that it is an over-reaction to the circumstances. People often suffer from a mixture of anxiety and depressive symptoms.

ANXIETY AND PHOBIAS

We are all liable to apprehension when faced with uncertainty, a challenge or possible danger. Most of us are anxious before an exam, an interview, or a visit to the dentist, for instance. In anxiety states, however, anxiety may be present all the time, causing persistent worry and a constant state of fear. Or it can be attached to dreaded situations such as being in a lift, boarding a plane, or being confronted by a cat, for instance. These are phobias and they cause extreme anxiety or panic. Sometimes an anxiety state takes the form of a panic attack, which may even be mistaken for a heart attack.

Around 30 per cent of the US troops who served in the Vietnam War later suffered post-traumatic stress disorder.

What are the main conditions in this category?

- **Generalised anxiety disorder** This is anxiety not focused on a particular event, but as a long-term reaction to everyday concerns such as problems at work or school. Symptoms include worry, tiredness, being tense and irritable, restlessness and inability to concentrate.
- **Obsessive compulsive disorder** (OCD, see page 147) Obsessional thoughts and compulsive, repetitive acts can dominate a patient's behaviour for hours at a time.
- **Post-traumatic stress disorder** (see page 151) Anxiety and other distressing symptoms as a reaction to a very stressful one-off incident or experience.
- **Panic disorder** The patient has a series of panic attacks that are not obviously linked to any one cause.
- **Phobias** (see page 149) These include agoraphobia (generalised irrational fear), social phobia (unreasonable fear of embarrassment) and specific phobias.

What are the treatments for anxiety?

Removing the underlying cause, if at all possible, is always the sensible starting point. Talking therapies, relaxation techniques and training in stress management are all helpful. Antianxiety drugs are only a short-term treatment because many have a high risk of addiction.

Examination stress
Today's society places a premium on good qualifications. When taken to extremes, the anxiety created by the pressure to excel in exams can lead to anxiety or depression, or a combination of both.

DEPRESSIVE DISORDERS

Depression after a loss, disappointment or frustration is perfectly natural and everyone has experienced it to some degree. Sometimes, too, we feel down for a day or so, for no obvious reason at all. In depressive mood disorders, however, this feeling is greatly increased, to the point where it blights everyday life. As well as a lowering of mood, sufferers experience pessimistic thinking, an inability to enjoy anything, slowness and reduced energy, and even thoughts of suicide.

What are the main conditions in this category?
- Depression (see page 142) This may range from mild to severe.
- Postnatal depression (see page 150) One in ten women develop depression after childbirth.
- Seasonal affective disorder (SAD, see page 153) This is set off by lack of light and so tends to occur in winter.
- Manic depression (bipolar affective disorder, see page 139) Sufferers swing between episodes of mania (excessive cheerfulness and activity) and depression.

Women are more liable to become depressed than men, but are less likely to commit suicide.

What are the causes?
Depression may be precipitated by stress, grief, poverty, unemployment or loneliness, or by being physically run down. It may accompany major illnesses such as cancer and heart disease, and also chronic disorders such as arthritis, bronchitis and stroke. Loss of the mother in childhood increases risk of depression as an adult. Genetic factors are more often seen in manic depression, in which there is often a family history.

What are the treatments for depression?
Depression and manic depression are likely to resolve eventually even without treatment (though it is hard to leave manic depression untreated). Unfortunately both are likely to recur. Talking treatments are useful for mild to moderate depression. Moderate depression also benefits from antidepressants (possibly alongside talking therapy). Antidepressants are essential in the treatment of severe depression. Manic depression responds to lithium and some antipsychotic drugs.

How anxious or depressed are you?

Many questionnaires have been devised to measure depression or anxiety. Two such are the Goldberg Depression Quiz and the Goldberg Anxiety Quiz, both developed by the eminent psychiatrist David Goldberg and associates for the British Medical Journal. These quizzes are in no way precise diagnoses, but if you answer 'Yes' to seven or more of the questions in one or other of the tests, you might want to consider consulting your doctor about possible symptoms of anxiety or depression.

THE GOLDBERG ANXIETY QUIZ
The nine questions each require a 'Yes' or 'No' answer. The more questions you answer with 'Yes' the more likely you are to be suffering from anxiety.

- Have you felt keyed up or on edge?
- Have you been worrying a lot?
- Have you been irritable?
- Have you had difficulty relaxing?
- Have you been sleeping poorly?
- Have you had headaches or an aching neck?
- Have you had any of the following: trembling, tingling, dizzy spells, sweating, diarrhoea or needing to pass water more than usual?
- Have you been worrying about your health?
- Have you had difficulty falling asleep?

THE GOLDBERG DEPRESSION QUIZ
Again, you are asked to answer 'Yes' or 'No' to nine questions, this time indicating possible signs of depression.

- Have you been lacking in energy?
- Have you lost interest in things?
- Have you lost confidence in yourself?
- Have you felt hopeless?
- Have you had difficulty concentrating?
- Have you lost weight (due to poor appetite)?
- Have you been waking early?
- Have you felt slowed up?
- Have you tended to feel worse in the morning?

Organic mental disorders

Organic mental disorders arise from diseases of the brain. This may be degeneration of the nerve cells, causing dementia, or bodily illness affecting the brain, causing delirium. Organic disorders nearly always affect mental awareness.

DEMENTIA

The common dementias are:

- **Alzheimer's disease** (see page 135)
- **Vascular dementia (multi-infarct dementia)** A lack of blood to the brain, perhaps resulting from a series of small strokes, leads to the brain being starved of oxygen and destruction of brain tissue.
- **Lewy body disease** This is similar to Alzheimer's and also arises from damage to brain cells. Hallucinations are common.

Less common dementias include:

- **HIV dementia** This occurs to some degree in about half of all AIDS cases. The cause is the human immunodeficiency virus.
- **Huntington's disease** Also called Huntington's chorea, this is inherited. The folk singer Woody Guthrie was a famous sufferer.
- **Creutzfeldt-Jakob disease (CJD)** This is caused by an infective agent known as a prion. Many experts believe that sometimes CJD is caused by eating beef from cattle infected by BSE (bovine spongiform encephalopathy).
- **Syphilis causing general paralysis of the insane (GPI)** This accounted for one in 20 admissions to mental hospitals in the UK a hundred years ago, but is now rare.
- **Dementia following severe head injury**
- **Dementia brought on by a blood clot or tumour in the brain** Sometimes the clot or tumour can be removed, after which the symptoms of dementia should subside.

What are the symptoms?

In dementia one of the first impairments is memory, particularly of things that have happened recently, this morning, or even a minute ago. People developing dementia forget what they have just heard or said, and repeat themselves. They answer the phone but forget the message, so don't act on it or pass it on.

As the disease progresses they forget where they are, with whom and the day, month and year. This is known as disorientation for place, person and time. Gradually more and more memory is lost. Sufferers forget that their parents have died, that they themselves are married and

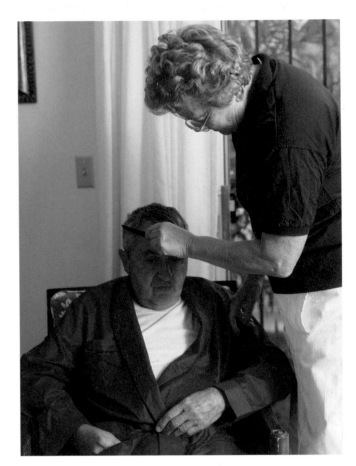

Dementia in old age
This man has Alzheimer's disease, the most common cause of senile dementia in old age. The disease produces a degeneration of brain tissue and as yet there is no cure.

had a job and then retired. In extreme (but not rare) cases an elderly person with dementia may not even recognise their spouse of many years standing.

Getting lost is a common problem in dementia: at first in less familiar surroundings (for example, on holiday) but later in the local neighbourhood, or even within the home. The tragic process of unlearning may continue until the ability to dress, use a knife and fork and wash is lost. Turning on electrical equipment or a gas cooker may become baffling, as may preparing a meal or laying a table.

Logic and insight are early casualties. Hasty or inappropriate decisions may be made about important matters, common sense gives way to irrational, impulsive behaviour and there may be serious inconsistencies, such as saying the season is summer when snow is falling. Because they are without insight into their condition, sufferers deny that there's anything wrong with them, but may blame others. Difficulty with calculation affects the handling of money. This, together with loss of judgement, means that people with dementia are easily exploited.

Language is another part of cognition affected by dementia. At first there is difficulty in finding the right word or putting a name to a face. Reading and writing skills dwindle. Gradually the meaning of words is lost, vocabulary becomes limited and sometimes speech becomes incoherent or nonsensical.

DELIRIUM

Because dementia involves the loss of brain substance, which cannot be replaced, the effects are lasting. Delirium, on the other hand, where the function of the brain is affected by bodily illness, runs over a course of days or a week or two at most. Full recovery from delirium is usual if the patient gets over the illness that caused it.

What are the symptoms?

Particular features include clouding of consciousness, confusion and visual hallucinations. Clouding of consciousness is reduced clarity of thought and awareness of the environment. Confusion is disorientation: not knowing where one is, what day or time it is, or being unable recognise close family members and friends. Hallucinations may be of people, insects and creepy-crawlies, and are generally alarming and unpleasant.

Who is at risk?

Those most at risk are the very old, the very young, the malnourished and alcoholics. Parents may recall nights with hot, bright-eyed infants chattering inconsequentially while in the throes of a fever. Very old people, especially those suffering from some degree of dementia, can become delirious with chest, urinary or skin infections, or following surgery, among other causes. Lack of vitamins contributes to delirium in people who are starving, or drinking alcohol rather than eating a balanced diet. The most dramatic alcoholic delirium is delirium tremens, caused by alcohol withdrawal. Deficiency of vitamin B_1 (thiamin) usually resulting from alcoholism can cause permanent severe loss of recent memory, known as Korsakow's syndrome.

" LIVING WITH ALZHEIMER'S DISEASE

My husband was diagnosed with Alzheimer's disease four years ago. The time will come when he needs full-time care in a nursing home but for now I am just about managing with him at home.

At first my husband's only symptoms were mild forgetfulness. Slowly this became worse and now, though he still recognises our children, he has difficulty with their names. He is mostly quite calm; occasionally he becomes restless and agitated but these moods pass. On a day to day

basis, I now have to do everything for him, including help him to wash, shave and dress in the morning. Thankfully he is not yet incontinent.

I don't have to stay in the same room as my husband but it's best to remain within earshot. I am careful to keep the front door locked because in the past my husband has wandered out of the house and not been able to find his own way back. Every week we have a trip out in the car; we both enjoy these excursions. I get very tired, and find it frustrating that I can't

leave the house without having to first organise someone else to be with my husband. I couldn't manage without the support of family and friends. Twice a week someone sits with my husband so I can get a few hours away – this helps me to cope the rest of the time.

"

Personality disorders

A personality problem is an aspect of someone's character that is troublesome enough to cause suffering to others or to the individual concerned. It usually involves ingrained patterns of behaviour that are difficult to change without some kind of professional help.

WHAT ARE PERSONALITY DISORDERS?

Personality disorder is a term applied to those people who have persistent difficulties in their relationships with other people. These difficulties can range from excessive, intrusive contact with other people to complete avoidance. The seriousness of the condition depends on the extent to which it produces impairment and suffering in the person who has the disorder, and for those exposed to the disorder. Evidence suggests that we all have some difficulties in our relationships with others, or at least show behaviour that is perceived as difficult. Because of this, there is no clear dividing line between people with and without a 'personality disorder'.

> **Personality disorders are commonplace, affecting about one in ten of the population.**

What are the main conditions in this category?

The principal personality disorders are (see also page 149):

- **Antisocial personality disorder** This refers to people who show aggressive or criminal behaviour.
- **Anxious (or avoidant) personality disorder** Someone suffers from anxious behaviour that causes them to avoid other people.
- **Borderline personality disorder** So named because those who suffer from this often have symptoms that border on other mental disorders, such as depression, suicidal behaviour and abnormal modes of thinking. Patients may be impulsive, unstable and self-destructive.
- **Paranoid personality disorder** Paranoid personalities live in fear of conspiracies from other people and act to anticipate them.

Other variations are:

- Dependent personality disorder – too submissive.
- Histrionic personality disorder – over-dramatic.
- Narcissistic personality disorder – feelings of superiority.
- Obsessive compulsive personality disorder – too rigid.
- Schizoid personality disorder – distant and detached.
- Schizotypal personality disorder – eccentric.

These represent very different types of problem so it is always important to qualify the description of a personality disorder. Those with more severe personality disorders often have several of the types described here simultaneously.

What are the causes?

Genetic and environmental factors interact to make every personality unique, and the same applies to personality disorders. In early life it is often difficult to detect those who will develop personality disorders, but people who have experienced abuse as children do appear to be at increased risk.

What are the treatments for personality disorders?

Different forms of psychotherapy have been found to be useful, depending on the type of personality disorder. Some drugs, including some antidepressants, also improve personality function.

What is the outlook?

Once established, often in late adolescence, a personality disorder may last for many years. Antisocial and related personality disorders tend to improve by the time the person reaches middle age. Some others can grow more marked with increasing age.

Is teenage antisocial behaviour a sign of a personality disorder?

In the 1960s – particularly in the USA – this was a fashionable theory and some teenagers ended up being treated in mental asylums who in other generations, before and since, would not have been. Often, what may appear to be symptoms of a personality disorder in fact turn out to be symptoms of the turmoil of puberty and largely disappear once the person reaches adulthood.

ASK THE EXPERT

Psychotic disorders

The core of a psychotic disorder is the patient losing touch with reality, and accepting an alternative, imagined reality instead. Symptoms can include false delusions and hallucinations. The most common psychotic disorder is schizophrenia.

WHAT ARE PSYCHOTIC DISORDERS?

A person suffering from a psychotic disorder in effect adopts another reality that becomes more real to that person than everyone else's reality. There is a defect in the processing and filtering of thoughts. Sufferers may be subject to illusions and fixed, often bizarre ideas, and are often not responsive to dissuasion or argument. Psychotic illness can occur at any time in life.

What are the main conditions in this category?

- **Schizophrenia** (see page 152) This psychotic disorder generally begins in individuals between the late teens and mid 20s, and may be divided into two types. In type I, delusions and hallucinations are prominent. In type II, symptoms such as lack of motivation and lack of self care tend to dominate.
- **Brief psychotic disorder** (see page 139) This is a psychotic mental disorder that, as its name indicates, lasts for only a few days or weeks.
- **Delusional disorder** (see page 141) Typically, someone with a delusional disorder has a rational grasp of reality over most things, but is suffering from an irrational delusion in one area. One example is erotomania, where the patient becomes convinced that another person, often of higher social status, is in love with them, despite lack of any evidence to support the belief.
- **Schizoaffective disorder** (see page 151) Sometimes, it is not easy to be sure whether a patient has schizophrenia or a mood disorder. In such circumstances, the diagnosis may be schizoaffective disorder.
- **Shared psychotic disorder** (see page 154) In very close partnerships, delusions may be infectious. In these so-called shared delusions, the partner who is not mentally ill may nevertheless become as equally convinced of the reality of the delusions as his or her mentally ill partner.

Evidence increasingly suggests that substance misuse earlier in life increases the risk of developing a psychotic disorder later on.

IT'S NOT TRUE!

'People with schizophrenia are usually dangerous and violent'

Studies have shown that about 8 per cent of those with schizophrenia display violent behaviour compared with 2 per cent of the general population. This means that the vast majority of schizophrenics are not violent. People with schizophrenia are far more likely to harm themselves – approximately one in ten eventually die by committing suicide.

What are the causes?

The causes of psychotic disorders are not yet fully understood. Genetics plays a part, but it is becoming clear that there is no single gene for psychotic disorders – many genes may be involved in various ways. People with schizophrenia are more likely to be born in winter and have a history of obstetric complications at birth, but the significance of these observations is unclear. Development in childhood and adolescence may be normal or abnormal, and no-one has yet succeeded in identifying any clear-cut environmental causes for psychotic disorders.

What are the treatments for psychotic disorders?

Although psychological, social and dietary treatments have been used in the treatment of psychotic disorders, the current mainstay is antipsychotic medication (see page 122), together with support from various mental health professionals, plus family and friends.

What is the outlook?

The outlook for an episode of a psychotic disorder is generally good. However, psychotic disorders are usually long-term relapsing disorders. Sometimes the disorder improves as the patient gets older, but this occurs only in a minority of cases.

FINDING OUT WHAT IS WRONG

Two out of every five visits to the GP involve problems to do with mental health. The first thing the doctor must do is find out if there is a physical cause behind a mental problem. It is also important to rule out prescribed medication or substance abuse as possible causes. The doctor will take a complete history of symptoms, followed by a physical examination. The next step is to use special diagnostic tests for psychiatric disorders. These often involve the use of questionnaires. In cases of dementia in particular, neuroimaging (taking a brain scan) can help with diagnosis.

Medical history and examination

At the GP's surgery, the doctor will ask about specific symptoms and general health, past and present, then carry out a physical examination. This done, the doctor will decide on treatment and/or referral to an expert.

TAKING THE FIRST STEP

The first step for anyone seeking help with a problem such as anxiety or depression, or any other suspected mental disorder, is generally to book an appointment to see the doctor. When patient and GP meet, how will the doctor reach a diagnosis? In what circumstances will the doctor refer the patient to a specialist, such as a psychiatrist or a psychologist?

Is the problem physical or mental?

Often, when the patient walks into the doctor's consulting room, a mental illness may not be uppermost in the patient's mind. The problem the patient describes may be tiredness, difficulty sleeping or poor concentration. Or there may be a relationship problem at home or at work. The doctor must first of all ascertain if the problem has a physical cause, such as an underactive thyroid gland, or has a mental basis. There are various steps towards reaching this decision.

Are mental disorders true illnesses in the same way as, for example, diabetes?

This is a difficult question to answer because of the wide variety of mental conditions. The term 'mental illness' may mean anything from mild anxiety to a psychotic disorder. At one end of this spectrum it would be something of an exaggeration to use the term illness, whereas at the other end there are mental conditions involving definite and serious chemical abnormalities within the brain. Severe mental illnesses (notably schizophrenia and bipolar affective disorder) usually require lifelong medication and are as disabling as physical illnesses.

ASK THE EXPERT

A typical questionnaire for depression

The patient is asked how many of these symptoms he or she has experienced in the past two weeks:

- A very sad mood that does not go away.
- Loss of enjoyment and interest in activities that used to be enjoyable.
- Tiredness and lack of energy.
- Loss of self-confidence or poor self-esteem.
- Feeling guilty when you are not at fault.
- Wishing you were dead.
- Difficulty concentrating or making decisions.
- Moving more slowly or sometimes becoming agitated and unable to settle.
- Having difficulty sleeping or, sometimes, sleeping too much.
- Loss of interest in food, or sometimes eating too much; changes in eating habits may lead to either weight loss or gain.

As a rough guide:

4 symptoms indicates possible mild depression
6 symptoms indicates moderate depression
8 symptoms indicates severe depression.

A THOROUGH HISTORY

Taking a patient's medical and psychiatric history is an essential part of the diagnostic process. Typically, a doctor will cover the following points:

- The patient is encouraged to describe the problem as fully as possible in his or her own words.
- The doctor asks specific questions designed to draw out detailed information about symptoms. When did each symptom begin? Do symptoms come and go? Are they progressively worsening?
- The patient is asked about his or her past medical and psychiatric history. A past history of mental illness, such as depression or an anxiety state, is predictive of current mental illness.
- The doctor asks about the medical and psychiatric history of the patient's family.
- What medications is the patient taking, if any? Does the patient smoke or use illicit drugs? What is the patient's alcohol intake?

Indications of a physical cause

The medical history may reveal symptoms that suggest a physical cause. For example, a patient who is tired and sluggish and feels the cold may become depressed, but it is possible that an underactive thyroid is the reason for the tiredness and the depression is secondary to that. A recent viral infection may cause prolonged debility and depression.

If alcohol intake is out of control, the patient is likely to feel depressed but again that feeling is secondary to the alcohol problem. Non-prescribed drugs, such as cannabis and cocaine, are thought to contribute to mental illness, especially in the young.

If a patient has serious worries, such as financial or domestic problems, this may lead to poor sleeping patterns, which in turn lead to feelings of tiredness and depression.

THE PHYSICAL EXAMINATION

From the beginning of the interview, the patient's overall appearance is carefully noted by the doctor. Are there obvious signs of a physical illness? Are there signs of self-neglect, a drug habit (such as needle marks) or self-harm (such as razor scars). Are there signs of excessive intake of alcohol?

The standard physical examination (heart rate, blood pressure, reflexes and so forth) may cause the doctor to suspect a physical cause, such as anaemia, underactive thyroid or heart failure, any of which can cause tiredness and depression. The doctor will follow up any suspicions by ordering further investigative tests.

BLOOD TESTS

A blood test is often useful at this stage of the investigation, as it can give the GP an early indicator of whether there is a physical cause behind a worrying mental condition. For instance, a blood count will show if there is anaemia, which can cause tiredness and consequent depression. A blood test for thyroid function

Questions to be ready for

The doctor will ask various questions aimed at drawing out details of specific signs and symptoms. It is a good idea for patients to think about the answers to the following before an appointment with the doctor.

- *When were symptoms first noticed? Was there one symptom to begin with, which was then joined by others?*

- *Are symptoms worsening? Do they come and go, or are they experienced all the time?*

- *Have you had these symptoms in the past? If so, when? Did you receive any treatment? What was the outcome?*

- *Has another member of the family ever had a similar problem? Again, what was the outcome?*

- *What medications do you take – prescription and non-prescription? How often and for what reasons?*

will indicate if the thyroid gland is not functioning properly. A blood test may show abnormalities that point to excessive alcohol consumption.

DIAGNOSTIC QUESTIONNAIRES

Taking a psychiatric history often involves the use of simple questionnaires, which may be written or verbal or both. A doctor can often make a fairly reliable diagnosis of depression, for example, by asking the patient questions such as:

- Do you feel depressed?
- Do you feel life isn't worthwhile?
- How well do you sleep – do you find yourself waking early (for example)?
- How good is your concentration?
- Have you noticed any change in libido (sex drive)?

There are also questionnaires that are much more specific (see page 111). Called psychological tests, these are generally used at a later stage in the diagnostic process by a mental health professional.

ASSESSMENT OF CAUSE, SEVERITY AND DURATION OF ILLNESS

This is most important, especially with a disorder such as depression. The condition may be of very recent onset, triggered by some short-term problem which is likely to be resolved in the near future. Or the condition may have been present for some time and is not clearly linked to a cause that is likely to disappear soon. This evaluation is fundamental to the choice of treatment.

TREATMENT OPTIONS AT THIS STAGE

Using the information gained, the doctor will decide on what treatment is best and/or refer the patient to an expert mental health professional.

Short-term counselling

In a mild case of depression of short duration, for example, a GP is likely to offer short-term counselling. The doctor may do this, or refer the patient to a counsellor either in the surgery or elsewhere locally. A counsellor, who will have been trained and certified by a recognised body such as the British Association for Counselling and Psychotherapy, will provide counselling over two or more sessions of 45 to 60 minutes each.

Drug therapy

If depression is more than mild, and the condition has been present for some time and is not clearly linked to a cause that is likely to disappear soon, the doctor may feel that talking therapy alone is inappropriate. An antidepressant may be necessary (see page 120). Such a drug will not work straightaway – it may take three or four weeks (or longer) for its benefits to be felt – and the patient will almost certainly have to take the drug for at least six months to reduce the risk of relapse.

REFERRAL TO A PSYCHOLOGIST OR PSYCHIATRIST

A GP is likely to refer a patient to a psychiatrist if the mental illness is severe (for example, if there is a risk of suicide) or if the condition has not responded to drug therapy prescribed by the GP. The psychiatrist will make a fuller assessment with a team that includes a psychologist. A whole range of treatments are available to psychiatrists including a variety of talking therapies, group therapy, more serious drug therapy (such as lithium) and electroconvulsive therapy (ECT).

Diagnostic tests

When a patient has been referred to a psychiatrist by the general practitioner, the next stage is to conduct further tests to reach as precise a diagnosis as possible, so that the most effective treatment can be decided upon.

WHAT TESTS MAY BE NEEDED?

More advanced diagnostic tests can be divided into two types: medical and psychiatric. Medical tests include brain scans and blood tests. Usually, the ultimate means of diagnosis is an interview between mental health professional and patient, in which a more comprehensive psychiatric history is taken, and diagnostic manuals are consulted. In addition, the patient may be asked to answer detailed questionnaires about symptoms.

BRAIN SCANS

Neuroimaging techniques are used to view the brain and visualise mental processes, in order to help the diagnosis and treatment of many diseases and disorders of the brain. Producing images of the brain is an especially effective way of investigating conditions arising from deterioration of the brain, in particular dementia, an organic mental disorder (see page 102).

Computed tomography (CT) and magnetic resonance image (MRI) scans have been commonly used as diagnostic tests in hospitals for some years. These scans are carried out by radiologists. There are also other methods of imaging the brain, notably positron emission tomography (PET), which are primarily used for research purposes at the moment, rather than to reach a diagnosis in individual cases.

Neuroimaging and dementia

Neuroimaging may reveal the atrophy, or thinning, of the brain's cortex or surface layer that is typical of Alzheimer's disease. This is typical also of other forms of dementia resulting from arterial disease and/or bleeding within the brain, notably vascular dementia and dementia following a severe head injury.

Computed tomography (CT)

Computed tomography produces an image of the brain by taking an X-ray of a cross-section – a 'slice' – of the brain. CT scans can show the differences in absorption of X-rays by areas affected by a brain tumour, or by blood as in cases of stroke or arterial disease (all can be causes of dementia).

Magnetic resonance imaging (MRI)

This is another way of producing cross-sectional images of the brain, in this case using magnetic fields to capture an image rather than X-rays. Images produced by MRI are much more detailed than CT scans (but also more expensive). MRI scans can detect evidence of brain disorders such as multiple sclerosis or stroke, as well as dementia.

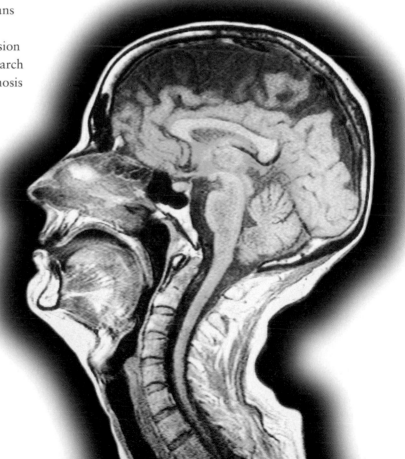

Signs of dementia on an MRI scan
This vertical section through the brain of a 50-year-old man, taken by means of a magnetic resonance imaging scan, reveals atrophy of the cerebrum. The affected area is coloured brown. Shrinkage and wasting away of tissue as shown here may indicate various disorders, including Alzheimer's disease and HIV dementia.

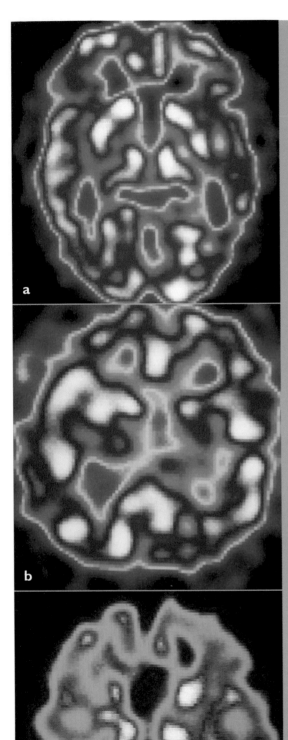

PET imaging of the brain

These PET scans all show the interior of the cerebrum, the largest and most highly developed part of the brain. They show a horizontal section through the brain, also called a transverse section. Areas of low metabolic activity are colour-coded blue and areas of high activity are shown as yellow. As a result, areas of metabolic activity (where chemical and physical changes are taking place) are depicted as yellow 'hot spots'. Here, a normal brain is contrasted with brains belonging to patients with schizophrenia and Alzheimer's disease.

a Normal

As shown here, normal brain metabolic activity produces a roughly symmetrical pattern.

b Schizophrenia

A PET scan shows up abnormalities of metabolic activity in the brain of a patient with schizophrenia.

c Alzheimer's disease

In this scan of the brain of a patient with Alzheimer's disease, the areas of 'hot spot' high metabolic activity are considerably fewer than in the scans above, indicating a much reduced level of brain activity overall. This image shows a case of advanced dementia.

Positron emission tomography

PET scanning uses radioactive tracers to locate and reveal abnormal metabolic activity in the brain. Having been injected into the bloodstream, the tracer travels to the brain, where it is drawn towards areas of metabolic activity. The scanner detects radiation given off by particles called positrons emitted by the tracer. This data is used to construct a cross-section of the brain. The level of radiation coming from each area of the brain is colour-coded to produce a map of metabolic activity.

PET does not show the brain's structure as clearly as CT or MRI, but gives more information on activity in the brain, and so can detect an abnormality in brain metabolism more quickly. PET scans have many uses – when investigating epilepsy or brain tumours, for instance – also for researching mental disorders such as dementia and schizophrenia. Tracers may be designed to bind to particular receptors in the brain, depending on the condition being investigated. For example, they are used to investigate dopamine receptor activity in cases of schizophrenia.

DIAGNOSTIC BLOOD TESTS

Occasionally, a doctor may consider a special blood test helpful for diagnosis of depression. In this test, called the dexamethasone suppression test, the patient takes dexamethasone (a corticosteroid) in tablet form at bedtime. A blood test is taken 18 hours later. A high level of cortisol (a 'stress' hormone) in the blood despite the patient having taken dexamethasone indicates depression.

GUIDELINES FOR PSYCHIATRIC EVALUATION

In order to diagnose a mental disorder when, as in most cases, there is no recourse to medical testing, psychiatrists and other mental health professionals turn to one of two official manuals: 'ICD-10' or 'DSM-IV'. They make a close study of the symptoms and history of the patient, then seek to match these with symptoms belonging to one of the many disorders described in detail in these manuals.

In Europe psychiatrists follow the guidelines relating to mental and behavioural disorders laid out in Chapter Five of the manual 'ICD-10' (the International Classification of Diseases and Related Health Problems – Edition 10) published by the World Health Organisation in 1992. In North America the manual used is 'DSM-IV' (the Diagnostic and Statistical Manual of Mental Disorders – Fourth Edition) published in 1994 by the American Psychiatric Association. Each manual differs a little in how they classify the many different mental disorders, but there are many similarities between the two. Both manuals use similar criteria to make a diagnosis. These fall into several categories.

- Symptoms that have to be present if a patient is to be diagnosed as having a particular disorder.
- Symptoms that are often present with the disorder but not always.
- Specific physical symptoms associated with the disorder.
- Indicators to do with age, gender and family background.

Is genetic testing relevant for any mental disorders?

With some diseases and disorders, genetic testing can be used to predict a person's chances of developing the disorder in the future, or to confirm a diagnosis. There are a number of mental disorders in which there may be an element of genetic inheritance. Major examples include dementia (Alzheimer's disease and Huntington's disease) schizophrenia and manic depression (or bipolar affective disorder). Accurate genetic testing is available for Huntington's disease. For Alzheimer's, genetic testing is only accurate in a rare subtype of this disease. There is as yet no genetic testing for schizophrenia or manic depression.

ASK THE EXPERT

When the American Psychiatric Association first published the Diagnostic and Statistical Manual of Mental Disorders (DSM-I) in 1952, this marked the first attempt to diagnose mental disorders through official, standardised definitions and criteria.

Diagnosing schizophrenia using the ICD-10 manual

To take the diagnosis of schizophrenia as an example, according to the ICD-10 manual symptoms must have been present for at least one month. Other criteria are whether the patient is hearing voices (auditory hallucinations) and believing unusual things (delusions). These are the most important symptoms. Other symptoms, which may or may not be present, include loss of interest in going out socially; lack of attention to personal care and appearance; and thought disorder, which may make it difficult to understand an affected person when he or she speaks.

PSYCHOLOGICAL TESTS

Psychological tests consist of sets of questions that have been carefully devised in order to give a numerical value to particular sets of symptoms (relating to psychosis, depression or anxiety, for example) or other human characteristics (personality, cognitive function, intelligence). They are usually administered by psychologists. These tests are sometimes used to help diagnose a disorder, but are more often carried out to monitor the effects of treatments or for research purposes.

Cognitive tests

Cognitive tests check the ability of the patient to acquire and process information. They assess cognitive processes such as reasoning, powers of concentration, memory and verbal ability. The tests vary considerably in complexity, from simple tests like asking the patient to say the months of the year backwards, to more complicated requests, such as asking the patient to list as many words as they can starting with a particular letter within one minute. Cognitive tests are particularly relevant when diagnosing dementia, attention deficit hyperactivity disorder (ADHD) and learning disabilities, and also when assessing psychosis and delirium.

CURRENT TREATMENTS

Treatment for mental disorders usually involves psychotherapy or prescribed drugs, or both. Often a combination of the two turns out to be the best solution. Electroconvulsive therapy is sometimes an option, if other treatments have failed. Surgery for mental illness rarely takes place today, but does happen occasionally. Complementary therapies such as aromatherapy and reflexology can be very helpful in reinforcing recovery attained by other treatment methods.

Talking therapies

Talking treatments vary greatly in duration and type, but in all cases the relationship between patient and therapist is vital to a successful outcome.

IT'S GOOD TO TALK

Most of us, when troubled, want to talk to someone. Usually this will be someone within the family – husband or wife, parent, sibling, son or daughter – or a close friend. If the problem is intimate or the family is too closely involved, however, we may look elsewhere. The important role of the priest as confidante has dwindled in our increasingly secular society, and has been largely replaced by the doctor. The GP's professionalism, experience, expertise and impartiality are valued, but the expectations of someone with a mental health problem may not be met by a short consultation followed by a prescription for medication – even though this may be appropriate. The idea that drugs can alter brain function for the better, though true, is often resented. 'Pills for personal problems' have had a bad press since benzodiazepine tranquillisers such as Valium (see page 119) were widely prescribed in the 1960s and 70s, and many people with personal or emotional problems prefer counselling or some other type of talking treatment to taking drugs.

How do you find the right psychotherapist ?

- A recommendation from someone you trust is the best way but this is often not possible. The British Confederation of Psychotherapists will provide lists of qualified psychotherapists (see the BCP website).
- Check the training and qualifications of possible choices – most are members of the BCP.
- Seeing the therapist for an initial consultation – or preferably more than one therapist so you can compare and choose – is a good idea before committing to a course of therapy.
- Ask them how much experience they have of working with people with similar problems to your own. A good therapist will be happy to answer such questions.

ASK THE EXPERT

Shared aspects of talking therapies

Experts suggest that all types of talking treatments have certain elements in common:

- Listening and talking (in that order)
- Release of emotion
- Giving relevant information
- Providing a rationale – helping the patient's problems to make some psychological sense
- Restoring morale so that the patient has the confidence to continue
- Suggestion, which may be of use in the early stages
- Guidance and advice, though ideally patients are encouraged to find the answers to their problems themselves
- A therapeutic relationship between therapist and patient – the 'therapeutic alliance'

WHEN TALKING TREATMENTS ARE USEFUL

Talking treatments have some place in almost all psychiatric disorders, and are of prime importance when treating anxiety states and some personality disorders. They are of less immediate value in severe mental illness, such as manic depression (bipolar affective disorder), psychotic disorders or dementia, but even here may be a useful adjunct to drug treatment when the acute phase of the illness has passed.

TYPES OF TALKING TREATMENT

There is a wide range of talking treatments, from support, sympathetic listening, reassurance, encouragement and relaxation, to sophisticated techniques that address particular symptoms or ways of thinking (cognitive behavioural therapy) or probe the unconscious mind (psychoanalysis, also sometimes called psychodynamic psychotherapy). The treatments may be brief or long, and work 'one to one', with couples, families or groups.

Taking a psychiatric history

The process of taking a psychiatric history may in itself be therapeutic. Over the course of an hour or so the skilled interviewer – often a psychiatrist or psychologist – asks about symptoms, how they arose and when, the course they have taken and how they affect the patient's

life. Questions are wide-ranging and may cover family and medical history, early family life, schooling and employment, housing and finances, delinquency, sex and marriage, children, friends and family, interests, religion, and use of alcohol and drugs. For patient and interviewer, this builds up a detailed picture of the patient.

The question 'Why have problems arisen now?' may then be answered by matching the start of symptoms to the patient's background, situation and life events. Such undivided attention from someone taking an active interest, hearing the patient out, yet by skilful questioning reviewing a lifetime within a single interview, can make the patient feel valued, understood and able to understand.

Active listening

Active listening by a sympathetic but sufficiently detached befriender, counsellor or therapist is the essence of supportive therapy. The skills required to sustain this should not be underestimated – it is quite difficult for the listener to refrain from handing out advice or chipping in with their own personal experiences.

COUNSELLING

Counselling is the most widely practised talking treatment. It is particularly concerned with solving problems, coming to terms with losses and taking difficult

Can talking therapies help people to lead happier lives?

Talking treatments demand a lot more from the patient than ordinary day-to-day chat. They take time and commitment from both patient and therapist. Therapy has to be contained within the time slots set aside for it (though there is often work to be done between sessions) and benefits are not immediate. Confronting phobias, trying to ignore negative thoughts and facing up to unwelcome aspects of oneself are all stressful. However, the rewards for those able to stay the course may include relief of symptoms, easing of problems, greater self-knowledge and feeling more in charge of oneself.

decisions. It starts with attentive, sympathetic listening, noting problems as they are revealed, then goes on to helping the client find answers to those problems.

Counsellors give advice sparingly, but restore a sense of proportion by taking a detached view of dilemmas which seem overwhelming to their clients. They encourage a positive, practical approach to difficulties. If there are no easy answers, counsellors support the client in accepting the inevitable with resignation and letting go of the past.

Counselling is not endless: a specific number of weekly sessions, lasting from half to one hour, is agreed at the outset – usually between six and twelve sessions. It seems that as many people want to be counsellors these days as need counselling, which is good, but counsellors need training, or there is a danger that their personal preoccupations and prejudices will distort their view of their clients' problems. Goodwill alone does not make an effective counsellor.

INTERPERSONAL THERAPY (IPT)

Interpersonal therapy is a structured treatment that aims to help with:

- bereavement or other loss;
- interpersonal disputes;
- role transitions – for example, marriage, motherhood, promotion, retirement;
- 'interpersonal deficits' such as loneliness or obsession.

Like counselling, interpersonal therapy is intended to be relatively short-term, involving between 12 and 20 weekly sessions, each lasting about one hour. It is of particular value where these problems contribute to, say, depression or an eating disorder. Specific situations in which these problems arise are noted, alternative ways of coping are considered, goals are set and progress is monitored. Patients are required to do homework along these lines, and every session starts with 'stocktaking' and ends with further goal-setting.

COGNITIVE BEHAVIOURAL THERAPY (CBT)

The aim of cognitive behavioural therapy is to enable the patient to alter patterns of thinking or behaviour that are causing problems. Changing how you think and behave also changes how you feel. The patient and therapist agree on treatment goals and the patient is asked to try things out between sessions.

Cognitive behavioural therapy is particularly useful for treating depression and anxiety states, but has applications to almost all psychiatric disorders, including schizophrenia. CBT lends itself to scientific evaluation, and its efficacy has been better demonstrated than that of any other talking treatment (though that doesn't mean that it is the best answer to every problem).

The conditioned reflex

Cognitive behavioural therapy derives from findings of the Russian scientist Ivan Pavlov on the conditioned reflex. In a series of famous experiments published in the 1920s, Pavlov began with the simple reflex of dogs that salivate when presented with food. By sounding a bell just before the food was given, he demonstrated that the dogs would salivate at the sound of the bell even if no food was forthcoming: this is a conditioned reflex. However, if the bell was sounded again and again and no food was forthcoming, the conditioned reflex was extinguished.

Operant conditioning

The other major form of conditioning is known as operant conditioning, and this strengthens or weakens conscious, voluntary behaviour. For example, attention-seeking behaviour may be reinforced by gaining attention, even if it takes the form of scolding or smacking, and eventually reduced by being ignored. Avoidance of phobia-inducing situations strengthens avoidance

TREATING PHOBIAS

Confronting a phobia through therapy that involves direct exposure to the fear is undoubtedly a nerve-racking procedure, but it has freed many phobia sufferers from debilitating anxiety. Phobia treatment is just one area of cognitive behavioural therapy.

Exposure to stressful situations is an important treatment of phobias. The patient and therapist first construct a hierarchy of feared situations, from the mildly disturbing to the frankly terrifying. Graded exposure then confronts these stresses either in real life (preferred) or imagination. For example, an arachnaphobic might start by looking at a photograph of a money-spider and end by stroking a tarantula. Relaxation is used at every stage to bring anxiety down to manageable levels. Often the therapist will need to spend time out and about with patients in order to be there when they confront their fears.

Treatment in action

In a real-life case, a patient had a crippling fear of witnessing a heart attack, which meant that he could not go near a hospital. Treatment involved graded exposure to the film 'All that Jazz' in which the main character has a heart attack at the start of the film and finally dies of another. Using relaxation techniques while gradually watching more and more of the film on video, the patient was eventually able to watch the entire film, and then visit his local hospital with hardly a qualm.

TREATMENT OPTIONS

- **Graded exposure in real life** The patient is exposed to the feared situation, first a very mild version, then, once familiarity and reassurance have made this tolerable, a less mild version. This continues until (hopefully) the patient has fully confronted and overcome the phobia.
- **Desensitisation in imagination** allows the patient to create and relax through a hierarchy of feared situations, perhaps as a prelude to confronting the real thing, such as a fear of flying.
- **Flooding** is a 'throwing in at the deep end' approach. The patient and therapist confront the stress at the top of the hierarchy head-on. After a highly fraught 15 minutes or so, the panic should subside into little or no anxiety. This can be effective, but it demands a lot of the patient.

behaviour by reducing anxiety, but often at a great cost to normal social living.

In an experiment, a class was able to manipulate its teacher by reacting with enthusiasm when the teacher approached pupils on the left side of the room and boredom when he approached those on the right. When the teacher started spending all his time in the left side of the room, they switched their response – and moved him over to the right.

Children learn fearful responses through operant conditioning by seeing how parents respond to certain situations. A frightened reaction to, say, a dog, may condition the child into a similar reaction, with this behaviour then reinforced by subsequent avoidance of dogs. The process may be reversed later by the child witnessing how a trusted person approaches and handles a dog with confidence and composure. Operant conditioning is at its most sinister in brainwashing.

TREATING DEPRESSION WITH CBT

In the treatment of depression, cognitive behavioural therapy is used particularly to address negative thinking. Aaron Beck, the originator of CBT, took inspiration from the Roman philosopher Epictetus, who said: 'Men are disturbed not by things but by the views they take of them.' Beck described three patterns of thinking in a depressed person – the 'negative triad':

- The person sees him or herself in a negative light, as defective, inadequate, diseased or deprived. The person attributes unpleasant experiences to this basic defect and believes that because of it he or she cannot attain happiness and contentment.
- The person sees the world as making excessive demands, and misinterprets dealings with the surrounding environment as defeats or deprivation.
- The person has low or no expectations of the future and expects to fail.

Thus depressed people come to the worst interpretation of their world. They fasten on a discouraging detail rather than the whole experience, exaggerate the bad things and overlook the good, and wrongly relate external mishaps and disasters to themselves. They use 'primitive' thinking, splitting their experiences into opposite categories – pure versus filthy, perfect versus flawed, saint versus sinner – always putting themselves at the worst pole. Beck contrasts this primitive thinking with the mature thinking that admits problems but offers hope. For example, the primitive view might be 'I always was and always will be a coward', in contrast to a mature view that 'my fears vary from time to time and from situation to situation'.

Cognitive behavioural analysis

All forms of CBT start with a cognitive behavioural analysis to note symptoms or problems, and when, where, for how long and under what circumstances they arise. Keeping a diary for a week at the outset of the analysis can be helpful in demonstrating the ABC of the problem:

- Antecedents
- Behaviour
- Consequences

It is then possible to set goals.

Suppressing and changing negative thoughts

There are two techniques for suppressing and changing negative thoughts: distraction, and challenging the logical errors in underlying assumptions.

- **Distraction** This involves deliberately attending to something else when a gloomy thought arises – counting birds, cars or trees, say, or stopping the negative thought by a sudden stimulus, such as pinching yourself or snapping a rubber band on the wrist.

Key terms used in talking treatments

DYNAMIC A term indicating forces that produce movement or change.

NEUROSIS A mental disorder that does not involve the patient having lost their sense of reality.

REINFORCEMENT The application or removal of a stimulus so as to increase the strength of a behaviour.

REPRESSION Threatening thoughts or memories of events are pushed out of consciousness so they are no longer remembered.

RESISTANCE The attempts of a patient undergoing therapy to prevent repressed impulses or conflicts from entering consciousness.

TRANSFERENCE When a patient redirects, or transfers, emotions previously felt for someone else towards the therapist instead.

TRAUMA An emotionally painful event that has damaging effects on the person who experienced it.

Sigmund Freud – the father of psychoanalysis

Sigmund Freud (1856–1939) was Austrian and lived in Vienna for most of his life. From the 1880s onwards, he developed the theories of the mind for which he became famous. His daughter Anna Freud also became a famous psychoanalyst. His nephew Edward Bernays took Freud's ideas to the USA where he applied them with enormous success to the advertising industry. In 1938 Freud, Anna and other members of the family were forced to leave Austria when the Nazis invaded. They settled in London, where Freud died the following year.

- **Challenging logical errors in underlying assumptions**
  Errors of logic include the belief that to be free from depression means being happy and successful all of the time: small setbacks are part of normal living. Patients are encouraged to remember their achievements and not just see themselves as being utterly helpless and hopeless.

The therapist's role in setting goals, homework and redressing the negative thinking balance is very important. There is good evidence that cognitive behavioural therapy plus antidepressant drug therapy for depression is better than either alone.

PSYCHODYNAMIC PSYCHOTHERAPY

Psychodynamic psychotherapy encompasses all talking treatments in which there is an attempt to explore the patient's unconscious mental state and bring about increased awareness, or insight. There are several different schools of psychodynamic psychotherapy, but they all have in common Sigmund Freud's concept of a dynamic unconscious. This is the idea that memories of thoughts or events from the first five years of childhood may be repressed because too emotionally charged at the time, but they are still active in our unconscious mind and can affect our conscious behaviour.

FREUD'S REVOLUTIONARY IDEAS

As Freud's daughter Anna wrote: 'We felt that we were the first who had been given a key to the understanding of human behaviour and its aberrations as being determined not by overt factors but by the pressure of instinctual forces emanating from the unconscious mind.' By analysis of what the patient said and interpretation of dreams and other manifestations of the unconscious, Freud aimed to recover the repressed memory of experiences – often from early childhood – in order to allow the patient to come to terms with these experiences and so be able to change unwanted emotions and behaviour. Freud talked about converting 'despair into common unhappiness', by changing what was a sick or maladaptive response to events in the patient's life to something that was more normal and consistent with ordinary experience.

Followers and successors of Freud

It was not long before followers of Freud began to take psychoanalysis in different directions. Carl Jung (1875–1961) and Alfred Adler (1870–1937) produced their own systems for understanding the mind. Adler pioneered the idea of the psychology of the individual, and developed the idea of the superiority and inferiority complex. Jung focused on a more spiritual dimension to the mind and thought in terms of how the individual's mind functioned as part of the collective mind of mankind. He wrote about his ideas of introvert and extrovert personalities, and made extensive studies of dreams. He investigated anthropology and the occult, which led to his theory of 'archetypes' – universal symbols present in the collective unconscious.

Since then psychoanalysts such as Karen Horney, John Bowlby and Harry Stack Sullivan have gone on to develop Freud's theories still further, and add insights of their own.

The influence of Freud's theories

Freud's ideas of the workings of the mind – his theories about the conscious and unconscious mind, the ego (self), the id ('animal' principle) and the super-ego (conscience) – have had an almost incalculable influence on modern thought. Concepts such as 'the unconscious' and 'ego' have become part of everyday life, but as with many everyday notions, problems show up when the harsh light of analysis is shone upon them. It is not easy, for example, to decide exactly what we mean by the term 'the unconscious'.

In the mid 20th century Freudian analysis was fashionable among those who could afford it. Nowadays, mental health professionals disagree among themselves in their assessment of its effectiveness.

PSYCHOANALYSIS

Psychoanalysis is the type of long-term psychotherapy promoted by the teachings of Freud and associated psychoanalysts such as Jung. Full psychoanalysis takes place over several years. Costly in terms of time and money, it is better suited to helping people with personality and relationship problems rather than those with major mental disorders, notably severe depression, manic depression (bipolar affective disorder) or a psychotic disorder. Examples of personality and relationship problems include: angry dependency, fear of commitment or disengagement, holding back from realising one's full potential for fear of competition, and being too aggressive in self-assertion.

BRIEFER THERAPIES

For practical purposes, briefer therapies based on psychoanalytic theory are more widely used, in which the therapist sits facing the patient and takes note of body language – looking away, trembling, twitching – as well as what is actually said. Such treatments last months rather than years and focus on specific problems rather than the whole personality.

Working together

Group therapy can be oriented towards either cognitive behavioural therapy or psychoanalysis. It can be used to help people with problems ranging from anger management to alcoholism to bereavement.

MORE THAN ONE-TO-ONE

There are types of therapy that deliver psychological treatments to more than one patient at a time.

Marital therapy

Marital therapy deals with the troubled couple as the patient, often examining how decisions are taken and who has the power.

Family therapy

This involves the whole family in dealing with a problem presented by one family member. It is used for disturbed and troubled children, for eating disorders and for any other condition in which the family's involvement seems highly relevant to the course of the disorder.

Group therapy

Groups of up to ten patients – usually of similar age and education and with like problems – meet weekly. The therapist usually avoids taking up individual issues but interprets the way the group deal with them as they arise in spontaneous discussion. Resistance from group members may be expressed in prolonged silence, lateness, informal meetings outside the group and 'ganging up', all of which are grist to the therapist's mill. Group therapy got a great boost during the Second World War, when it was used to tackle mental disorders arising from the stress of combat, which in the First World War had resulted in shell shock and long-term invalidism.

Antianxiety medications

*Drugs taken to combat anxiety are also known as minor tranquillisers
or anxiolytics. The main objectives of such drug treatment are to treat
nervousness or tension caused by stress or other psychological problems.
They are also given in emergencies in hospital to calm and relax patients.*

BENZODIAZEPINES

These are the most commonly used antianxiety drugs.
Well-known examples are diazepam (Valium) and
lorazepam. They are normally prescribed for a few weeks
only. Benzodiazepines work by damping down chemical
activity within the brain that is causing the anxiety.
At higher doses, most benzodiazepines cause drowsiness
(the majority of sleeping pills are benzodiazepines). Side
effects include dizziness and forgetfulness. Reaction times
may be slowed and so users should be warned against
driving or operating dangerous machinery.

Not for long-term use

When taken for a long period benzodiazepines not only
lose much of their therapeutic effectiveness but may also
produce a range of adverse effects. Patients can become
addicted to them, and they may cause psychological
impairment after long-term use.

Withdrawal symptoms commonly occur when the dose
is reduced or the drug is stopped abruptly. These
symptoms can include feelings of tension, restlessness and
panic, also poor concentration and impaired memory.
Physical symptoms can include a dry mouth, tremor,
sweating and sleep disturbance.

BETA-BLOCKERS

These are usually taken to control abnormal heart
conditions and reduce high blood pressure; examples are
atenolol and propranolol. In cases of patients suffering
from anxiety, they relieve the physical symptoms of
anxiety, such as palpitations, tremor and shaking. These
symptoms are caused by an increase in the activity of the
sympathetic nervous system. The chemical noradrenaline
is released by sympathetic nerves and stimulates the
digestive system, heart and other organs. Beta-blockers
block the action of noradrenaline in the body, and in this
way reduce the physical symptoms of anxiety.

Adverse effects

Beta-blockers affect many parts of the body and so there
are often unwanted side effects. By reducing airflow to

Addiction to Valium and other benzodiazepines

TALKING POINT

When the first and most famous
benzodiazepine – diazepam (trade name
Valium) – was first introduced in 1963
there was little awareness that those taking it could
become addicted. The drug was widely prescribed in the
1960s and 1970s – it is estimated that 2.3 billion Valium
tablets were taken by Americans alone in 1978. But
gradually the problems of withdrawal after long-term
use – problems that kept millions hooked for years at
a time – became known and publicised. In 1988, the UK
Committee on Safety of Medicines issued a warning
that Valium and other benzodiazepines should only be
used for short periods of time because there was a high
risk of addiction, and a serious withdrawal syndrome
after long-term use. It is thought that there are still as
many as half a million long-term benzodiazepine users
(tranquillisers and sleeping tablets) in the UK.

the lungs they may cause breathing difficulties in people
who already have respiratory diseases, such as asthma,
and for this reason they are prescribed with caution in
this group of patients. Other side effects are reduced
heart rate and cold hands and feet.

BUSPIRONE

Buspirone is an anxiolytic drug that may be prescribed
instead of benzodiazepines. Buspirone is not addictive
and there is no withdrawal reaction on abrupt
discontinuation of the drug. A disadvantage of buspirone
is that it takes at least two weeks to show an effect.
This limits its use if immediate action is needed and it is
therefore not suitable for treatment of acute or transient
anxiety states. Side effects such as drowsiness, dizziness
and headaches occur most commonly at the start of
treatment with the drug.

Antidepressant drugs

Prozac may be the antidepressant most people have heard of, but it is only one of the drugs for depression now available. The objectives of drug treatment for depression are to relieve distress, restore normal functioning and prevent the recurrence of depressive illness.

Drugs prescribed to treat depression mostly fall into one of two categories: the older tricyclics and the newer SSRIs (selective serotonin re-uptake inhibitors). Trials have shown no particular antidepressant is actually better at reducing the depression suffered by the patient than another. However, each drug has its own strengths, weaknesses and side effect possibilities, and so undoubtedly some antidepressants are more suitable for some patients than others.

Antidepressant drugs do not provide an instant effect – there is often a first response to treatment after two weeks but this may be even later, particularly if the recipient is elderly. Six months is generally recommended as a full course of therapy. If the depression recurs, it is possible that treatment may be continued indefinitely at the full dose. Treatment should always be withdrawn gradually over at least four weeks, to avoid withdrawal symptoms such as nausea, headaches and anxiety.

TRICYCLIC AND RELATED ANTIDEPRESSANTS

These have been available since the 1950s and, though very effective, are more toxic than newer antidepressants. They are relatively cheap in comparison with other antidepressants such as SSRIs. Their antidepressant effect was discovered by chance in the 1950s. Tricyclics raise levels of the chemical noradrenaline in the brain (and in some cases also serotonin), and by doing so reduce feelings of depression. They affect various chemicals in the brain and therefore produce a range of side effects;

among these are dry mouth, blurred vision, constipation and drowsiness. Examples of tricyclic antidepressants in use today are amitriptyline, imipramine (Tofranil) and dothiepin (Prothiaden).

SELECTIVE SEROTONIN RE-UPTAKE INHIBITORS (SSRI)

SSRIs decrease depression in patients by raising levels of serotonin in the brain – levels of serotonin in the brain have been shown to have an important influence on mood. They are mainly prescribed for the treatment of depression, obsessive compulsive disorder (OCD) and panic disorder.

SSRIs are just as effective as the older tricyclics and less dangerous in overdose. Also, they have fewer and less severe side effects and therefore fewer people on SSRIs discontinue their medication because of side effect problems. The main adverse effects of SSRIs are nausea and other gastro-intestinal problems. The chemical structures of different SSRIs vary, and therefore so do their clinical uses and their side effects.

- Fluoxetine (Prozac) is an antidepressant that is also used as an anti-bulimic agent, and a treatment for OCD. The doses for bulimia and OCD are a lot higher than

St John's wort (Hypericum perforatum)
St John's wort is a flowering plant native to Europe that grows as a weed in many countries. It is available over the counter as a herbal remedy for the treatment of mild depression. Its antidepressant properties relate to its ability to increase levels of serotonin, noradrenaline and dopamine in the brain. It is not effective against major depression and it must not be used with other antidepressants – a patient should always inform their GP that they are taking it.

the doses used for depression. Loss of libido is a possible side effect.

- Paroxetine (Seroxat) is useful for patients with depression accompanied by anxiety. It is also licensed for treatment of OCD, panic disorder, social phobia and post-traumatic stress disorder. Libido can be affected.
- Sertraline (Lustral) is licensed for the treatment of depressive illness and OCD.

MONOAMINE OXIDASE INHIBITORS (MAOI)

MAOIs increase levels of serotonin and noradrenaline in the brain by blocking monoamine oxidase, the enzyme that breaks these chemicals down. Doctors prescribe MAOIs less often than SSRIs and tricyclics because of the danger of problems when they are taken at the same time as certain foods and some other drugs.

In some cases, MAOIs are the best choice, however, and they are sometimes tried when other antidepressants have failed. If taken with certain drugs or foods rich in the protein tyramine, such as yeast extract, red wine, cheese and meat, they can cause very high blood pressure. People taking MAOIs are given a special card detailing banned drugs and foods.

Examples of MAOIs are phenelzine (Nardil) and tranylcypromine (Parnate).

- Reversible inhibitors of monoamines (RIMAs) These have fewer side effects than the older MAOIs. Prime example: moclobemide.

OTHER ANTIDEPRESSANTS

- Serotonin and noradrenaline re-uptake inhibitors (SNRIs) This type of drug increases levels of serotonin and noradrenaline. SNRIs are licensed for the treatment of depressive illness and generalised anxiety disorder. Prime example: venlafaxine (Efexor).
- Noradrenergic and specific serotonergic antidepressants (NASSAs) These drugs increase levels of noradrenaline and serotonin. Prime examples are mirtazapine and nefazodone. Mirtazapine can cause weight gain and have a sedative effect. Nefazodone hydrochloride can cause nausea, headaches and drowsiness.
- Noradrenaline re-uptake inhibitors (NARIs) This type of antidepressant increases noradrenaline levels only. Prime example: reboxetine, which is effective in treating patients who have mild to severe depression. Common side effects include constipation, insomnia and impotence.

LITHIUM FOR MANIC DEPRESSION

Manic depression (bipolar affective disorder) is usually treated with lithium salts. Lithium reduces the intensity of mania, reduces the frequency of mood swings and lifts depression.

History
Lithium was used in the 19th century to treat gout and epilepsy, and as a sedative. In the 1940s lithium chloride was used as a salt substitute in low-salt diets for patients with heart failure. The toxicity of lithium was discovered at this point, but sadly not before some patients had died. In 1949 lithium was first tried on patients suffering with manic depression and found to be an effective treatment. It also proved useful in preventing recurrent attacks.

How does it work?
Exactly how lithium works is still uncertain. It affects noradrenaline, dopamine and serotonin functions in the central nervous system. It also alters sodium and potassium transport across cell membranes. It may take three weeks before lithium starts to work, and so an antipsychotic drug may be prescribed with lithium at first to give immediate relief of symptoms.

What are the adverse effects?
Early effects that may not interfere with treatment include nausea and mild diarrhoea. Lithium can be toxic if levels of the drug in the blood are too high, so regular blood level tests are carried out during treatment. As the level of lithium rises in the central nervous system, side effects become prominent. These include tremor, drowsiness and giddiness, ringing in the ears and blurred vision. Prolonged use can cause hypothyroidism and kidney damage. Years of use should only be allowed if the benefits clearly outweigh the risks.

Antipsychotic drugs

The treatment of schizophrenia and other psychotic disorders has been revolutionised in the last few decades by the discovery of new, more effective drug therapies. These drugs are not cures, but they can still make all the difference for many sufferers of psychotic illness.

THEN AND NOW

Prior to the introduction of chlorpromazine in the 1950s there were no truly antipsychotic drugs – that is, drugs that reduce psychotic symptoms without impairing consciousness. Until then, management of schizophrenia and other psychotic illnesses was based on:

• the use of powerful sedative drugs, such as barbiturates;
• electroconvulsive therapy (ECT);
• physical restraint (including the use of straitjackets) and institutionalisation.

Nowadays, much more sophisticated drugs are the commonest treatments for psychotic disorders. Antipsychotic drugs help to suppress delusions, hallucinations and thought disturbances, and so are able to make everyday life for schizophrenics much easier than it would have been formerly. However, most have less effect on the other common symptoms of schizophrenia such as social withdrawal, apathy and lack of self-care.

Because they control symptoms rather than cure the psychotic disorder, it is important to keep taking antipsychotic medication exactly as prescribed. When a drug is stopped on medical advice, this is done by slowly reducing the dose. Sudden withdrawal of an antipsychotic drug can cause unpleasant side effects such as nausea, headaches and physical restlessness.

HOW ANTIPSYCHOTICS WORK

Psychotic symptoms are thought to be caused by an increase in communication between brain cells due to over-activity of the neurotransmitter dopamine, which can disturb normal processes and lead to abnormal behaviour. Standard antipsychotic drugs make brain cells less sensitive to dopamine and hence reduce psychotic symptoms. Some newer 'atypical' antipsychotic drugs work by affecting dopamine receptors in more specific parts of the brain and thereby reducing side effects.

How are they administered?

Antipsychotic drugs may be given by mouth, by injection, or in the form of a 'depot injection' that releases the drug slowly over a few weeks.

WHAT ARE THE CHOICES?

Individual antipsychotic drugs vary in their action and side effects – not only between themselves, but from patient to patient on the same medication. In general, approximately one in five people with schizophrenia are not helped by antipsychotic drugs. Listed here are some of the more common antipsychotics.

Standard antipsychotic drugs

• **Chlorpromazine** The first standard antipsychotic drug was chlorpromazine. When tests showed that it produced calm in patients without inducing unconsciousness, it became the drug of choice for

Depot injections

Depot injections eliminate the need for the patient to remember to take the right medication at the correct intervals. Instead, the patient goes to a clinic every few weeks and receives an injection. Such a procedure avoids the problem of patients not taking their medication properly. The antipsychotic is injected into a large muscle (often a buttock). The main disadvantage with depot injections is that if an adverse reaction occurs, it is likely to last as long as it takes for the drug to clear naturally from the body – usually over a month. This is a major concern with severe side effects such as liver or blood toxicity.

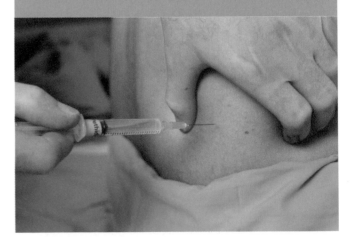

treatment of psychotic illnesses, and it remains the yardstick against which other standard antipsychotic drugs are measured, despite its sedative effect. In cases of schizophrenia, chlorpromazine reduces symptoms in about three-quarters of those treated.

- **Flupentixol** The action of flupentixol has a less sedating effect than chlorpromazine.
- **Sulpiride** This drug may act well against apathy when taken at low doses.
- **Haloperidol** The drug is effective for rapid control of hyperactivity, especially in older patients.

Unwanted side effects

The problem with taking standard antipsychotic drugs is the possible side effects. Since antipsychotic medication is often prescribed for many years, it is essential to minimise side effects by prescribing the drug best suited to each individual and keeping the dose to the minimum that is effective. Patients may well find themselves taking other prescription drugs as well, in order to lessen unwanted effects of antipsychotic medication.

The psychological side effects of drugs can be hard to differentiate from symptoms of the disorder being treated. They could include agitation, depression, drowsiness or insomnia, lack of energy or ability to concentrate.

Among the possible physical side effects are fine movement problems such as rigidity, tremor, restlessness, involuntary movements and muscle spasms. Other side effects could be dry mouth, blurred vision, constipation, reduced libido, low blood pressure, itchy or sensitive skin, and hormonal changes leading to breast growth or menstrual problems.

Atypical antipsychotic drugs

The 'atypical antipsychotics' introduced in recent years often have fewer side effects than standard antipsychotic drugs. They are now regularly prescribed for newly diagnosed schizophrenics, but changing to an atypical antipsychotic is not seen as necessary for someone already being satisfactorily treated by a standard antipsychotic. The atypical antipsychotics are clozapine, amisulpride, olanzapine, risperidone, quetiapine and zotepine.

- **Clozapine** The first of these new drugs and considered by many to be the most effective. However, clozapine can cause a steep decline in the number of white blood cells, and so is used to treat schizophrenia only in patients who do not get better with other antipsychotics.

Electroconvulsive therapy

It has been proved many times over that passing a mild electric current through the brain can relieve depression. But how and why this works is still not fully understood.

Electroconvulsive therapy (ECT) was first developed in the 1930s. Doctors had already discovered that inducing a convulsion (using drugs) helped to reduce symptoms of severe depression and mania. By the late 1930s it was realised that the best way of bringing on a seizure was to administer an electric shock.

How is it done?

The patient is given a short-acting general anaesthetic by injection, then injected with a muscle-relaxant drug. Next, two electrode pads are placed on or above the patient's forehead. A small and precisely calculated electric charge is delivered to the electrodes, causing an electric current to pass across the brain for a few seconds. This should induce a seizure lasting 20–50 seconds or so. Because of the muscle relaxant, the body experiences just a few, mild twitches of muscles in the face, hands and feet. Usually a course of treatments is prescribed: between three and twelve, taken twice a week.

Who can benefit?

The main beneficiaries are patients with severe depression (see page 142) or with manic depression (bipolar affective disorder, see page 139). ECT is also occasionally prescribed for schizophrenia and severe cases of obsessive compulsive disorder. Although drug therapy is now preferred over ECT in the vast majority of cases, ECT is still an alternative practised from time to time, normally for patients for whom drug treatments are not working, or who require a more rapid improvement in symptoms than drugs can give, perhaps because they are suicidal.

Are there any adverse effects?

Immediate side effects can include drowsiness, headache, nausea, muscle pains, mild confusion and some memory loss. All of these are temporary. There is debate over whether patients undergoing ECT risk irreversible memory loss or some more subtle form of brain damage, but there is no current evidence of permanent harm.

Psychosurgery

Surgery on the brain for the treatment of mental disorders is nowadays a much more precise science than it was once. Such operations rarely take place, but are still performed occasionally to help patients suffering from very severe anxiety or depression.

THE ROLE OF PSYCHOSURGERY

Psychosurgery, also called neurosurgery for mental disorder (NMD), is a treatment for extreme states of anxiety and depression, especially chronic anxiety, obsessive compulsive disorder and manic depression (bipolar affective disorder). Schizophrenia is no longer treated by pyschosurgery; neither are personality or addictive disorders. Nowadays just a few operations take place each year in the UK.

The treatment of last resort

Candidates for surgery are chosen with great care. Psychosurgery is generally the treatment of last resort – used when all other attempts at treatment have failed and the alternative is continued suffering for the patient.

Why does psychosurgery have such a bad name?

TALKING POINT

In the not so distant past, surgery on the brain for mental problems was sometimes carried out inappropriately. When Portuguese psychiatrist Egas Moniz introduced the lobotomy for severe mental disorders in the 1930s, it quickly became popular because there were so few alternative treatments. From the 1930s to the 1950s, around 50,000 lobotomies were carried out in the USA alone, for disorders ranging from schizophrenia to depression to uncontrolled aggression. The surgeon removed or disconnected part of the frontal lobe of the brain in order to reduce undesirable symptoms, especially those related to aggression; this could not be done with any precision and therefore the patient risked loss of brain function unrelated to the aims of the operation. This and overzealous and indiscriminate application of the operation led to a backlash in the 1960s against psychosurgery in general. Today, operations for mental disorders are much more precise, and performed only occasionally.

The patient must have consented to the operation. The idea is to remove or disconnect brain tissue with the aim of reducing anxiety, tension and compulsive behaviours. Surgical procedures aim to interrupt the nerve circuits within the limbic system in the frontal lobes of the brain; the limbic system is involved with the regulation and expression of emotions.

MODERN-DAY OPERATIONS

There are four types of surgical procedure in use today.

- Those that take place in the UK are chiefly the types called limbic leucotomy and subcaudate tractotomy.
- In the USA cingulotomy is often preferred.
- Surgeons in Europe have developed the anterior capsulotomy.

The operations all involve the creation of lesions (cuts) in the left and/or right frontal lobe. It is the positioning, size and number of the cuts that differentiates the operations. All of the different types of psychosurgery are irreversible.

Ensuring pinpoint accuracy

Surgery is carried out under general anaesthetic. Before the operation proper begins, a 'stereotactic' frame is attached to the patient's head. This is to keep the operation site absolutely still, and to allow the positioning of surgical instruments in the brain to be mechanically fixed and not dependent on the hand movements of the surgeon. X-rays plus CT imaging or MRI scans allow very accurate guidance (to within one millimetre) of the instrument to the target site within the brain. Cuts in the frontal lobes are generally created with a probe that uses either extreme heat or extreme cold to destroy unwanted tissue.

After the operation

Approximately three-quarters of patients experience an improvement in their mental condition after surgery. Improvements are not immediate, but emerge over the months following the operation. There is a risk of side effects such as apathy, weight gain and epilepsy.

Hypnotherapy

Hypnosis is a state of deep relaxation, artificially induced by a hypnotist, in which the mind is more than usually receptive to suggestion. Hypnotherapy is the process whereby a hypnotist attempts to use hypnosis to change patterns of behaviour in the patient.

When a patient's mind is in a hypnotic state, it may be possible for the hypnotist to introduce new ideas and positive suggestions that supplant old unwanted behaviour patterns. For a long-term effect on behaviour after hypnosis, a series of hypnotherapy sessions is often needed, to allow for repeated reinforcement of the new behaviours.

Many mental health professionals – including many who prescribe hypnotherapy – believe that it is possible to achieve most of what can be done through hypnosis by direct appeal to the conscious mind of the patient, that is, without the need for hypnosis. Certainly, how much the patient really wants to change is key to the success of any hypnotherapy. Generally, hypnotherapy is employed alongside other treatments, sometimes as part of cognitive behavioural therapy (see page 114).

The hypnotherapist should be a psychologist, psychotherapist or other qualified healthcare professional, or registered with the British Hypnotherapy Association.

WHAT HAPPENS DURING A SESSION?

The hypnotherapist starts the first session by taking a medical history of the patient and establishing the goals of the treatment – the nature of the problem and how the patient wishes to change. Hypnosis begins with the therapist guiding the patient into a state of relaxation similar to daydreaming. This is done by various means including deep breathing, muscle relaxation, counting down into deeper relaxation, and the use of imagery techniques (asking the patient to imagine a safe, stress-free place of their own choosing, for instance).

With the patient in a hypnotic state, the hypnotherapist attempts to teach the patient's subconscious mind the new ideas that the patient wants to learn, by such means as

Going under

The hypnotherapist is asking the patient to focus on a pen as the first stage of inducing a hypnotic state. Then the therapist will ask the patient to slowly count from one to ten, with the suggestion that the patient will become more relaxed with each number.

verbal suggestion and guided visualisation. The person being hypnotised is aware of what is happening at all times and cannot be made to say or do anything against his or her will.

When the session is over the patient 'awakes', and will usually feel relaxed and rested. A typical session is 40 minutes long.

Who might benefit from hypnotherapy?

Problem areas that might be helped include: anxiety and stress; obsessive compulsive behaviours; phobias; substance addiction, especially to nicotine; insomnia; eating disorders. Physical disorders, notably headaches (migraine or tension) and pain management can also be alleviated. However, some people are resistant to hypnosis and so are unlikely to benefit from this therapy.

Complementary therapies

Problems to do with stress, anxiety and depression respond well to light therapy, aromatherapy and treatments centred around touching. All are soothing, calming activities that work through the senses to benefit the mind as well as the body.

LIGHT THERAPY

Light plays a major role in your well-being. As the sun rises at dawn the light is recognised by the pineal gland located in the brain. This gland then secretes the neurotransmitter serotonin, which in turn reduces the production of the hormone melatonin. Melatonin helps you to sleep, while increased serotonin improves your mood and so boosts morning energy levels.

During the winter months, when there is less natural light available, some people experience a number of depression-related symptoms collectively referred to as seasonal affective disorder (SAD, see page 153). Not surprisingly, in people experiencing SAD regions of the central nervous system have been found to be deficient in serotonin. Bright light can be used to stimulate the production of serotonin, reduce production of melatonin and so alleviate symptoms of SAD. Light boxes and visors have been specially designed for use at home, providing full-spectrum light (the same as natural daylight) or bright white light that does not contain ultraviolet.

People who often work night shifts or travel a great deal between different time zones may also miss out on natural light and suffer the symptoms of SAD.

AROMATHERAPY

Aromatherapy can be defined as the inhalation and application of volatile essential oils from aromatic plants in order to enhance or restore health and well-being. The use of the medicinal properties of essential oil in plants has been documented as far back as ancient Egypt. Modern aromatherapy stems from research by a French chemist, Réné-Maurice Gattefossé, and other doctors in France, where essential oils are now sometimes prescribed in place of conventional medicines. In 1910, Gattefossé burnt his hand accidentally and applied lavender oil to it. He subsequently observed that the burn healed remarkably quickly, with little scarring. This led him to investigate the therapeutic qualities of other plant oils.

The body absorbs aromatherapy oils either through the skin in a massage or by inhalation, after a few drops of oil have been dropped into steaming water. Molecules of the oil are believed to enter the nervous system through the bloodstream, thereby affecting physical and emotional well-being. When inhaled, the scent released by the oils is captured by sensory receptor cells at the top of the nasal cavity, which act on the relevant parts of the brain to affect mood and stress levels.

Seasonal affective disorder

SAD is a syndrome characterised by recurrent depression, which occurs at the same time each year. During the winter months, when levels of sunlight are low, many people suffer from a variety of symptoms. These include increased appetite, weight gain, a drop in energy levels, reduced sex drive, disturbances in sleeping and waking patterns, reduction in the quality of sleep, body aches and pains, avoidance of social situations, decreased creativity, irritability, the inability to complete tasks, and even suicidal thoughts. Light therapy involves exposure to bright light one or two times a day for sessions lasting from 10 to 90 minutes. The main device used in phototherapy is a fluorescent light box that is often mounted on a stand.

Aromatherapy

To make an inhalation, add between five and ten drops of essential oil to a bowl of steaming hot water and then inhale the resulting vapour. The following is a list of popular essential oils and their therapeutic uses for the mind.

Oil	Therapeutic properties	Used to relieve
LAVENDER	Sedative; antidepressant	Tension; breathlessness due to nervous conditions; insomnia
ROSEMARY	Analgesic, stimulant	Nervous tension; mental fatigue; headaches; premenstrual tension (PMS)
SANDALWOOD	Sedative	Insomnia; depression
CLARY SAGE	Analgesic, sedative	Nervous tension; anxiety; depression; mental fatigue
GERMAN CHAMOMILE	Sedative	Nervous tension; headaches; PMS; insomnia

THERAPIES INVOLVING TOUCH

Touching, stroking and massage have been proved time and time again to have a beneficial effect on mental health, lifting and lightening agitation, anxiety and depression. There are many form of complementary therapy centred on the power of touch. Two of the most popular are Reiki and reflexology. Others include Swedish massage and Shiatsu massage.

Reiki

In Japanese, rei means 'universal' and ki means 'life energy'. Reiki is a way of promoting well-being, or 'healing', by the gentle laying on of hands. It was developed in Japan in the late 19th century and takes its inspiration from Tibetan Buddhism.

Each session lasts about an hour. The patient lies fully clothed on a treatment table and the practitioner places his or her hands on the patient's body in 12 set positions for about five minutes each.

Studies have shown how Reiki can assist in easing anxiety and decreasing depression by encouraging relaxation and increasing a sense of well-being. However, at present there are no conventional tests that can measure or ascertain how Reiki actually works. More research is needed in order to understand and quantify the physiological and psychological effects of Reiki.

Reflexology

Many forms of massage are calming to the mind as well as soothing to the body. Foot massage is said to have originated in China and reflexology is the practise of foot massage to treat ailments in all parts of the body.

Reflexologists believe that the feet and hands are a reflection of the body and that pressure placed on specific reflex points on the feet can affect corresponding areas of the body. There are around 7200 nerve endings in each foot. By applying pressure to specific points on the feet reflexologists believe they can stimulate better functioning of the circulatory and lymphatic systems. This in turn may be responsible for improvements in the patient's general health and sense of well-being. It is also possible that it is the effect reflexology treatment has on the nervous and hormonal systems that brings about the emotional and psychological benefits often experienced. Reflexology is reported to be a very effective for stress, tension and tiredness.

Reflexologists work on all parts of the foot; some reflexologists also work on the hand or ear. In a reflexology session the practitioner will start off by asking the patient about their past and present health and lifestyle. The practitioner examines the feet for any signs of existing or potential illnesses and may sometimes recommend that the patient has a medical check-up.

Creative arts therapies

Creative arts therapies – also known as expressive therapies – harness art and creativity to treat many different mental disorders and problems. They include art, music, dramatherapy and dance/movement therapy.

GIVING A VOICE TO WHAT CAN'T BE SAID

Creative activity can take a number of forms. Creating a painting or a sculpture, writing prose, composing or responding to music, dancing, drama and movement are all useful because they provide an alternative means of communication that can encompass or express emotions and experiences that are difficult to verbalise. This allows access to internal, unconscious, pre-verbal experiences and gives them a 'voice'. Creative activities also circumvent the defences usually put up during ordinary conversation to avoid direct emotional contact with the client's own self or with others.

Therapy sessions typically take place once a week for six months to a year. Each session lasts about an hour. Working individually or within a group, the client learns by building a relationship with the therapist and others, using the chosen creative activity. This enables the person to take control, make choices and make discoveries about themself and about other people. The therapist ensures a safe, non-critical environment, within set and understood boundaries. Beliefs, opinions and confidentiality are all respected.

Sessions are centred around the creative activity. The therapist observes the activity, together with the client's reactions, interactions, body language and responses, attitude and mood. Together, client and therapist try to discover where the client's behaviour may come from, when it may have begun and why, and the effect it has on the client's mood and life. Anyone calling themselves an art therapist, music therapist or dramatherapist in the UK must be state registered with the Health Professions Council (HPC).

Who benefits from creative arts therapies?

Creative arts therapies benefit people with many types of difficulties. They can help people who:
- have mental health problems, including eating disorders or substance addiction;
- are coming to terms with emotional or sexual abuse;
- are adjusting to a major life change such as bereavement or terminal illness;
- have learning difficulties;
- are autistic and therefore have major communication difficulties;
- have low self-esteem and lack confidence.

Mental health professionals, doctors, teachers, or other multidisciplinary team members may refer clients for treatment. Some people refer themselves.

a and **b** Art therapy
Clients are not expected to create a 'good' piece of art, they are simply encouraged to give expression to threatening or confusing emotions through the act of creation. Releasing such emotions in a safe environment is therapeutic in itself. Within the artwork there often emerges symbols similar to those that appear in dreams, which can lead to significant insights. Paint, crayons, clay, fabric and magazines for creating collages are some of the materials used.

c Music therapy

Reactions to music are often spontaneous and uninhibited and music therapy uses the act of making or responding to music as an alternative to communicating through words. Clients are not taught to play an instrument and musical knowledge is not necessary. Music is used initially to establish a trusting relationship between therapist and client, matching rhythms or repeating a tune to build the relationship and improve concentration. Further musical activity – improvisation, making up songs or copying rhythms – improves communication skills, listening skills and concentration.

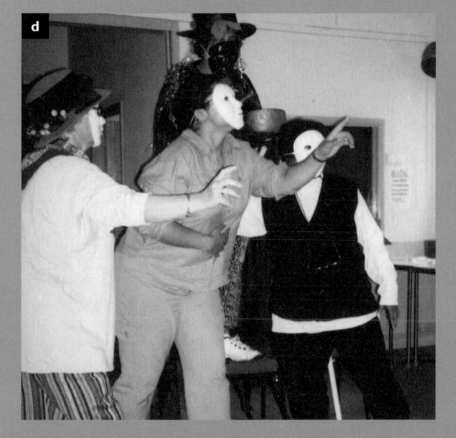

d Dramatherapy

This uses improvisation, role-playing, working with masks and puppetry to enable clients to tell their inner story and gain greater self-knowledge. Exploration of myths, texts and personal stories enables us to grasp how we become trapped within certain roles and expectations. Drama provides an opportunity to take risks in a safe environment. Feelings of isolation and confusion may be reduced, and new coping strategies and skills developed.

Psychodrama (not illustrated)

This is a form of group therapy in which one person acts out inner conflicts, thereby putting across feelings that are difficult to express in normal life. These personal dramas take place on a 'therapeutic stage', starting in the present and working back to childhood experiences. Acting out the drama provides an opportunity to learn and practice new, more appropriate behaviours and work through specific issues.

e Dance/movement therapy

Babies express themselves through their bodies long before they learn to talk. Their movements – such as wriggling for joy or kicking in anger – convey their emotions. As we grow up this direct link between emotion and movement is hampered and harnessed. Dance/movement therapy revives the natural link between movement and self-expression, enabling clients to express their thoughts and feelings, bypassing the conscious mind and making direct contact with their inner emotional landscape. Clients are encouraged to move freely, sometimes to music. Spontaneous gestures can be used along with formal dance steps. Some practitioners move along with the client, mirroring and supporting their moves, while others show support by observing.

Community care

The idea of care in the community for those with mental health problems originated in the 1950s and started to become a reality in the 1980s, with legislation to set in motion the closure of the large mental institutions in which people had lived, sometimes for most of their lives.

The aim of 'care in the community' for people with mental health problems was to treat them as people with rights and deserving of respect, rather than isolating them in asylums where life skills were frequently lost and institutionalisation common. Psychiatrists increasingly questioned standard treatments for some conditions, including schizophrenia, routinely treated with ECT and hospitalisation. The introduction of new drugs in the 1960s left the way clear for more people to be treated outside a hospital setting. In addition, patients were realising they had rights, and support groups and charities were becoming vociferous in detailing them. Legislation in the 1980s paved the way for the closure of the large mental institutions and the funding of community care.

Care in the community covers people between the ages of 18 and 65 with mental health problems and learning disability (arrangements for the over-65s come under the umbrella of 'care of the elderly'). The community mental health team coordinates individual written social and residential care packages. The teams are multidisciplinary, involving GPs, psychiatrists, psychiatric nurses, social workers, physiotherapists and occupational therapists. The care plan includes a named keyworker – often a community psychiatric nurse – to coordinate the plan, make sure it is working, and instigate regular reviews.

Alternatives to hospital may include sheltered accommodation, day centres, drop-in facilities and respite homes. Some sheltered accommodation involves a high carer to resident ratio to support those with severe problems; in other settings individuals are encouraged to live more independently; some short-stay hostels are seen as 'stepping stones' to the wider community; some people benefit from a short stay – usually a pre-agreed period of time – in a therapeutic community, where there is a resident psychiatrist and group therapy sessions. Community housing may be available through housing associations. Housing associations may also offer places in small, shared homes to those with particular problems, such as recovering alcoholics or those with learning difficulties. Alternatively, those with problems and their families are supported to continue to live at home.

Some day centres offer education and training, give support and encouragement to regain self-esteem, and teach basic life skills. Others are simply social, providing

Revising life skills
Those who have had a mental illness, or who have long-standing learning difficulties, may miss out on key life skills, such as sharing space, holding a conversation, or cooking a meal. Sheltered accommodation may offer the freedom to hone these skills in safety.

leisure facilities and perhaps meals, and the opportunity to share concerns with someone in a similar situation. These may be run by the local authority or a charity and there may or may not be a charge for attending.

Other support may include:
- Work schemes to help individuals who have never worked or who have not worked recently back into the work force;
- Physiotherapy to improve physical and psychological well-being;
- Occupational therapy to offer advice on all aspects of daily life.

NHS BACK-UP

A doctor or community health team who feel that someone would benefit from a stay in hospital can make a referral. Alternatively, anyone who feels their condition is getting out of hand can self-refer for inpatient treatment on the psychiatric ward of a hospital. The aim of this is to carry out a multidisciplinary assessment, offer medical treatment and aid rehabilitation, with the goal of returning patients to the community as soon as they are able to function there. Patients can sometimes be treated as day cases, generally following the same programme of group or occupational therapy as inpatients, but returning home at night.

ARE THERE DRAWBACKS?

Most people have a greatly improved quality of life living outside an institution. However, there can be drawbacks.
- Non-compliance in taking medication can make symptoms worse.
- There is still some social stigma attached to mental health problems. Inadequate housing, poor life skills and unemployment can make life difficult in the community for many people.
- Acutely ill patients may have difficulty getting a hospital bed – and may find themselves discharged too soon. Similarly patients who really should be in a psychiatric bed have to be accommodated on an acute medical ward.
- The involvement of the NHS, local authority and voluntary groups can mean that some people who need care slip through the net, and even for those who don't, the care can be patchy.
- Good community care is expensive: professionals argue that when working well it is far more expensive than the old-fashioned asylums.

Taking up residence

Residential care may be appropriate after a period in hospital, for example, to convalesce where there are carers on hand. It may also be useful when permanent carers need to take a break.

- There have been incidents in which a psychiatric patient in the community has committed assault or killed; more common are assaults on the mentally ill. Self-harm is also a problem. Violence to self and others is usually the result of not taking medication.

The Mental Health Act

TALKING POINT

The powers of the Mental Health Act (1983) can be used to compulsorily detain an individual who is judged sufficiently mentally unwell for assessment and treatment when it is in the interest of the health and safety of the individual or for the protection of others. Sections of the act allow for differing types and times of detention, which may be hospital or community based. Before a detention order is made, a patient must be assessed by a doctor who has prior knowledge of the patient, preferably the GP, and an approved psychiatrist. A third professional, always an approved social worker (ASW) who has had special training in mental health, must also be present. The Mental Health Act is currently under review.

Care for carers

Many people with mental health problems, in particular the forms of dementia associated with ageing, are cared for at home, usually by a family member. This places an enormous burden on the carer, who has to have adequate support.

It is easy for carers to neglect their own needs in their concern to attend to the needs of the person with problems. Putting themselves first some of the time is vital if carers are to be able to continue to fulfil this role.

Find out as early as you can what to expect of the progress of the condition which has been diagnosed, its symptoms, the side effects of any medication and so on. Ask your GP, social services or any relevant charity (see page 160) for advice. Social services have a duty to assess the needs of anyone diagnosed with dementia, and that assessment should include the needs of the carer. If you are working and have to give up either temporarily or permanently, check your financial and pension positions.

Discuss early what you both want to happen in terms of treatment (for example, at what point does the carer decide that coping at home is no longer an option).

Decisions made when a person is relatively well will help everyone to cope better later. Check which benefits you are both entitled to and appoint a power of attorney to manage finances when this is no longer possible. Carers should check their status regarding property ownership, finances and pension if residential care becomes necessary.

YOUR HEALTH

Carers have to look after themselves, too. Regular GP visits are a good idea, as is seeking timely advice for any niggling problem, no matter how trivial. Anxiety and depression are common in carers and easier to treat when they are in the early stages. Pay attention to your diet: if you cannot cope with cooking, ask for 'meals on wheels' and supplement these with fresh fruit and vegetables, low-fat protein and quality wholegrains at other times. Try to get some exercise, even a walk around the block in the fresh air is beneficial, and get enough night-time sleep (ask the GP's advice if your sleep is disturbed by a partner – medication may be an option for one or other of you). Remember: your health may make the difference between a person staying at home and moving into residential care.

TAKE A BREAK

You need time to yourself on a regular basis: aim for an hour a day, half a day a week and regular breaks of a few days. Ask friends or family to take over or find out what is available locally in terms of home care, day centres, lunch clubs and respite residential care. Social services should have details. It is important to keep up social contacts outside the home. Ask family and friends to call in or phone often so that your horizons do not become limited.

You can't do it all. Ask for help early and often, so that when you really need it later there is a team of tried and trusted people who can cope when you are not there.

Getting away
Caring for an elderly relative is exhausting and can put marital and parent-child relations under severe stress. Time away every few weeks or so can be important in keeping relationships strong, as well as broadening your horizons and putting yourself first.

A to Z

OF DISEASES AND DISORDERS

This section gives information on the main illnesses and medical conditions that affect the mind. The entries are arranged alphabetically and each is structured in a similar way:

What are the causes?

What are the symptoms?

How is it diagnosed?

What are the treatment options?

What is the outlook?

ALCOHOLISM

Alcoholism is the physical addiction to or dependence on alcohol. There are usually, but not always, abnormalities in tests of liver function in those who abuse alcohol. It is sometimes difficult to distinguish alcoholism from severe problem drinking.

What are the causes?

Alcohol is an addictive drug. Although it acts as a depressant, and its effects if abused are undoubtedly unpleasant in the longer term, it can be very effective in the short term in dulling the senses to unpleasant reality, and it dissolves social inhibitions. Alcohol has a rapid, direct effect on the brain and it is relatively easy to form a tolerance to it (needing a greater amount of alcohol to achieve the same psychological or physical effect).

There may be some genetic predisposition to dependence. Some people have suggested that some aspects of the personality, such as a dependence on reward, may predispose to alcohol dependence. Psychiatric disorders and other chemical variations in the brain have also been suggested as predisposing to alcoholism.

Family studies, looking at identical and non-identical twins, have suggested that there is a strong inherited component. However, these studies have significant flaws, not least of which is that the family members taking part are the children of people with alcohol problems.

Culture, too, plays a part. In cultures where abstinence is the norm, such as Moslems and Mormons, those who drink are at greater risk of problem drinking. Similarly where alcohol has been introduced to a previously abstinent population, such as the Native Americans, problem drinking is more common. Cultural aspects of drinking pattern, such as binge drinking, as opposed to intermittent social drinking – the 'Anglo Saxon' versus the 'Mediterranean' model of consumption – probably has little to do with this: alcoholism is common in Mediterranean countries as well as in more northerly European lands.

What are the symptoms?

Alcoholism forms a distinct syndrome. It is characterised by:
- narrowing of the drinking repertoire – not varying the kinds of drinks taken but focusing on the most cost-effective alcoholic 'hit';
- dominance or 'salience' of drinking, to the exclusion of other activities;
- withdrawal symptoms assuaged by alcohol – 'the hair of the dog' syndrome;

- increased tolerance of alcohol and rapid relapse after a period of abstention.

Severe problem drinking may have some of these features.

How is it diagnosed?

Diagnosis is primarily by the history of the symptoms. Some blood tests support the diagnosis, including the size of the red blood cells – the mean corpuscular volume (MCV) is high in alcoholism – and abnormalities in liver function.

What are the treatment options?

The short and medium term goal should be complete abstinence. A move to 'control' and reduce drinking may be feasible in some people, but it should be considered only when someone has negotiated a successful period (about six months) of complete abstinence. Simply cutting down, especially where there is dependence, is seldom effective.

There is no evidence that being admitted to hospital is superior to outpatient treatment, except in the most complicated cases. The initial form of treatment is 'detoxification' which covers the week or so of acute withdrawal symptoms after stopping alcohol. This usually involves the prescription of a drug, often a tranquilliser, to take the edge off the withdrawal symptoms.

Subsequently, most of the maintenance of treatment is by psychosocial treatments, such as group therapy. Drugs are available which interact violently with alcohol, and can underpin a person's determination to abstain. However, they require a highly motivated individual and are unsuccessful, even downright dangerous, if a person is not motivated to stop drinking.

Numerous groups exist to help with alcohol dependence, including Alcoholics Anonymous (p. 160) and various forms of the Alcohol Recovery Programme. As with many other treatments for addiction, these often follow ideological lines. There is nothing wrong with this, as long as people are able to sign up to the ideological approach. The likelihood of success with this treatment is small in those who cannot follow this approach. It pays to look around for a treatment that suits the individual.

What is the outlook?

The outlook depends on motivation. There is always pain associated with changing an habitual way of life. A person who is clear that the pain of changing is less than the pain of staying the same is more likely to be successful. Anyone who is not sufficiently motivated is unlikely to succeed, but the outlook for the motivated individual can be excellent.

ALZHEIMER'S DISEASE
The most common form of dementia.

What are the symptoms?
Alzheimer's erodes the memory, understanding, judgement, communication and competence. Eventually independence is lost, and a heavy burden is thrown on carers (generally members of the family), especially when there are behavioural problems. These include:
• wandering and getting lost;
• irritability and aggression;
• personality change for the worse;
• incontinence;
• reluctance to change clothes or wash;
• restlessness at night.
Alzheimer's is highly likely to end in institutional care (usually in a residential or nursing home) and shortens life. The course of the disease varies considerably, from a year or two to a decade or two; at its worst it ends in profound, speechless helplessness, but when more benign it may cause little more than endearing vagueness.

What are the causes?
Epidemiological studies show that one in 10 people over the age of 65 has the disease. The prevalence doubles every five years after 65, so that it is much more common in octogenarians than those in their 60s. The main risk factor is therefore ageing.

A family history of Alzheimer's increases the risk, especially for the presenile form, but only one in 50 cases is a genetic disorder passing from one generation to another. Genetic studies have found four genes that increase risk: amyloid precursor protein (APP) which contributes to the starchy amyloid plaques described by Alzheimer; presenilin 1 and 2; and apolipoprotein E. Apolipoprotein E comes in three forms – E2, E3 and E4. We inherit one of these forms from each parent, and there are six possible combinations: E2/E2, E2/E3, E2/E4, E3/E3, E3/E4 and E4/E4. There is a strong association of the E4/E4 combination with dementia, but there are too many exceptions to make apolipoprotein blood tests useful in establishing risk.

People with Down's syndrome (a form of learning disorder) are at considerable risk of Alzheimer's disease from their 50s onwards. Severe head injury increases the risk of Alzheimer's in later life, which may be relevant to footballers and boxers. A low intelligence quotient (IQ) and poor education may contribute to the earlier onset of the dementia. It now seems unlikely that aluminium in the water supply or from saucepans is a cause of Alzheimer's.

Two proteins – amyloid beta peptide and tau – are now known to damage nerve cells and their connections in Alzheimer's disease. This suggests possible opportunities for future treatment, including a form of vaccination.

How is it diagnosed and treated?
Few people want to know that they are developing Alzheimer's, but early recognition may enable them to have a proper say in their present and future care, including any form of residential or nursing care, and to make an enduring power of attorney so that if someone needs to handle finances and other affairs on their behalf it will be someone of their choosing. Short tests of memory, orientation, calculation, comprehension, writing and

Well-known sufferers from Alzheimer's disease include the former US president Ronald Reagan, former British prime minister Harold Wilson, actress Rita Hayworth and novelist Iris Murdoch.

Milestones
IN MEDICINE

Almost 100 years ago psychiatrist and neuropathologist Alois Alzheimer examined the brain of a woman in her fifties who had died after a dementing illness. He described shrinkage of the brain and, after microscopic examination, the plaques and nerve tangles that are characteristic of the disease which now bears his name. For many years Alzheimer's disease was regarded as a rare presenile dementia (coming on before the age of 65). Then, in 1952, the neuropathologist Jan Corsellis examined the brains of older people who had died with the diagnosis of senile dementia and found that most of them had the loss of brain substance, plaques and tangles of Alzheimer's disease too. This was the start of the recognition that senile dementia is not an inevitable consequence of ageing but a disease occurring much more often in older than younger people. In the past 40–50 years there has been a vast expansion in research and knowledge about Alzheimer's disease, which has also increased our understanding of how the brain works.

drawing a clock can help to indicate whether further investigation is required. The general practitioner can conduct these and then give advice.

Brain scans, using computerised tomography (CT) and magnetic resonance imaging (MRI) show up any shrinkage of the cortex or outer layers, enlargement of the ventricles (making the brain more hollow) and, in particular, the diminishing of the hippocampus, a structure on the floor of the brain somewhat resembling a seahorse, that is important for the laying down of new memories. SPET (single photon emission tomography) gives an accurate picture of the blood supply to the brain, and PET (positron emission tomography) is also valuable in research as it shows the metabolism of the brain (that is, not so much its structure, as what it is doing).

Biochemical and cellular studies established some years ago that those nerve cells in the brain which stimulate other nerve cells by the release of the neurotransmitter acetylcholine are particularly vulnerable in the early stages of Alzheimer's. Much research into how to keep up the supply of acetylcholine from flagging nerve cells has resulted in the discovery of anticholinesterases. Acetylcholine is removed from the synapse – the tiny gap between cells into which the neurotransmitter is released – by the enzyme cholinesterase. Anticholinesterases slow down this process, and enable acetylcholine to remain longer in the synapse, where it continues to stimulate the next nerve cell. Anticholinesterases are now available as drugs – donepezil, rivastigmine and galantamine – which can be given for early Alzheimer's. These often at least slow down mental deterioration for a year or so, and may actually improve memory and awareness for a while. They may also diminish the troublesome behaviour which makes Alzheimer's such an ordeal for carers.

The Alzheimer's Society (p. 160), founded by carers, is extremely helpful with information, advice and practical support, such as day centres and sitters who give respite to caring relatives. Social services can arrange care assistants, 'meals on wheels', financial allowances, sheltered housing and short or longer-term stays in homes, providing respite or continuing care. Old age psychiatric services, well established in the UK, have expertise in Alzheimer's and other dementias and can offer comprehensive assessment, drug treatments, community psychiatric nursing and occupational therapy. Reality orientation, reminiscence and validation therapies improve orientation, personal respect and awareness and empathy. Memory clinics are increasingly available, dedicated to the early diagnosis of dementia and its treatment. It is, of course, as important to take care of the carers as of the patients themselves (p. 132).

Can it be prevented?

Higher intelligence and good education seem to postpone Alzheimer's, but these are factors beyond an individual's control. Keeping the brain active with crossword puzzles, Scrabble and intellectual pursuits may help a little. There is some evidence that non-steroidal anti-inflammatory drugs (NSAIDs) such as ibuprofen and the oestrogen in hormone replacement therapy (HRT) have some slight protective effect against Alzheimer's, as may vitamin E, vitamin C (an antioxidant) and ginkgo biloba. Alcoholism damages the brain and contributes to dementia, but a glass or two of wine a day, especially red, may be beneficial.

ANOREXIA NERVOSA

Anorexia nervosa is one of a group of conditions in which an eating disorder is an external sign of emotional or psychological distress, or other internal dysfunction.

The term anorexia nervosa literally means loss of appetite because of nerves. This is inaccurate as an anorexic feels the hunger, but denies it. By doing so the affected person feels a measure of control over her life: by eating – or not eating – she blocks out painful feelings. Typical features are:
• an irrational fear of becoming fat;
• a preoccupation with food, its rituals and calorific values;
• starvation;
• compulsive exercising.
Menstrual periods stop – a sign of the devastating effect of starving on the body's physiological processes. Anorexia may lead to low blood potassium which can result in heart failure, a common cause of death in untreated anorexics.

Although most common in teenage girls and young women, anorexia can occur at any age and in either sex. Increasingly, pre-pubescent girls are developing anorexia.

What are the causes?

There is no single cause of anorexia. It may be to do with genetic makeup, or it may develop as a response to social pressures. High-achieving parents may deliberately or unwittingly pressurise their daughters to become high achievers. A vulnerable young person may then resort to abnormal eating behaviour as a way of dealing with these pressures and to try to regain control of her life.

Social influence may play a part. The media makes icons of women who are ultra slim. Successful models often have quite unfeminine shapes: their skinny bodies show an almost complete absence of breasts or shapely thighs. Other triggers for dysfunctional eating include:

- being bullied at school;
- abuse by parents;
- parental divorce;
- bereavement;
- concerns about sexual inclinations, such as being gay.

How is it diagnosed?

Diagnosis is made mainly on the history and physical examination. Family members often report their concern about the ill person's excessive weight loss or obsession with body image or odd eating behaviour. The diagnosis is suspected from a history of persistent weight loss in the absence of another medical cause. Reports from the family of altered body image make this diagnosis likely. If the woman's weight is less than 85 per cent of the expected weight for her height, if other causes of weight loss have been excluded as far as possible, and especially if her periods have stopped for more than three months as a result of the weight loss, anorexia nervosa is the most likely diagnosis.

About 1 per cent of women in the UK between the ages of 15 and 30 suffer from anorexia nervosa, although it also occurs in older and younger women and in men.

What are the treatment options?

Treatment is often difficult. One-third of anorexics will eventually die of their disorder and only one-third will be 'cured'. Not only doctors, psychologists and dietitians but friends, relatives and support groups all play an important part in helping an anorexic. The aim of treatment is to help the ill person to embark on and maintain a programme of nutritious and regular eating, while at the same time dealing with the underlying psychological problems that have caused her dysfunctional behaviour, by learning new and healthy coping strategies.

ASPERGER'S SYNDROME

A developmental disorder present from early childhood.

Asperger's syndrome has commonly been considered to be part of autism, but it is perhaps better regarded as part of a spectrum of developmental disorders, with autism at one extreme and Asperger's towards the 'normal' end of the spectrum. Boys are six times more likely than girls to have the disorder which occurs in one or two per 10,000 children. Asperger's syndrome is named after Hans Asperger, the Viennese physician who first described it in a paper in 1944.

What are the symptoms?

A child with Asperger's syndrome is usually of normal intelligence. The problems are of social interaction, with awkward body language, failure to develop friendships or close relationships with peers, a lack of spontaneous seeking to share enjoyment or interests with others, and a lack of social or emotional reciprocity. In other words, people with Asperger's syndrome show a poor understanding of social cues and are poor in giving appropriate social cues. They often have idiosyncratic hobbies. For example, many children collect stamps. For most children this is a normal, transient phase, and even people who carry on with the hobby in later life are sharing their interest with thousands of like-minded people around the world. A person with Asperger's syndrome will collect, for example, the serial numbers on telegraph poles, or bus timetables, or all the top ten pop records since the 1950s. There will be little sense of sharing this interest with others, although they are often more than happy to discuss their particular hobby in considerable detail to anyone prepared to listen.

What are the treatment options?

Medication has no place in the treatment of Asperger's syndrome. If recognised, children can be taught social skills, or at least to appreciate inappropriate social behaviours. They can be given counselling and, as they are frequently subject to bullying, be protected in this regard. They often require career counselling, so that their interests may be directed into more congenial activities. Because they are usually of normal intelligence, there is no reason why someone with Asperger's should not settle to a rewarding and normal career, as long as it is in line with his or her interests. In such cases the outlook is good.

ATTENTION DEFICIT HYPERACTIVITY DISORDER (ADHD)

The most common psychiatric disorder in children.

Children are prone to many learning and behavioural problems but comparatively few amount to a full-blown psychiatric disorder. ADHD is one such disorder.

What are the causes?

There is some evidence that ADHD runs in families. However, because it is very common anyway, it may well occur more than once in larger families, without there necessarily being a genetic component. Some, albeit controversial, studies in the United States suggest that up to 10 per cent of children have ADHD, with boys three times more likely to be affected than girls. Adults can also be affected by the condition.

What are the symptoms?

Persistent symptoms of inattention can be seen in:
- an inability to concentrate in work or play;
- a tendency to lose things;
- inability to follow through instructions;
- lack of organisation or perseverance.

The child (or adult) will show evidence of hyperactivity and impulsivity, such as fidgeting, distractibility, inability to keep sitting, restlessness, ceaseless energy, and being overly talkative. The condition comes on before the age seven and the symptoms carry over from school or work to home.

How is it diagnosed?

Diagnosis is entirely on the history. There are few, if any, objective measurements or tests that can be done. Inattention, hyperactivity and impulsivity can be more formally measured by psychological testing, but these are not objective diagnostic tests.

What are the treatment options?

These are controversial. Medication, in the form of the amphetamine-like compound methylphenidate (Ritalin), has been used widely in the United States and increasingly in Britain and Europe.

Many people are concerned at the administration of such powerful drugs to children in the absence of controlled studies of the effect of their long-term use in young people. Such medication sceptics prefer an educational approach, perhaps with individual remedial training, recognising that some children are not able to work effectively within a class, but nevertheless respond well to individual treatment. While such an approach has considerable merit, there are many studies and persuasive personal reports of the dramatic effect of medication on a child who had been otherwise entirely unmanageable.

Many other treatments have been suggested for the disorder, including psychological treatment, dietary manipulation, herbal treatment and biofeedback.

While there is still a lack of convincing evidence that any of these treatments work, all may be worth trying in individual cases.

What is the outlook?

The outlook is reasonably good if the condition is correctly recognised and treatment, whether educational or medical, is instituted early enough. Children with ADHD are at high risk of early brushes with the law and of having problems with alcohol and drugs later on. ADHD may be a significant, but not inevitable, contributor to subsequent dissocial or psychopathic personality disorder.

AUTISM

Autism is a pervasive developmental disorder. It usually manifests before the age of 30 months and is more common in boys.

What are the causes?

No one knows what causes autism. There is evidence that it runs in families, with relatives of an autistic child showing, if not autism, then some of its symptoms, such as delayed language. The mother of an autistic child may have experienced complications during pregnancy and the baby's delivery.

There is no evidence that parental behaviour has any influence on the development of autism, although the reverse is undoubtedly true: having an autistic child can place considerable strain on parental health.

Historically, autism has occurred in 3–4 per 10,000 births. It appears to have increased in frequency in recent years up to seven-fold, a frequency that has, arguably, paralleled the use of the combined measles, mumps and rubella (MMR) vaccination. This has led to intense speculation that the MMR vaccine causes autism. However, this suggestion is highly controversial. The majority of established public health and epidemiological research refutes the idea, but some individual scientists, usually virologists, suggest the possibility that there may be a causal link. One of the problems is that the MMR vaccination is usually initiated at about the time when autism would become evident in the first place. The child may often appear normal, then develop autism at around the age of two. This can also be when the first MMR vaccines are given. There is no robust evidence to link the two conditions, but it is important to keep an open mind.

What are the symptoms?

The basic symptoms are abnormal and delayed language and social ability. An autistic child is almost unaware of the separate existence of other people, does not usually enjoy being cuddled, and may not make eye contact with anyone, including his mother. The child tends not to use gestures to communicate, and is often unable to enjoy make-believe play. He or she may also develop strange mannerisms, and is typically highly resistant to any sort of change.

The majority of children with autism have below average intelligence. Occasionally, autistic children develop unusual abilities, almost always involving mechanical tasks and feats of memory or calculation, rather than true creativity.

How is it diagnosed?

Diagnosis is on the history. There are no objective tests of autism, although psychological testing may formalise some of the symptomatic deficits seen. Brain scans are contradictory. Some indicate abnormalities deep in the brain in the temporal lobes, together with abnormalities in the cerebellum. Other studies have failed to do so. Although the balance of the evidence is currently that autism is associated with brain abnormalities, there are no sure biological markers for the condition.

What are the treatment options?

There is no evidence that medication helps. A few people with comparatively mild autism are not recognised as such and may, during their teenage years, be mistaken for people with schizophrenia. They may receive antipsychotic drugs which may actually make them worse.

Treatment is along educational lines, usually with intensive one to one behavioural education.

What is the outlook?

The outlook for autism is mixed. Although some treatments have claimed substantial success, it remains that for most people with autism, the outlook is gloomy. People with milder cases, though, may be amenable to treatment and enjoy a comparably improved outlook.

BIPOLAR AFFECTIVE DISORDER
Depression with mania, or manic depression.

Unipolar affective disorder, depression without mania, is ten times more common than bipolar affective disorder.

What are the symptoms?

Sustained elation, boundless optimism, restless overactivity and extreme talkativeness, occurring at different times, characterise mania. Nearly everyone who experiences mania also suffers from depression, but by no means everyone who experiences depression suffers from mania.

Mania can be associated with creativity in its early stages, and being 'high' through the illness can be compared with being 'high' on drugs. But when mania hits its stride it is devastating. Money is spent like water, sometimes leading to financial ruin. Lack of inhibitions can cause great offence, loss of employment and charges of sexual misconduct. Grandiose delusions lead to intolerance of discouragement and restraint. Exuberance can turn to anger, paranoia and aggression. Compulsory treatment may be warranted, for the patient's safety and that of others.

What are the causes?

There is a strong genetic component to bipolar affective disorder. Individual episodes may arise 'out of the blue', but often follow life stresses.

What are the treatment options?

Mania is unlikely to respond to talking treatments and antipsychotic drugs and lithium carbonate are needed. These are often effective within a week or two. Lithium carbonate is a mood stabiliser that may also be useful in preventing the recurrence of depression and mania. Long-term treatment is thought to be more effective than intermittent treatment.

Electroconvulsive therapy (ECT, p. 123) is effective for severe depression, mania and/or mixed episodes. However, doctors and their patients and families should discuss the potential benefits and risks of ECT, and of available alternative therapies, before considering this treatment.

What is the outlook?

Both depression (p. 142) and mania are likely to resolve eventually even without treatment (though it is hard to leave mania untreated). Both, however, are likely to recur.

BRIEF PSYCHOTIC DISORDER
Psychosis of rapid onset, usually following major stress.

The episode is always time limited, lasting from a day to a month. Generally, the faster the onset, the quicker the recovery.

What are the causes?

The causes are not clear. The condition has been considered to be a reaction to a significant life event, particularly a culture change or culture shock. Brief psychotic disorder has also been associated with drug use. Particular culprits include amphetamines, cocaine, crack cocaine, painkillers such as Pentazocine and hallucinogens such as Ecstasy.

What are the symptoms?

The symptoms are those of a psychotic disorder, namely delusions, hallucinations, incoherent speech and grossly abnormal behaviour.

At first glance, brief psychotic disorder resembles an acute schizophrenic episode. However, by definition a brief psychotic disorder resolves after a short time, usually about five to seven days. This is likely to be true with or without treatment, although medication is commonly required to reduce the distress caused by the psychotic symptoms.

Sometimes, a brief psychotic disorder may be an early form of schizophrenia. Individuals may have several brief psychotic episodes but return to a level of functioning slightly below the status quo each time. There may then be an episode from which they do not recover spontaneously and for which they require long-term treatment.

How is it diagnosed?

It is diagnosed from the history and symptoms. It is worth obtaining a blood or urine estimation of drugs, but their presence or absence does not clinch the diagnosis. There are no other objective tests for the disorder.

What are the treatment options?

Brief psychotic disorder resolves spontaneously within five to ten days and there is no need for continued treatment. However, if the episodes become repetitive, longer term treatment, which will include antipsychotic medication, is most likely to be effective. During the early phase, when a person may be very disturbed, antipsychotic and sedative medication is used.

What is the outlook?

The outlook varies. Many people will have only one, or at most two, episodes, usually associated with extreme stress or a binge on drugs. They recover spontaneously, return to their normal level of functioning and the prognosis is excellent. However, where episodes are repeated and coalesce into longer and longer episodes with the development, perhaps, of schizophrenia, the outlook is less good.

BULIMIA NERVOSA

Bulimia nervosa is an eating disorder typified by recurring periods of binge eating, during which huge amounts of food are consumed in a short period of time, followed by episodes of purging.

Bulimia nervosa often goes undiagnosed. It affects many people – probably at least one in 50 women – and whereas anorexia nervosa is typically a teenage condition bulimia affects slightly older women. Men are affected too but relatively rarely.

The typical bulimic knows that her eating is out of control and is frightened that she will be unable to stop. She is afraid of being fat and may feel depressed and guilty after a binge. Typically a binge is followed by self-induced vomiting or the use of a laxative or a diuretic (or both), or a period of fasting. Unlike anorexia, in bulimia weight is generally normal or even a little above normal and often varies by several pounds between binges and fasts.

What are the causes?

Often thought of as a slimmer's disease, bulimia is much more than an obsession with being slim. Certainly, media and fashion pressures to be slim make many women feel the need to diet which can lead to an eating disorder, and bulimics often feel that happiness depends upon being slim. But often bulimia nervosa is the physical way of coping with difficult emotions arising, for example, from being abused as a child or being in a difficult personal relationship. Bulimics often clearly remember the first time they made themselves sick which, at the time, gave a huge emotional release. Sometimes there is no obvious cause.

How is it diagnosed?

There are no clinical signs apart from weight fluctuations. The diagnosis depends almost entirely upon the symptoms reported by the affected person. There are several characteristic features, especially the recurring episodes of binge eating. An episode of binge eating is when an amount of food much larger than most people would eat – sometimes as much as 15,000 or 20,000 calories – is consumed in a short time, such as two hours. The bulimic cannot stop eating or control what she eats. She tries to compensate for overeating by self-induced vomiting, using laxatives, diuretics or enemas (or a combination of these), or fasting or excessive exercise. The episodes occur typically at least twice a week and, for the diagnosis to be made, these must have been going on for at least three months.

What are the treatment options?

A variety of self-help books offer strategies for improving eating behaviour and describe ways to avoid situations in which you are likely to binge. A doctor should be consulted as soon as possible and may recommend talking therapy. This may be counselling or cognitive behavioural therapy, both of which can help a sufferer to assess why the condition has developed and what can be done to deal with the underlying emotional needs.

COMPULSIVE OVEREATING

Compulsive overeating, also known as binge eating disorder, is a relatively recent diagnostic term in the group of eating disorders.

Whereas the features of anorexia nervosa, the best-known of the eating disorders, were first described in the 12th century and the condition was labelled by Laseque in 1873 and Gull in 1874, binge eating disorder was first defined as recently as 1994. It is similar in many ways to bulimia but has important differences. It is characterised by recurrent episodes of binge eating but, unlike in bulimia, there is no self-induced vomiting or use of laxatives.

Binge eating disorder is probably the most common eating disorder. Most people with this problem are overweight or obese, although people of normal weight may also have the disorder. At least one in 50 adults has the condition. About one in eight people who are significantly overweight and who are trying to lose weight have binge eating disorder. The disorder is even more common in people who are severely obese. Unlike in the other eating disorders such as anorexia and bulimia a lot of men have the condition – about two men for every three women. People who are obese and have binge eating disorder often became overweight at a much younger age than those without the disorder, and they also tend to lose and regain weight (the yo-yo effect) more often.

What are the symptoms?

- Recurring episodes of binge eating. An episode of binge eating is when a very large amount of food, often containing several thousands of calories, is consumed in a relatively short period of time, for example two hours.
- Unlike in bulimia, binges are not associated with compensating behaviours such as self-induced vomiting or the use of laxatives or diuretics.
- Severe distress because of the binge eating.

- The sufferer loses control of eating during the binge, feeling unable to stop eating or control what is eaten.
- The binges are associated with at least three of the following: eating much more quickly than normal, eating until feeling uncomfortably full, eating large amounts of food even when not hungry, eating alone because of feeling embarrassed by how much is being eaten, and feeling disgusted, depressed or guilty after overeating.
- Binges occur on average twice a week and, for a diagnosis to be made, have been recurring for at least six months.

Apart from the guilt and depression that go with the condition, people who are overweight and have binge eating disorder are more likely to develop a range of conditions including diabetes, heart disease, high blood pressure, high blood cholesterol levels, gallbladder disease and some forms of cancer.

What are the treatment options?

Professional help is necessary. A GP may refer a patient for a talking therapy such as cognitive behaviour therapy, and may discuss whether antidepressants are suitable. Those with the best prognosis tend to be those in whom the condition is recognised and treatment started early, and who have a good support network. Ultimately, unchecked compulsive overeating can cause premature disability or death from complications such as heart disease and diabetes.

DELUSIONAL DISORDER

Delusions are fixed, culturally inappropriate ideas that are not amenable to argument or correction. Deluded people 'know' that their ideas reflect reality.

Delusional disorder is diagnosed when a person has essentially normal ideas about most things, but entertains bizarre delusions about one particular matter. An uncommon example is erotomania (de Clérambault syndrome) where the affected person 'knows' that someone else, usually of higher social status, is in love with him or her (usually her), despite the lack of any evidence. Another, more common, example is of a person who may have reasonable views on most things, but may 'know' that his neighbour is pumping poison gas through his floorboards.

The distinction between delusional disorder and other psychotic disorders such as schizophrenia is that in schizophrenia, the delusions are accompanied by other symptoms, including hallucinations.

Treatment is with antipsychotic medication; however, since a person often does not accept that there is a problem, sticking to a treatment regime is a challenge. Even if a patient does take the medication and accepts other forms of treatment, fixed delusions are notoriously difficult to treat.

DEPRESSION

At its worst, depressive illness is the extremity of human suffering, causing utter despair, hopelessness and suicide.

Depression is our natural response to disappointment and loss, and remains with us until we are able to 'let go' and put the past behind us. We may also have days of depression that cannot be easily explained: a 'bad hair day', or we have 'got the hump'. But in depressive illness, as in anxiety and mood disorders in general, depression is sustained, severe and out of proportion to whatever may seem to have caused it.

Depression is extremely common. At any one time one person in eight is significantly depressed, and at least a third of us will suffer depression at some time in our lives. Children can suffer from depression too.

What are the symptoms?
The chief symptoms of depressive illness are:
- feeling low, hopeless, suicidal – especially at the beginning of the day;
- looking miserable – a blank, unhappy face, down-turned mouth;
- loss of interest, enjoyment, motivation and sexual desire;
- loss of self-esteem;
- guilt, self-reproach and a sense of futility;
- loss of concentration, conversation and sociability;
- anxiety and agitation;
- doubt, indecision and irritability;
- fatigue, slowness of speech and movement;
- loss of appetite and weight;
- sleep disturbance, particularly early morning waking.

Depressed people think the worst of themselves and expect others to have the some opinion. They dismiss their past achievements as spurious or of no importance. In very severe depression they may believe that they are utterly wicked, doomed and damned, and that everyone knows how evil they are, is talking about them and even planning their (deserved) removal from the world. Other delusions reported by depressed patients include believing that they are contaminated or ruined, that their insides are blocked, or even that they are already dead. In the worst cases there is appalling agitation, a seeking for reassurance which cannot be accepted, or slowing down to the point of immobility and saying, eating and drinking nothing: this stupor is a medical emergency.

Depression affects memory, especially in older people, partly by slowing thinking, partly by impairing attention, partly by gloomy preoccupation. The fear of dementia is then added to the depressive symptoms: 'My mind's going!' Memory can be so badly affected that there is a pseudodementia, from which, happily, recovery can be complete.

The great talents of Virginia Woolf and Sylvia Plath did not save them from losing their lives to deep depression, while Winston Churchill was haunted by his 'black dog'.

Physical symptoms accompanying depression include pressure on the head and headache, palpitations, pain in the face, neck, back, chest and abdomen, and feeling tired all the time. In milder depression these symptoms are the basis for fears of bodily illness. In more severe depression a fatal disease may seem welcome.

One in seven sufferers from severe depression commits suicide. In this event the question is often asked 'How could she/he do that, with two lovely children and such a nice husband/wife?' The answer is that feelings of affection and attachment are numbed by depression, and in such an extremity of suffering and misery, feeling too bad to stay in the world, the action is understandable. In particularly tragic cases, a deeply depressed father, say, decides to take his wife and children with him and kills them before taking his own life. Men and older people are more likely to commit suicide, women and younger people to attempt it, though there has been an increase in the rates of suicide in younger people in recent years.

What causes depression?
A distinction can be drawn between predisposing and precipitating causes. Predisposing factors include:
- **Heredity** More important in bipolar (manic depression) than unipolar depression (no episodes of mania), and when depression first develops in younger rather than in older people.
- **A pessimistic, introverted, or obsessional personality** Pessimists acquire 'the power of negative thinking', which looms large in depression.
- **Being female** A classic study by sociologist George Brown showed that women with three children under 14, an unsupportive partner, no one else in whom to confide,

poor housing and with no employment outside the home are at significant risk of depression. Menstruation, childbirth and the menopause all carry risks of depression. And women, more able to admit how they feel than most men, are more likely to be diagnosed as depressed.

- **Loss of the mother before the age of 11** through death, illness or desertion.
- **Occupation** Farmers and doctors are among those most at risk of depression and suicide, but unemployment is a greater risk factor.
- **'Learned helplessness'** Experiments by psychologist Martin Seligman showed that when people are placed for a long time in a situation which they can neither influence nor escape – like an old person stuck in hospital or a refugee passed on from one camp to another – the chances of depression are much increased.
- **Physical infirmity and illness** Chronic, disabling conditions like arthritis, severe bronchitis, Parkinson's disease and heart failure cause isolation, dependency, insecurity and depression.
- **Brain and body chemistry** Certain neurotransmitters that carry messages from one nerve cell to another seem to be depleted in depression, notably serotonin, noradrenaline and dopamine. Antidepressants probably act by restoring levels of these chemicals to normal. Hormones may also be important – for example, fluctuating female sex hormones, reduced or increased thyroxine in thyroid disease, too much cortisone in Cushing's syndrome, melatonin (a sleep hormone) in SAD (p. 153).
- **The biological 'clock'** We are adapted to a 24-hour day, and our biochemistry normally fluctuates accordingly. Levels of cortisol – produced by the adrenal glands on top of the kidneys under the influence of the pituitary gland in the brain – are normally high in the mornings and drop in the afternoon, but in depression they are high all day.
- **Medication** Some of the early drugs for high blood-pressure caused serious depression through lowering levels of brain neurotransmitters. Steroids, contraceptive pills and beta-blockers (used for anxiety and for high blood pressure) may also bring on depression.

Precipitating causes are often losses – of a person through death, illness or the end of a relationship, of a job, a cherished hope, or life expectancy through a heart attack or a diagnosis of cancer. Rather mysteriously, certain infections such as influenza, glandular fever, typhoid and brucellosis seem liable to cause depression.

How is it diagnosed?

Deep, disabling depression lasting for a month or more is likely to be clinical depression. It must be distinguished from other causes of debility such as like anaemia, thyroid disease and myalgic encephalitis (ME), and from other mental disorders – schizophrenia in younger people, dementia in older, as well as anxiety states, obsessive-compulsive neurosis, eating disorders, alcoholism and drug dependency. All these conditions may be associated with depression, but it is secondary to them.

There are many questionnaires and rating-scales designed either to reveal depression or measure it. The nearest thing to a laboratory test is the Dexamethasone Suppression Test, based upon the sustained high level of cortisol in depression (see above); it has been used more in research than ordinary clinical practice.

What are the treatment options?

The treatments are psychological, pharmacological and physical.

- **Psychological treatments** are nearly always appropriate and applicable. Counselling may include sympathetic, non-judgmental listening, identification of problems and possible solutions and regular support, reassurance and encouragement. Interpersonal therapy gives structure to this process, and cognitive behavioural therapy particularly addresses the negative thinking that accompanies and may even cause the depression. Psychotherapy considers how repressed or suppressed anger may be expressed as depression (suicide is thought to be an expression of anger turned on the self) and seeks to bring it to light and deal with it.
- **Pharmacological (antidepressant) treatments** These may complement psychological treatments, or temporarily take their place in patients who become too preoccupied, agitated, retarded or demoralised to cooperate with a 'talking' treatment. Placebo-controlled trials have repeatedly found antidepressant drugs to be effective in moderate to severe depression. They were first discovered in the 1950s, when it was noticed that certain drugs used in the treatment of tuberculosis lifted the depression associated with that disorder. The early drugs (tricyclics) worked, but had some troublesome side-effects such as a dry mouth and sedation among them. Then, years later, came Prozac, a serotonin-specific reuptake inhibitor (SSRI) and all at once antidepressants were news. SSRIs are not more effective than the earlier drugs, but they tend to be better tolerated. Antidepressants, contrary

to popular belief, are not addictive, nor are they 'happy pills': they work by raising lowered levels of neurotransmitters, notably serotonin and noradrenaline, in the brain to restore a depressed mood to normal. They are cumulative, so take weeks to work and should be continued for at least six months. They do have side-effects, but these are bearable and tend to wear off.

- **Physical** An effective treatment for severe depression is electro-convulsive therapy, or ECT. Nobody quite knows how it works, but it is thought that the convulsion (fit) is therapeutic. Today, the fit is safely induced under anaesthesia, by passing a current briefly across the temples; the effects of the fit on the body are reduced to a slight twitching by the use of a muscle relaxant. Usually a course of 6–8 treatments is given over a period of three weeks. Psychiatrists are often criticised for using this treatment but continue to do so because it is the quickest and most effective way of relieving the anguish of severe depression. Where food and drink are being refused it is life saving, and it is a valuable resource for that minority of patients who do not respond to antidepressants, with or without talking treatments.

What is the outlook?

Recovery from an episode of depression is the rule, though some patients with treatment-resistant, or 'refractory', depression are not easily cured and may be left with residual symptoms such as not feeling really right till the afternoon. Severe depression is associated with reduced life expectancy, not only from suicide but self-neglect.

Unfortunately, having suffered from depression increases the risk of doing so again. The risk may be reduced by psychotherapy or cognitive behavioural therapy to improve how the person copes with subsequent stress; by continuing or resuming antidepressants that have proved effective in the past; or by the use of mood regulators such as lithium carbonate, carbamazepine and valproate.

DRUG DEPENDENCE

Drug dependence is a physical dependence on or addiction to a drug. It means that there are repeated failures to stop using the drug concerned.

The most common drugs involved in dependence are opiates such as morphine and heroin, in addition to barbiturates, cocaine and benzodiazepine tranquillisers. However, addiction to nicotine and caffeine can involve as much dependency as drugs such as heroin, perhaps more in the case of nicotine, although the social and criminal consequences are different.

What are the causes?

Drug taking has always been a common behaviour of humans of all ages. Experimental or recreational use of drugs is widespread among adolescents and young adults. Psychological factors, including peer pressure, the 'buzz' of illegal behaviour, and a sense of rebellion play a part. However, the drugs themselves are addictive and act on the 'reward' pathways in the brain that depend on the neurochemical dopamine.

What are the symptoms?

Symptoms are similar to those of alcohol dependence (p. 134) with the relevant drug substituted for alcohol.

What are the treatment options?

As with the treatment of alcoholism, motivation is everything. Without strong motivation, a dependent person is unlikely to achieve long-term abstention.

One important factor is that a person who has become addicted to drugs, especially if these are obtained illicitly, has generated a range of contacts from which to obtain drugs and may be dealing to fund their habit. If, on leaving an in or outpatient programme, they return to their former environment, they will soon hook up with their former associates and find it very difficult to continue to abstain.

The medical treatment of drug addiction has been controversial. In the case of heroin and other opiate addictions, there has been an attempt to use the opiate Methadone which induces a long 'high' and, because it is taken orally, avoids the risks associated with injected drugs. In many cases, however, this has simply substituted one addiction for another. The opiate drugs such as Burprenorphine, which seemed to have less addiction potential, have also been used.

More controversial still has been the suggestion that for some people who are intractably addicted to heroin, the most effective option is to maintain their habit, but to do so legally by prescribing injectable heroin for them. There is also an accent on harm minimisation, as shown by schemes to ensure that addicts have clean needles with which to inject, and therefore not spread diseases such as hepatitis and AIDS. These measures may appear sensible, although they are not an option in prisons, where there can be significant drug problems.

There have been suggestions that natural compounds such as ibogaine, a plant derivative from West Africa, may eliminate drug cravings after one or two doses. Ibogaine is attracting attention from researchers, but in its natural form it is associated with a significant, sometimes fatal, side-effect. It is unlikely, therefore, to become mainstream.

Lofexidine is a non-opiate treatment used to help patients undergoing opiate detox to cope with withdrawal symptoms. Other rapid forms of detoxification or treating drug addiction have been tried. Their proponents believe in them, but they have yet to become mainstream. Treatment of addiction to other drugs, such as cocaine and crack cocaine, is more problematic. There is frequently a rebound depression on the cessation of drug use (especially with crack) and some people treat the withdrawing addict with antidepressants. The bulk of the treatment options, however, are not medical but psychosocial, depending as always on the person's motivation.

Treatment on an inpatient basis is fairly common.

What is the outlook?

Given sufficient motivation on the part of the user, the outlook is excellent. However, there are many physical and psychiatric complications of drug misuse and addiction, some of them serious and potentially fatal. Apart from the dangers of infection or overdose, other problems inherent in the lifestyle of drug addictions include violent crime and accidents.

FALSE MEMORY SYNDROME

Our memories are unreliable. We forget a lot, but sometimes remember things that never happened: this is false memory.

Memories of our childhood can be particularly faulty, because without adult understanding we may misinterpret what we have perceived, or our very perception may be affected by our being young and little. It is a common experience that 'the house where I was brought up' seems much smaller if we go back there in later life, because it was then so much bigger than we were. Strong emotions like fear, sorrow and ecstasy can considerably colour and distort memories, as can powerful beliefs such as prejudice and superstition.

Witnesses to crimes and accidents can give surprisingly different accounts of what they have seen even from the same vantage point, but the particular importance of false memory syndrome has been in some accusations of rape and allegations of abuse in childhood elicited years later in adulthood by enthusiastic therapists.

Freud found that patients in his middle-class clientele in Vienna around 1900 described (during psychoanalysis) sexual activity involving their parents, but he attributed this to forbidden fantasies emerging under hypnosis or by free association. Recently, however, there has been a tendency to attribute many psychiatric and personality disorders to child abuse, even when the patient at first can remember nothing of the kind: the incest survivor syndrome. A popular book *The Courage to Heal* (Laura Davis and Ellen Bass) has stimulated many women to embark on recovered memory therapy, in the course of which some of them recover memories which, it is proposed, have been repressed. Techniques include dream work, art therapy, drug-induced 'reliving' of repressed emotion, abreactions (an automatic response to a stimulus whch reminds a person of an experience, such as abuse), hypnosis, 'survivors' groups' and 'age regression'. Subsequent denunciations have disrupted families and led to criminal charges and compensation claims. The counter-accusation is that therapists committed to their hypothesis have imposed a false memory on their patients through the power of suggestion.

Parents accused of abuse in this way are naturally drawn to the 'false memory' interpretation, but a number of those who 'recovered' their memories in therapy have now realised and admit that they were overpersuaded.

The Royal College of Psychiatrists (UK) claims that there is no evidence to support the belief that memories can be 'blocked out by the mind'. They go on to say that 'recovered memories differ from other forms of forgotten and remembered events in being built up over time. They resemble narrative rather than memory, with more being added at each attempt at recall, often becoming increasingly elaborate and bizarre . . . Therapist and/or patient expectations, reinforced by guided reading, particular techniques and survivors' group expectation may distort any existing memory or implant a wholly new one.'

LEARNING DISABILITY

A significant impairment of intelligence and social functioning acquired before adulthood.

'Learning disability' is the preferred term for what used to be known as mental retardation, developmental disability or intellectual disability. It affects about 2 per cent of the population. Although the degree of disability is not the same over the whole range of skills, impairment in most intellectual skills is common. Disability is somewhat arbitrarily subdivided into mild or moderate (IQ 50–70); severe (IQ 20–50); and profound (IQ below 20).

What are the causes?

The cause varies according to category. In mild learning disability, there is often a history of social and economic deprivation with poor or absent parental care. Family size may be large and overcrowding probable. The environment may have been unstimulating and language development not promoted. Parental intelligence is not necessarily in the disability range, but it is often lower than average.

Specific medical causes include chromosomal abnormalities (such as Down's syndrome and fragile X syndrome) and birth injury. It is often associated with other conditions such as epilepsy, hearing and visual impairment and autism. Malnutrition, either of the mother during pregnancy, or the child, may also result in mild learning disability, as may toxins such as alcohol or, more controversially, lead in the environment.

Most children in the more severe categories of moderate to profound disability (IQ less than 50) have physical brain abnormalities. This is not to say that social effects are irrelevant, however. Chromosomal deficit accounts for approximately 40 per cent of learning disability in this group, of which Down's syndrome is the most common, followed by fragile X syndrome, sex chromosome abnormalities and other, rarer chromosome abnormalities.

Genetic defects, such as metabolic disorders (galactosaemia and phenylketonurea) account for a significant minority of moderate to profound disability, together with events in pregnancy such as infection (rubella, toxoplasmosis and AIDS), alcohol or drug abuse or dependence, and problems after birth, including head injury.

How is it diagnosed?

Assessment involves determination of the level of mental function; identification of associated problems, including psychiatric problems; investigation of the cause of the disability; and assessment of the family's ability to cope.

What are the treatment options?

Treatment depends on the severity of disability. Children with profound disability may not be able to perform activities of daily living, such as feeding and toileting. Children at the mild end of the spectrum may usually expect to lead independent and fulfilled lives. They may need special education, and it is down the educational pathway that most treatment will be found.

However, as psychiatric and neurological disorders are common, there may also be a role for medication. Sometimes, behavioural therapy or psychotherapy may complement or supplement educational treatment.

How can it be prevented?

Good female health before conceiving and during pregnancy and education can go a long way towards preventing learning disability. The identification of families at particular risk of having members with problems is a social priority, and, since chromosomal defects are more common in children born to older mothers, screening for such deficits at an early stage of pregnancy is desirable. Techniques exist to test for Down's syndrome, for example, by taking measurements from early ultrasound scans. Other tests include amniocentesis, where a sample of the fluid surrounding the developing baby is analysed, and chorionic villus sampling, when cells from the placenta are studied. Both tests identify cells in which there are chromosomal abnormalities. This is a technique not without its dangers, as haemorrhage and miscarriage may be induced. The newer, less invasive, tests based on scans are likely to become more popular.

MILDER MEMORY DISORDERS
The inability to remember everything an individual would wish to.

We all forget things. Despite our remarkable brains, our memories are fallible. Most of what we forget is what we don't need to remember. We may not bother to remember things when the information is easily available: many people will look at their watch or a newspaper to discern today's date. What we were doing last Thursday, the Thursday before that, a Thursday last month or a year ago, we are less and less likely to remember unless it was some special occasion like a birthday or other anniversary or the date of a dramatic event, like '9/11'. Most of us have some vivid memories of childhood (which may or may not be accurate) but they are relatively few and far between. There are various sorts of memory:

- **Sensory memory** is part of perception: because the picture we see on the cinema screen is momentarily stored, we see a film, not a rapid succession of images.

- **Working (short-term) memory** holds information long enough for us to reply to a question or dial a phone number we've just been given.

Longer-term memory needs permanent storage in the brain by encoding as one or a combination of:

- **Semantic memory**, concerned with general knowledge, language, history, science, literature and geography.
- **Episodic memory** – our memory of ourselves and personal circumstances.
- **Procedural memory**, which is to do with such activities as cycling and swimming, and is fairly durable.

There are, very basically, three stages in memory:

- **Registration**, that is, perceiving what is to be remembered.
- **Retention**, storing the information – short or long term.
- **Recall** – retrieving the information.

We may fail to register something properly because of inattention, impaired perception (deafness, poor vision), preoccupation (other things on our mind), distraction (too much going on at the same time) or befuddlement by drink or sleeplessness.

Failure to retain registered information usually means brain disease such as dementia or Korsakow's syndrome, in which a nerve centre in the mid-brain is damaged by vitamin B_1 deficiency: working memory is intact but long term is devastated, so that what is happening now cannot be recalled at all in two minutes' time.

Recall is much affected by emotion: anxiety, for example, causes 'exam nerves' which may hinder recall, while depressed people may only be able to recall unhappy memories. Recognition is easier than recall, and shows that the memory had been stored even if it was hard to access.

What are the causes?

Though we are more likely to forget what is trivial and unimportant to us, we may also forget things we want to remember – where we left our keys or glasses or parked the car, for example, or the word for someone who sells wine, or the name of the old school friend we bumped into in the street. These difficulties occur at all ages, but probably more often from the age of 50 onwards, often called 'senior moments'. Older people may worry about developing Alzheimer's disease, but there are other explanations:

- Age associated memory impairment (AAMI), mainly due to a slowing of the memory in later life. It varies a great deal between individuals, is mild and rarely gets worse.
- Stress and depression causing preoccupation and distraction.
- Sensory impairment, particularly deafness.

- Physical illness, such as heart failure, small strokes, thyroid disease.
- Alcohol, sleeping tablets and several other drugs, including prescribed drugs.

What are the treatment options?

While medication may help to slow the progress of more serious diseases that affect memory, there is no magic pill to improve a person's memory. There are, however, several self-help techniques that people have found useful:

- Pay attention – this is vital to effective registration.
- Get organised: 'a place for everything and everything in its place'.
- Use diaries and calendars; make lists.
- Use aides memoires: the knot in the handkerchief, the note on the back of the hand, morning and/or evening pills by the toothbrush.
- Keep fit: *mens sana in corpore sano* – a healthy mind in a healthy body.
- Use your mind – don't be a couch potato. Read, learn, play bridge, Scrabble, do puzzles. Maintain outside interests and hobbies.
- Reality orientation: rehearse the day and date, where you are and what's going on; if going to a reunion dig out old photos and think about who might be there.
- Mnemonics – memory tricks – work for some. They generally use visual imagery to make something more memorable, or association to link a new memory to something that is already established.

Bridge players need to plan ahead, use their working memory, organise cards, and respond to others' moves, all of which can help to keep the mind active.

Finally, forgetfulness isn't necessarily due to getting older. Young people forget a lot, and put it down to their hectic lifestyles. Nobody's perfect!

OBSESSIVE COMPULSIVE DISORDER (OCD)
A potentially disabling anxiety disorder which can persist throughout a person's life.

The disorder ranges from mild to severe. A sufferer is locked into a pattern of repetitive thoughts and behaviour to the extent that work, home or school commitments all suffer. Once thought uncommon, from American estimates OCD is now believed to affect 2 per cent of the population, many of whom keep their behaviour secret and do not seek help or treatment.

What are the symptoms?

Persistent fears of harm, fear of contamination or an obsession with doing things correctly predominate, leading to permanent anxiety and then compulsive, repetitive behaviours such as hand washing or rearranging objects. Rituals are common.

Some people with OCD are aware that their obsessions and compulsions are unnecessary and meaningless, especially when they are not actually performing them, but others believe them to be valid. Many sufferers can control their behaviour for months or years, but for others OCD takes over, making life outside the home difficult. Many sufferers do not seek help until the disorder has taken over their life – and those of family members – to a considerable degree.

What are the treatment options?

Medication or behaviour therapy, or both, may be helpful. Drugs that affect the neurotransmitter serotonin (SSRIs) can decrease the symptoms of OCD in more than three-quarters of sufferers. Medication may need to be continuous, although at a reduced dose, to avoid relapse.

Behaviour therapy may be helpful. For example, in a controlled setting, a sufferer may be encouraged to touch an object that they believe contaminated and then resist washing. This approach requires considerable support from family and friends as well as motivation on the part of the individual, but gradually many patients become less anxious about obsessive thoughts and resist their compulsions. Studies from the USA show that up to three-quarters of those helped by behaviour therapy do not relapse once the therapy is ended.

PARANOIA

Paranoia is a state of morbid suspicion, and a feature of several mental illnesses, including schizophrenia, mania, depression, delirium and dementia. It can be drug induced, or may take the form of a personality disorder.

What are the symptoms?

Paranoid personalities are chronically mistrustful, quick to see faults, take offence, complain and go to law. They have a 'chip on the shoulder' attitude to life, and feel that if they are not vigilant they will be slighted, passed over, 'done down', exploited and betrayed. If they form relationships they tend to be touchy, jealous and exacting, so they are likely to end up alone. They are difficult workmates, appalling customers, and though their cynicism and

scepticism may occasionally be entertaining, their total lack of empathy and a sense of humour are not. There are many paranoid personalities among so-called vexatious litigants.

Paranoia may emerge in mood disorders. In severe depression there may be 'mood-congruent' paranoid delusions: 'Everyone's saying I'm rotten and ought to be exterminated – and they're right!'. In mania, frustration at those who oppose the patient's exuberant but wildly unrealistic plans may erupt in paranoia and aggression.

Paranoid schizophrenia tends to develop in 18–30 year olds, and persecutory delusions are typical. Paranoia may develop in the course of delirium. Acutely confused people easily misinterpret what is being done for them as being done to them and feel that they are being wrongfully imprisoned, restrained or even tortured. The delusions are usually fleeting but can cause very vigorous protests and resistance to rational management.

The commonest form of paranoia in dementia is the belief that someone is stealing things that the muddled person has mislaid. Very often the person so blamed is the carer, already burdened and distressed.

Paraphrenia is a form of paranoia in older people, often isolated, perhaps prickly people who develop delusions about their neighbours. Paraphrenia is not a form of dementia, but it can be more disruptive.

A rare form of paranoia, most often encountered in early dementia, is Capgras syndrome, where the delusion is that a person or people in the patient's environment have been replaced by alien doubles.

Abuse of amphetamines can lead to paranoid delusions.

A particularly tragic version of paranoia is morbid erotic jealousy, the so-called Othello syndrome, in which the patient becomes convinced that his or her sexual partner is being unfaithful and goes to extreme lengths to prove or prevent it – searching clothing for stains related to sexual activity, questioning closely about any deviations from the usual daily timetable, or demanding repeated sex in order to satiate. Alcoholism, which impairs sexual performance, may be a factor in morbid jealousy. As in Shakespeare's play, the disorder may ultimately lead to violence and murder.

What are the treatment options?

Paranoid personalities cannot be cured, as a rule, and must simply be endured. However, paranoia as a part of mental illness will respond, to a greater or lesser extent, to antipsychotic medication. The trouble is that many sufferers from paranoia lack insight into their disorder and do not seek or refuse to take the treatment offered.

If the case is bad enough, compulsory treatment may be needed – which brings to reality some patients' paranoid fears.

PERSONALITY DISORDERS
A range of conditions in which behaviour lies outside social norms.

ANTISOCIAL PERSONALITY DISORDER
This is the most severe of the personality disorders in creating distress and suffering as it tends to affect a larger number of people than other personality disorders. It is the most common personality disorder in the prison population, affecting nearly half of all prisoners. It overlaps considerably with those whom in the past were often referred to as 'psychopathic'. This describes a constellation of features, including abnormal irresponsibility, superficial charm, callousness, lack of remorse, impulsivity and aggression, the absence of any long-term goals and a history of criminal behaviour from an early age. There is no specific treatment for antisocial personality disorder but it tends to improve with advancing age. What is described as 'dangerous and severe personality disorder' in a recent government White Paper (although that definition has no medical or legal basis) includes some of the most serious forms of antisocial personality disorder.

ANXIOUS (OR AVOIDANT) PERSONALITY DISORDER
People with this type of personality disorder are troubled by meeting other people unless they know them extremely well. They are anxious and find any form of uncertainty threatening. As a consequence they tend to wall themselves off from others unless they can be absolutely certain that they will be safe and untroubled in their company. Such people tend to live restricted lives, but within these boundaries they are often able to function quite well, provided that there are no unexpected events or unfamiliar faces to disturb the equilibrium. People with anxious personalities tend to have more stress-related illnesses such as peptic ulcers and irritable bowel syndrome than other people, and are frequently prone to depression and worries about their health. There is some evidence that treatments for anxiety and depression such as cognitive behaviour therapy and antidepressant drugs may be effective if they are given for longer periods, rather than just targeted at relieving symptoms.

BORDERLINE PERSONALITY DISORDER
Borderline personality disorder describes a complex condition which causes a great deal of distress to the sufferer and which therefore leads to more treatment than is common with other personality disorders. A person with borderline personality disorder is very changeable, with periods of animation and optimism interspersed with intense boredom, despair and uncertainty about aims and direction in life. This may lead to self-harming behaviour, instability of relationships and a crisis of identity. The rapid fluctuations make it difficult to treat, but there is now good evidence that psychological treatment, particularly when focused on self-harming behaviours and when consistently applied, is helpful. Some drugs that are able to control impulsive behaviour, including some of the newer antidepressants and atypical antipsychotic drugs, have also been shown to be of value. The outcome of borderline personality disorder is generally good in the longer term, but in the short term it is disruptive and can be difficult to manage.

PARANOID PERSONALITY DISORDER
Paranoia, or intense suspiciousness of others with fears of conspiracy, is at the heart of this disorder. Paranoia is common in some other conditions, particularly schizophrenia, but in paranoid personality disorder these features are ingrained and part of normal functioning, not of disease. The person with a paranoid personality tends to have very few close acquaintances and is very secretive in behaviour, finding sinister explanations in the simplest of failures to achieve stated aims or targets. Joseph Stalin and Adolf Hitler were both paranoid dictators who retained control by eliminating all opposition at an early stage and mistrusting everyone around them, even those who appeared to be loyal friends. Unfortunately, very few people with this disorder seek or want treatment. Not only do they not see that they have a problem, but they would be predictably suspicious of any intervention.

PHOBIAS
An intense irrational or inappropriate fear of a person, animal, object or situation that makes normal life difficult. More than 100 phobias have been identified.

The causes of phobias are unclear. There may be a hereditary aspect, with phobias running in families. Children may learn them from a parent. Phobias tend to be more common in women than men. Symptoms include:

• Immediate anxiety – sweating, rapid heartbeat, difficulty breathing – when faced with the object or situation, or perhaps simply a photograph or thought of it.
• A strong desire to avoid what is feared.
• Inability to carry out normal activities.

Medication or behavioural therapies, or both, may be suggested. Beta-blockers depress some of the signs of anxiety such as a racing heart and raised blood pressure. Antidepressants can reduce anxiety, while sedatives aid relaxation. Relaxation techniques may be useful. Desensitisation therapy – gradual exposure to the cause of the phobia – can be successful. Cognitive behavioural therapy, involving working with a therapist to change the way the feared object or situation is viewed, can be helpful.

POSTNATAL DEPRESSION (PND)

The 'happy event' of childbirth is quite the opposite for a number of mothers who find the days, weeks or even months after giving birth a time of great distress.

To some extent this could be understandable, if the child is unwanted or unwell, or the mother's circumstances are wretched – a hostile or absent partner, poverty, poor accommodation, loneliness and lack of support – but in most cases there doesn't seem to be such an obvious reason. The baby is wanted and normal, the home seemingly happy, the partner and parents supportive, yet there is an awful feeling of anxiety, misery and inability to cope. This is postnatal depression, which affects one newly delivered mother in ten.

Two other conditions may be classed with PND:
• The 'baby blues', sometimes termed the third or fourth day blues, since that is when they tend to start.
• Psychotic puerperal depression.

The baby blues are very common, affecting half of all new mothers, and last no more than a day or two. Tearfulness, anxiety about the baby (often related to feeding), moodiness, poor concentration, forgetfulness, brief disenchantment with the partner, weariness, insomnia and headache are commonly reported symptoms. It is probable that the sudden drop in levels of hormones like oestrogen and progesterone contribute to the blues, but soreness and qualms about getting to know the baby may contribute.

Psychotic puerperal depression is a very severe depressive illness coming on within six weeks of giving birth and affecting one in 400 new mothers. The depression is profound and associated with delusions of guilt.

There are risks both of suicide and infanticide, but recovery after treatment (usually involving admission to hospital, ideally in a mother-and-baby unit) is the rule.

What are the symptoms?

Depression is the chief symptom – feeling low and wretched most of the time. Some mothers feel worse in the mornings, others in the evenings – many have better and worse days. On a bad day life may seem hardly worth living.

• **Anxiety**, often expressed as fear of being left alone wholly responsible for this helpless infant, and unwillingness to let the partner leave home.
• **Irritability**, mainly with the partner, also towards any other children and occasionally with the baby.
• **Fatigue** is so extreme that the depressed mother feels there may be something physically wrong, such as anaemia.
• **Sleeplessness**, even after dropping gratefully into bed, exhausted, and whether or not the baby needs feeding.
• **Loss of appetite**, eating too little, then feeling 'tetchy' and run down. Less often there is over-eating, then guilt.
• **Loss of enjoyment of life**, including pleasure in the baby and the partner's company, which can put the relationship under strain.
• **Not coping** – too little time, doing nothing well, unable to do anything about it.
• **Delay in bonding with the baby**

What are the causes?

There is no known single cause for PND, but these are the 'risk factors':
• a previous episode of depression, especially PND;
• lack of support from the partner;
• a premature or ailing baby;
• the mother's loss of her own mother as a child;
• an accumulation of misfortunes – bereavement, housing and money problems, and so on.

It seems likely that hormonal changes play a part, but evidence is lacking. There is no greater drop in oestrogen, progesterone or other hormones in women with than women without PND, but they may be more vulnerable to change.

How is PND diagnosed?

Mothers may not be willing to disclose their misery when everyone expects them to be very happy. But if the GP and health visitor know how common and serious the disorder is, they will be on the alert for it. A good question is: 'Have you felt depressed since you had your baby?' If the answer is 'Yes' it is not too difficult to explore the possibility of

PND. A 1- item questionnaire, the Edinburgh Postnatal Depression Scale, given within four to six weeks of the birth by the GP or health visitor, has improved diagnosis.

What are the treatment options?
Recognition is the first requirement. It helps to be told: 'You've got postnatal depression'. At least, then there is a reason for feeling so bad, and it is not something worse – like 'going mad' or a brain tumour. Most women have heard about PND from magazines, newpapers, TV and the radio. They can be reassured: 'You will get better, but it may take time, so we'll see that you get help until it does.' With the patient's consent, the partner then needs to be put in the picture. He may have been bewildered and distressed, even resentful, at the change in the new mother since the baby was born; he too is likely to be grateful for a diagnosis and an indication of how he can help. Patience, affection, readiness to listen, being positive and giving practical help in the home and with the baby are of great value. Family – mother, mother-in-law, sisters in particular – and friends and neighbours should be enlisted where possible. Further, professional support may be provided by the Health visitor, GP and, if the psychiatric services are called upon, a psychiatrist and a community psychiatric nurse. Voluntary organisations of women who have recovered from PND can offer valuable information and personal support (p. 160).

'Off-loading' to a sympathetic, understanding, uncritical listener – friend, volunteer or professional – can be a great relief and release. Group therapy conducted by trained health visitors has been shown to help. Antidepressants and antipsychotics have an important place, though many patients are reluctant to try them and need reassurance that they are not addictive and will not make them feel more ill, although a woman may be advised to stop breastfeeding. Hormones appeal to many women more than antidepressants because they seem more 'natural'. However, the evidence that progesterone works better than a placebo is doubtful, and oestrogen may add to the risk of thrombosis.

What is the outlook?
Recovery is the rule even without treatment, but can be lengthy. By this time, however, irreparable damage may have been done to family relationships.

Can PND be prevented?
Up to a point. It is wise to reduce commitments and stress as the time of birth approaches, not to move home while

pregnant or until the baby is at least six months old, to enlist future babysitters, identify a confidante, and for the partner to attend antenatal classes too.

POST-TRAUMATIC STRESS DISORDER
An anxiety disorder that develops following a event or ordeal characterised by real or threatened physical harm.

Many traumatic events can trigger post-traumatic stress disorder, including assault such as rape or mugging, disaster such as flood or hurricane, bombing, accidents including road or rail crashes, or active service with the armed forces. Troops, rescue workers, refugees, survivors and witnesses, are all at risk, as are members of their families.

What are the symptoms?
It is usual to re-experience the ordeal as memory, nightmare or flashback, especially when exposed to a potentially similar experience (getting back on a train, for example, or being in a crowded or dark street). The anniversary of the event may trigger symptoms. Other symptoms include:
• sleep disturbance;
• anxiety;
• irritability;
• anger;
• guilt.
Symptoms can develop immediately or there can be a delay of months or even years before their onset. A diagnosis is made when symptoms last for more than a month.

What are the treatment options?
Cognitive-behavioural therapy, group therapy and exposure therapy in which, under controlled conditions, a sufferer relives the trauma may be helpful. Medication can help to ease depression and anxiety, and improve sleep patterns when these are factors. Counselling after a traumatic event may be helpful, if started quickly, but some families in the wake of atrocities such as the Omagh bombing of 1998 and Dunblane in 1996 found community support as useful.

SCHIZOAFFECTIVE DISORDER
A condition in which schizophrenic symptoms and mood disorder coexist to an equal degree.

The causes of this disorder are not known, but its symptoms are those of a combination of schizophrenia and mood disorder, either mania or depression. Neither mood component nor schizophrenic component predominates. One problem with this is that there are no objective tests for this comparatively unusual disorder. Treatment is as for schizophrenia, although antidepressants and mood stabilisers such as lithium are commonly employed as well. The outlook is essentially that of schizophrenia, perhaps slightly worse.

SCHIZOPHRENIA
Schizophrenia is a chronic relapsing illness which can be emotionally devastating.

The term was coined by the Swiss psychiatrist Eugen Bleuler during the early years of the 20th century, built on the slightly older concept of the German psychiatrist Emil Kraepelin, who described 'dementia praecox' in terms of a deteriorating condition, characterised by poverty of thought, a loosening of associations between thoughts, apathy and what he termed 'autism', not to be confused with autistic disorder, but expressing a morbid absorption and preoccupation with the self.

What are the symptoms?
Schizophrenia is currently divided into two broad syndromes, with separate ranges of symptoms.
- Type I ('positive') schizophrenia is characterised by florid psychotic symptoms, including bizarre delusions, hallucinations and abnormalities of the thinking process. The mood is often abnormal, and a person's appearance and behaviour may be strange, too: they may have a perplexed look and may seem to respond to hallucinations, either by look, gesture or speech. Type I schizophrenia is usually of sudden onset.
- Type II ('negative') schizophrenia more closely equates with Kraepelin's description of dementia praecox. Type II schizophrenia is characterised by 'negative' symptoms. It is commonly of gradual onset and, paradoxically, is the condition that family and friends find more difficult to cope with than the more florid and bizarre type I schizophrenia. This is because in type I the person is more obviously ill; the main symptoms of type II are apparent laziness, lack of motivation, loss of ability to communicate, inability to perform everyday tasks like getting out of bed and washing, and changed sleep patterns such as sleeping all day while being awake and active all night.

Schizophrenia affects one person in every 100 at some point in their lives. Although some patients continue to need medication, others make a full recovery.

What are the causes?
There are numerous causes. Genetics play a part, and the condition often runs in families. Close relatives may not have schizophrenia, but they may have oddities or eccentricities that are reminiscent of the affected individual.

In sporadic cases there may have been an injury at birth. Some have suggested that infections in the pregnant mother, notably influenza, may also contribute to the development of schizophrenia. There is no evidence that parenting approach or attitude causes schizophrenia.

Schizophrenia is more common in men than in women. Also, it has a slightly earlier age of onset in men – during the late teens and early twenties – compared to onset in women during the mid to late twenties.

There are abnormalities in the dopamine system within the brain, but we now realise that more chemical systems are involved as well. The so-called dopamine hypothesis forms the basis of action of many antipsychotic drugs, but these drugs have actions on a range of neurochemical systems, all of which probably contribute in some way to their antipsychotic effects.

How is it diagnosed?
Diagnosis is on the basis of the history. There are no objective tests for schizophrenia, nor does it cause obvious structural abnormalities in the brain. The continued symptoms reinforce the diagnosis.

What are the treatment options?
Treatment is a multidisciplinary affair, involving doctors, nurses, psychologists, occupational therapists, social workers and so on. Where there has been a movement of care into the community (p. 130), the aim has been to reintegrate the individual into society, and the treatment of schizophrenia may be thought of in phases. In the acute phase, the aim is to treat the psychotic symptoms and minimise the patient's distress. This usually involves the use of antipsychotic medication, but may not involve admission to hospital.

The second phase of treatment involves treating symptoms, but also the beginning of the process of reintegration into society. Prevention of relapse depends in large measure on compliance with medication, but is by no means the whole story. Social support, ideally from the family, is essential.

Not all support is good, however. Some ground-breaking studies have looked at the ways in which families interact with a member who has schizophrenia. If the family shows high expressed emotion, such as over-protectiveness, incessant criticism and over-involvement with the affected person, this is generally associated with a higher rate of relapse, especially if the person does not take medication – perhaps at the instigation of his family. On the other hand, if the family is more tolerant of the affected person, allowing personal space and not getting over-involved in symptoms – in other words, shows low expressed emotion – this is associated with a significantly better outcome. Outcome is best, therefore, where there is full compliance with medication and low expressed emotion.

People with schizophrenia often find social situations difficult, so their choice of accommodation is important. Care in the community is of no value if the 'care' amounts to little more than being left to cope alone in deprived circumstances. In such cases, relapse is almost inevitable.

Other proposed forms of treatment include the use of dietary manipulation and food supplements. Perhaps the least controversial of these methods is the use of high doses of fish oils that contain EPA amino acids. Oily fish are rich in these compounds, but usually supplements in the form of cod liver oil or fish oil capsules are used. There is some evidence to suggest that this can improve symptoms over the longer term. There appear to be few, if any, side-effects and therefore it is generally worth trying. Other forms of dietary manipulation, including the use of vitamin B_3 (niacin), are more controversial.

What is the outlook?

Perhaps a third of patients with schizophrenia will, given the appropriate care, regain a considerable amount of their original function. Many people with schizophrenia are able to work, sometimes in high level and demanding occupations. Returning to the world of work is, however, a slow process which needs to be graded in difficulty if success is to be achieved. A significant proportion, perhaps a third, of people with schizophrenia will simply remain the same for the foreseeable future, and some will deteriorate.

About 25 per cent of people with schizophrenia are not responsive to ordinary medical treatment, and are described as 'treatment resistant'. Until comparatively recently there were few options for such individuals. However newer drugs, most notably Clozapine, have changed the outlook for many of these patients. There remains a hard core, however, that are resistant to any form of treatment, and

for them the outlook is indeed gloomy. The rate of suicide in schizophrenia is high – about 10 per cent, or roughly 10 times that of the population as a whole. Depression commonly coexists and its recognition is important. The depression is treatable with antidepressants and the outlook for such depressive symptoms is very good.

SEASONAL AFFECTIVE DISORDER (SAD)

Three per cent of the UK's population suffer 'winter depression': spirits drop as the days shorten, remain low through the dark and cold of the winter months and only rise again as the days lengthen with the spring. This condition is seasonal affective disorder, or SAD.

What are the symptoms?

The main symptoms of SAD are low mood, lack of energy, irritability, anxiety, poor concentration, reduced interest in sex and unsociability – all typical of depression at any time. However, there is also a tendency to hypersomnia (sleeping too much, with sleepiness by day) and to eat more, especially chocolate and other carbohydrates, thus putting on weight: these features are rather like hibernation in other mammals.

One theory to explain SAD is that it could be due to overproduction of a hormone, melatonin, secreted by the pineal gland in the brain. Melatonin is normally only produced at night, and helps to induce sleep. Bright light (not much in evidence in the depths of winter) suppresses the secretion of melatonin, and seems to be of some benefit in SAD in the form of phototherapy (p. 126).

What are the treatment options?

The main treatment is phototherapy and the following points apply:

- It requires much brighter light than is usual indoors.
- It is effective whatever time of day it is given.
- A dose of four hours' exposure is the most effective.
- The effective strength of the light stimulus is in the range of 2,500–3,500 lux at a distance of a metre. Most of our homes, as a comparison, have a light intensity of 250–300 lux, while a bright office may have a level of 500 lux; light levels may reach 20,000 lux on a bright spring morning and 100,000 at the height of a summer day.
- It works through the eye, not through the skin.
- It works within days, but the effects soon wear off if the treatment stops, so treatment must be regular and ongoing.

Another technique is dawn stimulation. The patient, while still asleep, is exposed to white light of gradually increasing brightness from 4.30 am, peaking at 250 lux after 90 minutes. This appears to be more effective than bright light, even though the level in dawn stimulation is relatively low and the eyes are closed. Probably ensuring that patients wake at 6 am is beneficial in helping them to overcome daytime sleepiness and develop a regular sleep schedule.

SELF-HARM
Self-inflicted pain or injury.

The most common form of self-harm is probably cutting, although burning, punching or hitting the body against something may also be tried. The condition includes destructive behaviours such as drinking and overdosing on medications. Most eating disorders have an element of self-harm. More women than men self injure, and research suggests that it is more common than generally believed.

24,000 teenagers are admitted into hospital annually following a self-harm episode. They represent about 13 per cent of all self-harmers.

Self-harm is not always a cry for help, nor is it a suicide attempt. For most affected individuals, self-harm is a way of surviving deep emotional pain, where other people might resort to drink or drugs, or other risky behaviours. Self-harmers may hurt themselves for years. Self-harm may be a means of releasing tension, or it may help a person to feel in control of life. Some self-harmers may have been abused or overly criticised as children.

Talking therapies tend not to be helpful unless directed at the underlying distress. Staff in accident and emergency departments are urged by support groups to be sympathetic and will offer psychiatric counselling, which may be refused by the patient. Given the right support and understanding, however, particularly from non-judgmental family and friends who are prepared to listen, many self-harmers can overcome the condition. The key seems to be resolving the underlying pain.

SHARED PSYCHOTIC DISORDER
Shared psychotic disorder was first described in the 1870s as 'folie à deux'.

The basic feature is that mental symptoms are transmitted from one person to another, rarely more than one other, who are part of the original sufferer's immediate circle.

They share the same delusional ideas. The commonest partnership in delusion is husband and wife, and the extent of the sharing depends on who is the dominant partner. If, therefore, the psychotic individual is the dominant partner, then the other person is more prone to experience this 'infectious' delusion.

What are the symptoms?
The delusions are usually persecutory or hypochondriacal. The original, or primary, patient usually suffers from a mood disorder and transfers the delusions to his or her partner. The delusions in the second person may persist even if he or she is separated from the primary patient.

What are the treatment options?
Treatment is as for any other psychotic disorder. It should be acknowledged that the great majority of people living in an intimate relationship with a psychotic person do not develop his or her delusions. Shared psychotic disorder is thus rare and can be difficult to treat. It is sometimes necessary to admit both the sufferers together, but close long-term follow-up is necessary. Separating the sufferers can cure the partner in whom the delusion was 'induced' without the need for medication. In almost half of cases, the partner's delusions will resolve satisfactorily.

What is the outlook?
If the situation that gave rise to the original psychotic disorder is restored, it is likely that the psychotic disorder will return, too. However, the outlook can be good if medication is taken as directed.

SPLIT OR MULTIPLE PERSONALITY
The idea that different 'individuals' coexist within the same person who moves from individual to individual is attractive in fiction, but of dubious clinical reality.

In some 'dissociative' conditions, the affected person feels as if particular actions were performed by someone else, by another, distinct, individual. This represents an extreme form of a more common psychological defence mechanism in which part of the individual denies traumatic events.

This was described well by Robert Jay Lifton in his tales of concentration camp guards from World War Two. These individuals behaved during their working days with the most sadistic brutality towards their charges, but were able to return home and lead normal and affectionate family

Acknowledgments

Carroll & Brown Limited would also like to thank:

Picture researcher
Sandra Schneider

Production manager
Karol Davies

Production controller
Nigel Reed

Computer management
Paul Stradling, Nicky Rein

Indexer
Jill Dormon

3-D anatomy
Mirashade/Matt Gould

Illustrators
Andy Baker, Jacey,
Kevin Jones Associates,
Mikki Rain

Layout and illustration assistance
Joanna Cameron

Photographers
Jules Selmes, David Yems

Photographic sources
SPL = Science Photo Library

1 SPL
7 Manfred Kage/SPL
8 *(top left)* BSIP, Sercomi/SPL
9 Lascaux Project/ Eurelios/SPL
10 Sheila Terry/SPL
11 *(right)* Getty Images
12 *(bottom)* BSIP, Sercomi/SPL
13 *(top)* James King-Holmes/SPL
14 *(centre)* Getty Images
15 Getty Images
16 *(top)* Dr Jeremy Burgess/SPL
16/17 Getty Images
20/21 Robbie Jack/Corbis
21 *(top)* SPL
22/23 David Turnley/Corbis
26 Alfred Pasieka/SPL
28/29 Biophoto Associates/ SPL
30 *(right)* Will and Deni McIntyre/Corbis
31 *(centre)* Steve Prezant/ Corbis
32 Getty Images
33 Getty Images
34/35 Lawrence Lawry/SPL
35 Getty Images

36 *(top left)* Neil Bromhall/SPL *(bottom left)* Getty Images *(bottom right)* TempSport/Corbis
36/37 Alfred Pasieka/SPL
37 *(top left)* Science Pictures Ltd/SPL *(bottom left)* Getty Images
38 *(top)* Getty Images
39 *(centre)* Getty Images
40 *(left)* Getty Images
41 Getty Images
42 *(right, 2nd, 4th from top)* Getty Images
43 Getty Images
45 *(centre, bottom left)* Getty Images
46 *(left)* Getty Images
46/47 *(background)* SPL
52 Getty Images
53 Getty Images
54 *(top, bottom left, bottom right)* Getty Images
55 *(top left, top right, centre left, centre right)* Getty Images
56 *(right, 3rd from top, bottom)* Getty Images
66 Getty Images
70 Getty Images
71 Getty Images
72 *(top, bottom left, bottom right)* Getty Images
73 *(left)* John Henley/ Corbis *(right, 2nd from top)* Getty Images *(6th from top)* Michael Keller/Corbis
74 Getty Images
77 *(centre)* Getty Images
78 Getty Images
82 *(left)* Powerstock
83 *(left)* Getty Images
85 *(top right)* Getty Images *(bottom left)* Michael Keller/Corbis
88 John Henley/Corbis
89 Getty Images
90 *(left)* BSIP Boucharlat/SPL *(centre)* Custom Medical Stock Photo/ SPL *(right)* Tim Beddow/ SPL
91 Damien Lovegrove/SPL
94 Ariel Skelley/Corbis
97 Damien Lovegrove/SPL
98 BSIP Boucharlat/SPL
99 Ed Young/SPL

100 Mug Shots/Corbis
102 Custom Medical Stock Photo/SPL
103 Will and Deni McIntyre/SPL
107 BSIP, Chassenet/SPL
109 Simon Fraser/Royal Victoria Infirmary, Newcastle upon Tyne/ SPL
110 Tim Beddow/SPL
113 Jim Varney/SPL
115 *(top)* Pierre Perrin/ Corbis Sygma *(bottom)* Kent News & Picture/Corbis Sygma
117 Bettman/Corbis
118 Will and Deni McIntyre/SPL
120 Gusto/SPL
121 Manfred Kage/SPL
122 Mediscan
125 Philip Reeson/Retnauk
126 Pascal Goetgheluck/SPL
127 David Aubrey/Corbis
128 Carroll & Brown
129 *(top)* Barry Plummer, courtesy of Nordoff-Robbins Music Therapy *(centre, bottom)* Dr Sue Jennings
130 Getty Images
131 Mauro Fermariello/SPL
132 Ronnie Kaufman/ Corbis

Front cover
Carroll & Brown

Back cover
(centre) Getty Images
(right) BSIP, Chassenet/SPL

Contact details

Alateen
020 7403 0888
www.al-anonuk.org.uk

Alcohol Concern
www.alcoholconcern.org.uk

Alcoholics Anonymous
08457 097555
www.alcoholics-anonymous.org.uk

Alzheimer's Society
020 7306 0606
www.alzheimers.org.uk

Anti-Bullying Campaign
020 7378 1446
www.bullying.co.uk

Association for Postnatal Illness
020 7386 0868
www.apni.org

Brook Advisory Centres
020 7284 6040
www.brook.org.uk

Childline
0800 1111
childline.org.uk

Citizen's Advice Bureau
www.nacab.org.uk

Drinkline
0800 9178282

Eating Disorders Association
01603 621414
www.eduk.org

Lesbian and Gay Switchboard
020 7837 7324

Mencap
0808 808 1111
www.mencap.org.uk

Mental Health Foundation
020 7535 7439

MIND (Association for Mental Health)
08457 660163
www.mind.org.uk

National Autistic Society
0870 600 8585
www.nas.org.uk

National Drugs Helpline
0800 776600
www.ndh.org.uk

NHS Direct
0845 4647
www.nhsdirect.nhs.uk

NHS Drinkline
0800 917 8282

NHS Quitline
0800 169 0169

Relate
0845 130 4010
www.relate.org.uk

Samaritans
08457 909090
www.samaritans.org.uk

Sane
0845 767 8000
sane.org.uk

Scope
0808 800 3333
www.scope.org.uk

Sexwise
0800 282930

Shelter
0808 800 4444
www.shelter.org.uk

Women's Refuge
0870 599 5443